A GUIDE TO THE PUBS OF LONDON

KNOWN TREASURES & Hidden Gems

PETER HAYDON

Author: Peter Haydon
Design: Rob Howells
Cover artwork: John Dunne
Typeset by T&O Graphics, Broome, Bungay, Suffolk
Printed in Great Britain by Ashford Colour Press

Published by CAMRA Books, Campaign for Real Ale, 230, Hatfield Road, St Albans, AL1 4BW.
Tel: 01727 867201 Fax: 01727 867670
Managing Editor: Mark Webb

First published 1996

Contents

How to use this guide

All pub or beer guides traditionally start with a section entitled 'How to use this Guide.' This is because such sections are pretty indispensable and for that reason alone this guide will stick to the convention.

As the title of the guide suggests this book is about 'Known Treasures and Hidden Gems'. So there are no prizes for guessing that the pubs in the guide are classified according to whether they are treasures or gems.

In point of fact there are three classes of pub in the guide:

1 **Known Treasures:** Pubs that are famous in their own right, or which are popular due to their proximity to important locations.

2 **Pubs that are near tube or railway stations,** and which are good pubs in their own right. They are also good places for meeting people.

3 **Hidden Gems:** Pubs that are a little tucked out of the way, which can be a little hard to find, and which tend to be all the better for it.

Pubs are arranged alphabetically by postcode within the areas of East, North, South East, South West and West London with outer area postcodes coming after main area postcodes. Pubs within each district are listed alphabetically.

In all but a few instances information about a nearby station and local bus routes is provided. Unless the pub is a *near station* pub the station may not necessarily be very near and a bus ride may be needed in addition. Similarly not all bus routes will drop you outside the pub, but they are major routes that pass within easy walking distance. We have not given complex directions to pubs, as we appreciate that our readers will either have an A-Z London guide map or be better served by asking the locals.

A pub's regular real ale range is displayed in the body of the text but if the pub takes guest ales this fact is indicated. However, the number and type of guests a pub takes may vary week to week. A pub owned by a non-brewing operating company is not a Free House unless the landlord has 100 per cent discretion in the choice of his real ales. In practice this situation hardly ever occurs as the pub-owning firms use their total purchasing power to negotiate discounts. Free Houses shown in this guide, therefc are, to the best of our knowledge, genuinely free. But even some of these may have a loan tie, ie the owner may have gained a loan at favourable rates from a brewery in return for taking their beer. Where a pub is owned by a pub-operating company or a brewery, or is tied to a brewery, the owner is identified.

Opening hours are given as 'normal' in the majority of cases, ie the pub opens for the full number of permitted hours. These are 11am to 11pm, Monday to Saturday and 12 noon to 10.30pm on Sunday. Where they differ from this (usually with respect to Sunday opening hours, or weekend closing in the City of London) the variations are given. The times are given first followed by initial letters indicating the day(s).

If food is offered, then these details are included but only by session. Increasingly pubs tend to offer food throughout the day but the hour at which food service ends at night can vary widely as pubs frequently alter hours to suit the demand of the moment.

Finally, we indicate whether the pub has a garden or outside seating area, family room, car park or disabled access. Unfortunately few pubs in the guide have dedicated facilities for disabled people. This tends to be a result of the age of the pubs, for where new pubs are opened or where refurbishments of old buildings allow, disabled facilities are almost always included. Family rooms, however, are still few and far between.

SYMBOLS

FR Family room – an area where parents can sit with their children
G Garden or outside drinking area, often a patio
CP Car park
DA disabled access
R Restaurant
ML Meals lunchtime
ME Meals evening
SL Snacks lunchtime
SE Snacks evening

A FEW FACTS AND FIGURES

The 400+ pubs in this guide have been selected by CAMRA members from all over London. They represent a cross section of some of London's best pubs. There is no bias towards any particular brewer and it is fair to say that all brewers have both good and bad pubs.

Nearly 20 per cent of the pubs included in this book are genuinely Free Houses, ie not owned by any chain whatsoever. Certain chains – notably Wetherspoons – describe themselves as Free Houses. They are not and do a great disservice to real Free Houses by doing so.

Thirty-six per cent of the total number of pubs take at least one guest beer. This rises to 45 per cent when Free Houses are excluded. This is a most encouraging figure, but it remains the case that too many pubs take their guest beers from approved lists, and the beers on the list are virtually national brands as a result. Marston's Pedigree and Wadworth 6X are the perennial guest beers. However, the beer most widely available in the Guide is Fuller's London Pride. Bass too appears frequently and Tetley, from Yorkshire, is also readily available but, according to many Yorkshire drinkers, has lost something on its travels south.

The average London pub has three real ales, excluding guest ales, whilst over 120 beers are regularly available in the pubs in the guide. A number of brewers: Fuller's, Young's, Whitbread, McMullen's and Greene King, produce seasonal beers, so the number of beers on offer does fluctuate slightly.

Real Ale Growth in London

Around 1974, when CAMRA was first founded, a list of pubs that served real ale in London was produced and circulated. It had around 200 names on it. These were not the best real pubs in London, these were *all* the pubs that sold real ale in London. They represented something under five per cent of all the capital's public houses. Today, the reverse is true and it is only around five per cent of pubs that do not serve some form of real ale.

This impressive statistic is only the tip of the iceberg as far as the story of real ale in London goes. It does not say anything about the quality of the beer currently on offer. Nor does it say anything about the range or origins of the beers. When one starts to analyse these aspects of London beer's recent history, a very fascinating story emerges.

Most noticeable is the decline of Bass Charrington as a real ale force in the London market. This is due, in part, to a reduction in the size of their estate in London as a result of the government enforced sale of pubs initiated in 1992. But even before this, Bass Charrington houses were gradually losing favour as the drinker turned away from Charrington IPA, believing it not to be the beer it once was. Charrington was the quintessential East End brewer. In the 1870s the heir to the brewing family fortune F.W. Charrington, having witnessed an act of alcohol-induced violence underneath a painted sign bearing his own family name, became a prominent temperance campaigner

He maintained cordial, if distant, relations with his brewing family, who never disowned him.

The family firm of Young's are today's standard bearers of the honourable tradition of brewing eccentricity. When, in the 1970s, other London brewers like Fuller's and Courage did not want publicans to take cask ale, Young's kept the faith. Never more than a small London estate, there has been a decline in Young's percentage share of real ale pubs due to their traditional concentration in South West London. Young's have not expanded their estate as well as their London rivals, Fuller's, which has probably enabled the Wetherspoon pub chain to cash in on South London.

There has been a small, and welcome, increase in representation amongst the home counties regional brewers like Shepherd Neame, McMullen and Greene King. However, the main picture is one of little change. Fuller's have been steadily increasing their tied estate but in 1974 it supplied real ale to barely more than 10 of their London publicans, who insisted on it. Today they have won more CAMRA Champion Beer Awards than any other brewery.

In 1976 Scottish & Newcastle had no real ale outlets in London at all. Their last real ale house, the Three Compasses in Holborn, had ceased serving Younger's Bitter and No.3 a year or so before. Allied produced nothing and both London brewers, Watneys and Truman, sold no real ale. Then, as now, the champions of the cause of the discerning drinker were a handful of Free Houses, the Anglesea Arms in Kensington (q.v.) McMullen's Admiral Mann (q.v), the Packenham Arms and the great and wonderful Becky's Dive Bar. Becky's was a legend in its lifetime. The squalor of the place was notorious. The stairs were so rotten, regulars knew which ones to step over. A visit to the ladies' toilet would stir a swarm of flies from the duck boards. To ask for a sandwich was enough to stop all conversation amongst clients and staff alike, yet Becky sold a little-known brew called Theakston's, Thwaites, and a beer called Shepherd Neame Imperial.

One of the first CAMRA successes was in persuading Whitbread to replace its deleted real ale from Chiswell Street (ceased brewing in 1975) with Wethered's from Marlow (axed in 1988). Although Whitbread's tried to hold out and sell only keg Trophy, Wethered's took off as soon as it was introduced.

In the low point of British drinking, London drinkers had a very small choice of pubs in which they could hope to find real ale. These were mainly pubs serving

Charrington IPA, Young's, a few Courage houses selling London Ale and a handful of Fuller's and Free Houses. In the late seventies, the brewers had to respond to consumer demand. Where the big brewers responded, they did so by reintroducing London-brewed beers for the London market. Watney's brewed Stag, Antler, Hamilton Stout, Coombe Bitter and Fined Bitter, that real ale drinkers joked was so named because it was so hard to 'find'. Truman's produced the superbly hoppy Sampson and Truman's Best Bitter but all these beers had very short lives. Just as it became apparent that cask ale was going to stay, the London brewers ceased brewing London beers.

In 1986, Watney acquired the widely respected Rutland firm of Ruddles and developed their two brands County and Best into national brands to their instant detriment. They reduced the number of beers they brewed in London, replacing them with Ruddles. By 1988, Truman's Sampson had gone the way of Coombe's and the same year, the Mortlake brewery ceased brewing cask ale. The next year, the Brick Lane brewery closed and Truman Best moved briefly to Usher's in Trowbridge before disappearing.

Bass did the same with Charrington IPA which moved around a number of breweries before it was axed in 1995. In its last incarnation it was actually contract brewed for Bass by Shepherd Neame!

What has happened is that the numbers of pubs selling real ale has increased but the number of beers on offer from the big brewers has declined. For example, Allied, which in 1976 had only four real ale pubs in London, increased its presence in the capital over the last two decades but has cut its beer portfolio by 23 per cent since 1989. The beneficiaries of the growth in real ale have been the big brewers who have channelled their efforts into national brands. This is why London pubs serve no London beer other than Young's and Fuller's but serve plenty of beer from Manchester and Yorkshire.

Other companies have gained from the vacuum left by Bass's abandonment of London, notably Fuller's but brewers like Sam Smith's, Brakspear, Adnams, Marston's and Greene King have increased their presence in London; although only the first and last have any estate. The main beneficiaries, however, have been Free Houses and these are the pubs which offer the widest choice to consumers.

The big brewers have used the guest ale provisions of the supply of beer orders to augment the choices of beers available in pubs but actually reduce the numbers brewed by themselves. There are around 100 beers in this guide that are classed as regularly sold in a pub and there are probably another 200 which survive as guests. The choice of real ale in London is growing at the bottom end of the market as fast as it is contracting at the top end. Sadly the growth of real ale in London has been matched by the decline in the real ale of London.

Poor Quality Beer and Service

It may happen, even in the best of pubs, that you find that the pint you have ordered is not of the quality you expect. Even the most competent of landlords will end up with a poor pint at some time. Real ale is a living product and, like all living things, can be cantankerous at times. However, the regularity of poor beer and how any quality complaint is handled, reflects on the abilities of a landlord.

Bad beer can usually be prevented by good cellar management. It frequently occurs because some publicans do not care; do not fully understand real ale; or have experience of a regular brand and do not know how to treat others. The behaviour of real ales in the cellar varies immensely from beer to beer; an experienced cellarman will know the 'personalities' of a large number of beers. It is obvious that increased cellar training would eliminate many of these causes, but only a handful of breweries and pub chains offer fully comprehensive training schemes. It costs money.

Unfortunately London is probably the worst region of Britain for poor quality beer. London is also the region with the greatest competition between pub operators and which has seen the greatest amount of turmoil. High rents have meant that many good publicans have left the trade in recent years and many new publicans do not have the necessary cellar skills.

There are a number of conditions that can cause bad beer:

Poor Hygiene. Cellars should be clean places. Even the walls, floors and ceilings should be clean in order to reduce the potential for sites of micro-organism growth that will increase the chances of airborne infection of the beer.

Oxidisation. The beer has been in contact with air for too long. This is likely to lead to problems of haze as the protein in the beer reacts with the oxygen in the air. Often, it is a sign that the cask is near the end and should be changed. If there is still a considerable amount of infected beer left it would suggest that the cask has been selling too slowly and the beer has been in the cellar too long. The simplest remedy is to reduce the size of the cask (and maintain high standards of cellar hygiene). This will reduce the ratio of air to beer in the cask and reduce the risk of airborne infection.

Poor temperature control. A pub cellar should be maintained at the correct temperature (13-14C, 55-57F), and that temperature should not be allowed to fluctuate. Temperature affects the condition of the beer. Condition refers to the liveliness of the beer, i.e. the amount of dissolved CO^2. The ability of the beer to hold gas depends on its temperature. Cold beer is too gassy, warm beer is too 'flat'. Warm cellars produce beer like dish water.

Lack of maturation. Real ale undergoes secondary fermentation in the cask, although some beers are designed to undergo the minimum possible amount. Secondary fermentation provides the final condition and finesse to the beer. It adds around 0.1 per cent ABV but is a more subtle process than the heady, busy fermentation in the brewery and produces the complexities that give real ale its superior taste. Serving beer before it has had time to undergo secondary fermentation will produce a sharp, 'green' pint and prevents the beer developing its full flavour. Too often, taste is sacrificed for a fast turnover.

Deterioration in lines. In between sessions or if a beer is selling very slowly, a beer may sit too long in the line. Here it may be subjected to an increase in heat or may sit on yeast deposits in the lines if they are not properly cleaned. The result will be a warm, flat, tainted pint. If beer is left to sit in the lines for any length of time, the lines should be cleared and pulled through with water and the beer thrown away. If lines are not cleaned regularly, the beer can be subject to yeast and mould infections. The presence of 'floaters' (lumps of coagulated yeast), drifting around the bottom of a pint, is a sign that the pipes need cleaning.

Wrong use of spiles. During secondary fermentation a soft spile is inserted into the shive. The soft spile is a porous plug allowing CO^2 from secondary fermentation to escape but preventing foreign bodies from entering the beer. Once fermentation has stopped, a hard spile (impervious plug) must be used. A hard spile should be firmly in place at all times when the cask is not in use.

The tragedy of the bad pint is that it is entirely counter productive. The drinker who has a bad pint will forsake the pub. The drinker will, in future, buy his drink from the off licence, or supermarket, and stay at home. The pub loses, the community loses and the government loses, as tax on take-home drink is lower than on pub drink.

Poor quality beer in the nation's pubs will only be eradicated when pub owners recognise that they cannot continue to demand ever-increasing rates of return from their retail outlets and, at the same time, instigate proper, regular training. The fault lies much more squarely with them rather than with the publican who has just poured you a sour, cloudy pint.

A Full Pint Please

Unfortunately, it is not only beer quality that suffers from poor training. In 975 AD King Edgar decreed that a pot should contain a standard measure and that this should be a quart (two pints). This standardisation was reinforced by countless pieces of legislation throughout the centuries, including the famous Magna Carta of 1215. In 1987 the government included in the Weights and Measures Act a section (no.43 to be exact) which stated that the froth on the top of a beer was not part of the pint. However, this section was not to be enacted until a minister said so. To date, ministers have refused to ratify the right of a Briton to a full pint, which had had the force of law for one thousand years.

Legitimisation of short measure came at a time when short measure was becoming an ever more widespread problem. A 5-10 per cent shortfall is not unusual. If you receive a short measure, you are entitled by law to ask for a top-up. It is unfortunate that the onus is on the customer not the pub to ensure that they serve a full pint. Only a handful of London pubs use oversized glasses, which is the only real way to ensure a full pint. You will, of course, find them at all CAMRA's beer festivals.

EC1

Angel

73 City Road

Allied Domecq

ML SL

Opening Hours: normal m-f closed s-su

Station: Old Street

Buses: 43, 76, 141, 214, 221

Eldridge Pope Dorchester, Tetley Bitter, Ind Coope Burton Ale

Moderately sized, airy but busy City pub, on the famous City Road. Semi-circular bar maximises bar area and food serving space. Friendly bar staff and fast service make it a pleasant pub to drop into, especially for those waiting for a report to come from Companies House. The Honourable Artillery Company and John Wesley's (1703-1791) Chapel and museum are very close. Very much a pub to service the needs of city workers, but one that does so a little more comfortably and less perfunctorily than most of the main road pubs do.

Bishops Finger

9-10 West Smithfield

Shepherd Neame

G SL SE

Opening Hours: 11-11m-f 11-3s closed su

Station: Farringdon

Buses: 56, 63, 259

Shepherd Neame Masterbrew, Shepherd Neame Spitfire, Shepherd Neame Porter, Shepherd Neame Bishop's Finger + Guest Beers

This small pub, opposite St Bartholomew's Hospital, has a downstairs bar and an upstairs function room. It is one of the oldest established of the small but growing number of Shep's Houses in central London and is one which does the whole range of beers. Its proximity to both Bart's Hospital and Smithfield Market means it enjoys a slightly later trade than many nearby pubs. On a Monday night, for example, singers from the Bart's Hospital Choir can often be found soothing their tired throats before wending their way home. The pub is somewhat functionally furnished and the food downstairs is rather more in the 'grub' line of food than the haute cuisine more fashionably served in many pubs these days.

Britannia

94 Lever Street

Whitbread
ML ME SL
Opening Hours: normal
Station: Old Street
Buses: 4, 43, 55, 56, 214, 243, 505, X43
Boddingtons Bitter, Fuller's London Pride, Flowers Original, Marston's Pedigree

Popular locals' pub with a professional trade at lunchtimes. The single room pub has a walk round island bar. The sandstone chimney and domestic gas fire gives the place a bit of a feel of a suburban front room, which is no bad thing in a pub. However, it probably loses some of that atmosphere on Friday and Saturday nights, or the occasional Wednesday when there is an eclectic range of live music on. And if you were in a suburban living room you probably would not want the Britannia's darts teams in there with you either (Women: Tuesday; Men: Thursday). There is a big difference between the lunchtime and evening trade but a lot of the office workers like to come back in the evenings, so it must be a good pub.

Crown

43 Clerkenwell Green

Nicholsons
ML SL
Opening Hours: normal
Station: Farringdon
Buses: 55, 243, 505
Adnams Bitter, Tetley Bitter, Ind Coope Burton Ale, Young's Ram Rod + Guest Beers

Recently refurbished Nicholson's house, that, thankfully, is no different than prior to attention. Vestiges of multiple partitions are still present, which gives the pub plenty of nooks and corners without making it claustrophobic. A wide range of real ales is available. Right in the heart of Clerkenwell Green, which is the City's only real London village – London is merely a collection of villages that run into each other – Clerkenwell is not only one of the most historic parts of London but has a strong community feel to it. Popular as a lunchtime venue and in summer when drinkers spill out to the forecourt on the Green. There is no grass, but there is a horse trough and a fine view of the Middlesex Sessions House. The pub is handy for the offices of the Guardian and the Guardian on Sunday (Observer) newspapers, as well as the recently restored old London prison, the House of Correction.

Fox & Anchor

115 Charterhouse Street

Allied Domecq
ML SL
Opening Hours: 6.30am-9.30pm m-f closed s-su
Station: Farringdon
Buses: 45, 46, 63, 259
Tetley Bitter, Ind Coope Burton Ale + Guest Beers

Built in 1897, the original frontage is one of the most distinctive and attractive in London. In 1993 the pub won the prestigious English Heritage and CAMRA sympathetic restoration award – frequently unawarded. The back of the pub consists of a number of small eating booths of slightly varying character. An original booth on the left, with stained glass doors and partition, feels rather like an Edwardian pantry, the one on the right is narrower and with the luggage racks above feels like an early railway carriage. The black and white tiles give away the fact that prior to restoration this was the gents toilet. The origin of the pub's name is uncertain – its being opposite Fox & Knot Street is an added confusion. One likely theory is that the first licensee Mr Fox, only managed to open the pub by taking up a licence from a vacant pub (The Anchor) elsewhere in the City. This would sit nicely with known licensing activity at the time. There is evidence to suggest that it was then known locally as Fox's Anchor. Its art nouveau frontage and Edwardian interior are very unusual, and the fact that in its heyday it had a female publican adds to its mystique. It is one of the few London pubs to have and use a market licence (the others nearby are the Hope, the New Market and the Cock Tavern), which enables it to open at 6.30am. Worth a visit for breakfast.

Hat & Tun

3 Hatton Wall

Bass
ML SL
Opening Hours: 11-11 m-f closed s-su
Station: Chancery Lane
Buses: 63, 243, 259
Greene King IPA, Worthington Best Bitter, Fuller's London Pride

A very homely one-room pub with light wallpaper, prints, plates and a dresser at the end of the bar that gives the whole the feel of a Victorian parlour. The bar runs down one side of the pub, with a fine bar stillion behind. The rubber plant on the dresser should more properly be an aspidistra to complete the feel and the piped music is unobtrusive but nevertheless not a bonus. The pub is made by the odd items of household furniture around the room, the dumb waiter and the foot of a bed screwed to the wall. The head of the bed doubles as the menu board. Rather tucked away on quiet Hatton Wall, just off busy Hatton Garden, the pub makes a fine and pleasingly different retreat from the busy city bustle.

Kings of Clerkenwell

7 Clerkenwell Close

S&N
ML SL
Opening Hours: 12-3, 5.30-11m-f closed s-su
Station: Farringdon
Buses: 55, 243, 505
Webster's Yorkshire Bitter, Ruddles Best, Morland's Old Speckled Hen

Small one-room and highly eccentric pub. Decor includes a stuffed rhinoceros head and numerous papier maché models and sculptures which give the whole a strangely surreal effect. The pub itself is quite dark, despite opening out onto the street and gaining a view of St James Church, Clerkenwell. The exterior is a very restrained, East End-style with original Mann, Crossman and Paulin windows, which dates them to pre-1958. The inn sign is in three dimensions, which represents a novel departure and acts as a warning that there is a little Bohemian quarter in the straight-laced City.

Mitre Tavern

Ely Court (off Ely Place)

Allied Domecq
SL SE
Opening Hours: 11-11 m-f closed s-su
Station: Chancery Lane
Buses: 8, 17, 22b, 25, 45, 46, 171a, 243, 501, 521
Tetley Bitter, Friary Meux Best Bitter, Ind Coope Burton Ale

Part of the Diocese of Ely, the pub is in an alley which was originally closed off by Beadles of the Bishop of Ely, though this practice ended fifteen or so years ago. A cherry tree built into the corner of the pub dates back several centuries and marks the boundary of the diocese. The small public bar and the larger saloon to the rear have a Tudor feel resulting from the dark wood panelling. White aproned bar staff add a gentlemanly and professional air to the pub.

Old Fountain

3 Baldwin Street

Whitbread

G ML ME SL SE

Opening Hours: 11-11m-f 11-3, 5-11s 12-3, 7-10.30su

Station: Old Street

Buses: 43, 214

Boddingtons Bitter, Fuller's London Pride, Flowers Original + Guest Beers

The exterior of this pub is bright white, but on stepping in the woodwork is as dark as wood can be without actually being ebony. The wallpaper is a quite striking design, and an invitation to pub designers to be a little more adventurous in their choice of decor. Mouldings and wall coverings below the dado rail are original and a large aquarium in one corner of the slightly raised rear room lends a bright and therapeutic focus to the pub. The front bar is the main food area and meals will be prepared on order even if it looks as though all has been cleared away. Guest beers, usually two or three at a time, are rotated every three months or so. The pub has won several awards for its flower arrangements and Whitbread company awards for quality of service. The subdued lighting may be due to its proximity to the Ophthalmic Hospital nearby.

Sekforde Arms

34 Sekforde St

Young's

ML ME SL SE

Opening Hours: 11-11m-s 12-4su

Station: Farringdon

Buses: 153, 279

Young's Bitter, Young's Special, Young's Winter Warmer

Small attractive corner pub, popular with supporters clubs of several non-London football teams. A funny shaped pub, formed by a fork in the road, the pub is split into two areas by the chimney piece. The front area is a more normal stand-at-the-bar area, whilst behind the chimney, as it were, is a seating area. The pub concentrates on food, which is served till quite late at night and the menu is quite extensive. Upstairs there is a restaurant, that doubles as a function and meeting room in the evenings and which is quite heavily used. Decor is traditional Young's, and so is the clientele. The Sekforde borders marks the edge of Clerkenwell. To the South are a number of good pubs, to the north, very few, so pop in for sustenance, should you be heading North.

Vaults

42 Chiswell St

Whitbread
ML ME SL SE
Opening Hours: 11-11m-f closed s-su
Station: Moorgate
Buses: 43, 76, 141, 214, 271, X43
Flowers IPA, Boddingtons Bitter, Fuller's London Pride + Guest Beers

The Vaults really are vaults, and as old city style wine and ale houses go this one panders to a broader appeal and less 'gentlemanly' image than some of the more sober (sombre) traditional cellar pubs. Directly under the Brewer's House and across the road from the Whitbread HQ, the Vaults are almost the Brewery Tap. A main passage, lined with old pipes, runs the length of the pub, with individual vaults in bare brick running off to the right. A large amount of old drink-making artefacts fill the alcoves, from champagne racks to presses, but milk churns, cartwheels and knife sharpeners – as well as the ubiquitous casks – are also in evidence. Any and each of the five vaults can be hired for private parties and functions and, towards Christmas, are increasingly busy. There is a pool table in a side room and the pub has two exits to the street at either end of the long main passageway. The Vaults themselves may be authentic, the fixtures themselves are rather too bogus, with the effect of over gilding the lily. A fine place for an office party however.

Viaduct Tavern

126 Newgate Street

Nicholsons
ML ME SL SE
Opening Hours: normal
Station: St Paul's
Buses: 8, 22b, 25, 56, 501, 521
Tetley Bitter, Ind Coope Burton Ale + Guest Beers

Fine old Victorian pub across the road from the Old Bailey which was built on the site of the notorious Newgate Prison in front of which executions took place until 1876 when they retreated behind the prison walls. The Victorian ceiling, glass and painted murals, as well as decorative marble and glazed tiles, are amongst some of the finest surviving examples. The pub was obviously partitioned in the past, as can be seen by the glazed tiles along the wall which now forms the steps down to the toilets. At one time these tiles were obviously the wall of a corridor. A popular gossiping corner for journalists covering Old Bailey trials, the customers also include postmen from the sorting office behind the pub and staff from St Bartholomew's Hospital three minutes walk away, towards Smithfield Market. A great example of the style that became known as 'gin palace' though true gin palaces never looked like it!

EC2

Bricklayers Arms

63 Charlotte Road

Free House
R ML ME SL SE
Opening Hours: normal, m-f closed s eve-su
Station: Old Street
Buses: 5, 43, 55, 243, 505

Old-style corner pub that has been turned into a hybrid French style cafe-pub. Fine Whitbread glass mirrors in the bar stillion are offset with a more Continental style Kronenbourg sign. Meals are served upstairs and the rear of the pub is devoted to pin tables and table football, very French. A few tables are squeezed onto the pavement, in what is still quite an 'artisanal' part of the city. All seven real ales are guests and a wider range is on offer than in many pubs. Not all attempts at creating this type of pub are successful, this one is very successful. A good real ale pub.

Princess Royal

76-78 Paul Street

Whitbread
R ML ME SL SE
Opening Hours: normal m-f closed s-su
Station: Old Street
Buses: 43, 76, 141, 214, 271, X43
Flowers IPA, Boddingtons Bitter, Whitbread Castle Eden, Fuller's London Pride, Flowers Original

Crowded wood-lined corner-street location with quite a close knit feel for a city office pub, with a sizeable locals contingent too. An à la carte restaurant upstairs is reached via a cleverly space saving spiral staircase in the front corner of the pub. In summer, a few chairs are squeezed onto the pavement. Decor has some art nouveau features, which actually work quite well. Quite a wide range of real ales from the Whitbread stable, but nothing too strong, as most trade is lunchtime and early evening.

EC3

East India Arms

67 Fenchurch Street

Bass

SL SE

Opening Hours: 11-10m-w 11-11th-f closed s-su

Station: Fenchurch Street

Buses: 40, 100, D1, D11

Worthington Best Bitter, Fuller's London Pride, Draught Bass + Guest Beers

Just around the corner from Fenchurch Street station, the pub dates back to 1815 and takes its name from the East India Company, which was established in 1600 and was for many years Britain's most important trading concern, at various times having virtual monopolies over various commodities such as gunpowder and tea. The headquarters of the company were in Leadenhall Street until 1862 on what is now the site of the Lloyds Building. Despite a refurbishment that is attractive for being highly inept, the pub retains an intangible eighteenth century feel. This is imparted by the architectural proportions rather more than by the decor – the neck-high wood panels are a nice feature, the wallpaper above them is not. This impression is enhanced by the arched windows and shop style door which gives a slight coffee house appearance to the pub.

Hoop & Grapes

47 Aldgate High Street

Bass

ML ME SL SE

Opening Hours: 11-11m-f closed s 12-3su

Station: Aldgate

Buses: 15, 25, 42

Worthington Best Bitter, Fuller's London Pride, Draught Bass

This Grade II listed building is the only remaining timber framed structure of its kind in the City of London. These structures were forbidden by Parliament after the Great Fire of London in 1666, as were the traditional Tudor style of gabled, overhanging buildings, hence the scarcity of the timber framed house. That said, it is only fitting that it should be a pub. It would also be fitting if the brewery had some idea of history itself, before refurbishing the rear dining area in the fashionable, but bogus, style of hammering off all the plasterwork to reveal bare brick. The front of the pub is delightful, so it is recommended that you sit in the front with your back to the rear and enjoy the sight of London passing by through crooked windows. The pub serves a large range of Belgian fruit beers as well as a larger range of guest ales than is frequently to be found.

Lamb Tavern

10-12 Leadenhall Market

Young's
ML SL
Opening Hours: 11-10m-f closed s-su
Station: Fenchurch Street
Buses: 8, 22a, 22b, 26, 35, 47, 48, 149
Young's Bitter, Young's Special

A famous City boozer with a large bare floored bar that allows plenty of space for the predominantly male clientele to come and down a swift pint or two in the limited time available. In this respect, it is very faithful to the old ethos of the City alehouses of the eighteenth century. A spiral staircase leads to an upstairs seating and dining area. On high days the custom spills out into the arcades of Leadenhall Market, an old London meat and fish market now devoted to shops and sandwich bars. The Lamb is said to date to around 1780. The pub has a very handsome frontage with fine etched windows. Downstairs is a 'dive bar' with green and white glazed tiles to shoulder height and with some caustic aromas escaping from the pub cellar, it feels a bit like a swimming pool. However it is a pleasant area to get away from the bustle above and it is available for private functions. Many of the pub's customers will work in the insurance markets and it is only a matter of yards from the famous Lloyds Building.

EC4

Blackfriar

174 Queen Victoria St

Nicholsons
ML SL
Opening Hours: 11-11m-f
Station: Blackfriars
Buses: 4, 11, 15, 17, 23, 26, 45, 63, 76, 172
Brakspear Bitter, Adnams Bitter, Tetley Bitter, Wadworth 6X

A unique treasure of a pub. London's only true art deco pub, built in 1902, the pub takes its name from the

Dominican Priory that was on the site as early as 1278. Designed by Henry Poole RA, there are three separate drinking areas, all with a different character. A fireplace welcomes the visitor in one of the front areas but it is the back 'Grotto' area that is the most striking. It is a rich mixture of many types of marble with relief scenes and mottoes of suitably uplifting character such as 'Wisdom is Rare', 'Industry is All', 'Don't Advertise Tell a Gossip'. The pub also has mini-beer festivals where 2-3 extra selections are available.

Ye Olde Cheshire Cheese

145 Fleet Street

Sam Smith's
ML ME SL SE
Opening Hours: 11-11m-s 12-3 su
Station: Blackfriars
Buses: 11, 15, 23
Sam Smith's OBB

In business since 1667, the Cheese in Wine Office Court, takes its name from the Office of Excise (which was there until 1665). It was not one of the great London taverns of the eighteenth century. It is, however, a survivor and herein lies its fame. The Cheese has a list of illustrious visitors including Dr Johnson, Garrick, Pope, Conan Doyle and Thackeray, to name but a few. The Cheese has another claim to fame. Each year a plum pudding has been prepared at the Cheese. Each pudding contains a small piece of its predecessor, ensuring that the same pudding has been eaten for years. Almost as famous was the Cheese's celebrity talking parrot, Polly, who lived to the ripe old age of 40. When she died in 1926, obituaries appeared in newspapers all over the world. The Cheese has been extended in the rear in a spectacularly uninspiring fashion and the authentic parts of the pub tend to be closed during the afternoons. The Cheese is still one of London's good pubs but under Sam Smith's management can no longer be said to be the truly great pub it once was.

Clachan

Old Mitre Court

S&N
ML SL
Opening Hours: 11-9m-f closed s-su
Station: Temple
Buses: 11, 15, 23
Theakston's Best, Theakston's XB + Guest Beers

A small upstairs room which leads to a larger room downstairs which closes between 3-5 in the afternoons. The Clachan is very much in the London style, with bare board floors upstairs, half panelling and plenty of 'City' scene prints. The pub very much exists to serve the liquid needs of the lawyers of the Inner and Middle Temples – advocacy, after all, can be thirsty work. The pub is only 20 yards off the busy strand in Old Mitre Court but the sounds of traffic are effectively silenced. The Clachan stays open as late as there is custom, which usually means till around nine o'clock Monday to Wednesday and slightly later as the weekend approaches. The windowless downstairs room has the lunchtime's food servery and a large wood-panelled carpeted lounge containing a bar billiards table for those who like a more sedate game with a cue.

Cockpit
7 St Andrew's Hill

Inntrepreneur
ML ME SL SE
Opening Hours: 11-11m-f closed s-su
Station: Blackfriars
Buses: 4, 11, 15, 17, 23, 26, 76, 172
Courage Best Bitter, Marston's Pedigree, Courage Directors

A hotch-potch of mock Tudor features is arranged below a false gallery, giving the pub a bit of a Shakespearean theatre feel, which is accentuated by the pub's corner location and the odd shape this imparts. Why the walls are painted pink is a bit of a mystery. The name is taken from an old cock fighting pit and pictures and motifs of cockerels are much in evidence. The pub sports a large collection of whisky water jugs. A pub that was clearly once part of the street life and these connections can still be imagined by watching the city pass on a warm day.

Horn Tavern
29 Knightrider Street

Eldridge Pope
Opening Hours: 11-9m-f closed s-su
Station: Blackfriars
Buses: 4, 11, 15, 17, 23, 26, 76, 172
Eldridge Pope Thomas Hardy Country Bitter

A traditional pub meets wine bar style city pub. The emphasis very much on quality food, wine and beer. A small range of fine beer is balanced by a large range of fine wine which is arranged around the back of the bar where the stillion is more usually found. Wood panelled with convincing, if not original, old style booth and settle seating, an impressive row of which stretches down one narrow limb of the pub, very much after the fashion of the old city Chop Houses. Downstairs is a restaurant, again very much in the city style, windowless but with glass panes opening onto nothing. The 'Sommelier Menu' is both reasonable and imaginative. A hard pub to find but one that entirely dominates Knightrider street. Convenient for St Paul's.

Punch Tavern
99 Fleet Street

Nicholsons
ML SL SE
Opening Hours: 11-11m-s 12-3, 7-10.30su
Station: Blackfriars
Buses: 11, 15, 23
Brakspear Bitter, Tetley Bitter, Worthington Best Bitter, Draught Bass, Ind Coope Burton Ale

A large highly ornate pub, unlike any other in the city. Very much a lost soul these days since the demise of Fleet Street as the home of the best and the worst of the world's press. The walls are decorated with scenes from the famous satirical magazine Punch, which folded at the start of the 1990s after 150 years of lampooning our national figures and our way of life. The Punch is abundantly done out in a handsome style with plenty of original features, a fine ceiling and wall mirrors, the intrusion of video games and piped music in place of the gossip of journalists betrays its loss of raison d'etre. The entrance lobby is in classical London style, with plenty of glazed faience, of which very few such fine examples now survive. The pub still has the daily papers on display for customers, but if the walls could talk what stories they could tell.

Vintry

Queen Street

Fuller's
ML SL
Opening Hours: normal
Station: Mansion House
Buses: 149
Fuller's Chiswick Bitter, Fuller's London Pride, Fuller's ESB

A fair example of how modern materials and workmanship can still create a traditional pub that works. The Vintry is a richly dark wood pub in an odd shape and with a lovely high ceiling which prevents it being oppressive. One for the designers, with lots of corners, angles and interesting shapes, producing an overall good use of the space. The whole is done in wood except for a little side area, which doubles as the lunchtime dining area. Original tiling and ironwork features are spaced amongst the modern fittings. The whole effect is a good example of sympathetic treatment of the 'traditional City' theme.

E1

Alma

41 Spelman Street

Free House

ML SL

Opening Hours: 11-11m-f 11-4, 7-11s 12-4, 7-10.30su

Station: Aldgate East

Buses: 25, 253

Young's Bitter, Fuller's London Pride, Young's Ram Rod

Do not be put off by the slightly stern frontage the pub presents to the street – it's that sort of neighbourhood. Inside the pub is a hidden gem. A warm atmosphere and cluttered bar belie the exterior. Every spare inch of wall space is covered in pictures which seem to have no one theme, rhyme or reason. The bar area is covered in bank notes and club badges, whilst the white painted wooded front walls make the pub light and cheerful. The back dining room, an obvious extension, is devoted to Jack the Ripper, who terrorised the streets nearby. The walls are covered with pictures, by a local artist at a guess, of Ripper victims – spot the spelling mistake on the picture of Elizabeth Stride – investigators and likely suspects and displays a thorough knowledge of the extensive Ripper literature. Evening food is served if ordered in advance and the menu consists of honest pub grub which is reasonably priced.

Artful Dodger

47 Royal Mint Street

Free House

ML SL

Opening Hours: normal

Station: Tower Hill

Buses: 15, 25, 100, D1

Webster's Yorkshire Bitter, Courage Best Bitter, Fuller's London Pride

On the edge of the city, the Artful Dodger (named after the Dickens' Character from Oliver Twist) is a Free House where the City and the East End rub shoulders, not something they do fairly often it must be added. Windows on two sides make this one room house a very bright airy pub. A bar billiards table to the rear offers entertainment. Upstairs is a function room and dining room; food is served from 12-3. The pub, with its jaunty colour scheme of green, pink and brown (it looks much better than it sounds) has that casual air of nonchalance that only Free Houses can achieve and which is one of their endearing characteristics. The food is excellent value and is definitely in the pub grub style, and why not?

Brown Bear

139 Leman Street

Allied Domecq
ML SL SE
Opening Hours: 11-11m-f closed s-su
Station: Aldgate East
Buses: 5, 15
Adnams Bitter, Tetley Bitter, Young's Bitter, Marston's Pedigree + Guest Beers

Spoilt slightly by games machines, this busy pub is nevertheless older than a first glance would suggest. Original decorative mouldings and a general absence of right angles and true planes suggest an old building. The walk round bar and mirrors from Allsopp's and other brewers give the game away. The pub has been tarted up to appeal to a younger clientele but at the same time serves a good range of real ales. The bare floored bar, subdued lighting, lots of dark wood and proper pub coloured walls gives a darkish atmosphere, which is not very much in vogue these days – outside the City at least. The effect is one that contrives to prolong the visit as the interior remains inviting whilst the harsh light from outside, or indeed the growing gloom, looks ever more uninviting. Psychology has its place in pub decor. That extra ounce of resolve is needed to leave a pub like this.

Dickens Inn

St Katherine's Dock

FR DA R ML ME SL SE
Opening Hours: normal
Station: Tower Hill
Buses: 100, D1
Greene King XX Mild, Adnams Bitter, Courage Best Bitter, Wadworth 6X, Courage Directors, Ruddles County

This busy pub which is made of European Redwood has an equally exotic clientele. Large numbers of tourists, with and without cameras from all four points of the globe, locals and those with business in or who have come to enjoy the tranquil setting of the marina. The pub is handy for the Tower of London, Tower Bridge and other riverside attractions.

Hollands

7-9 Exmouth St, Brayford Square

Young's
ML SL
Opening Hours: normal
Station: Shadwell DLR
Buses: 5, 15, 40
Young's Bitter, Young's Special

Hollands is perhaps the best example of what an old East End boozer used to look like. In 1974, the pub was listed and changed its name from the Exmouth Arms to Hollands, in recognition of the five generations of landlords of the same family. The main bar fittings date back to 1843 and the opening of the pub by William Rubin Holland. The cast iron mantelpieces and bar date from this time. Changes were made by John Partridge Holland around 1881 but the pub remains largely unaltered to the present day, with the exception of some rather nasty wallpaper in the dining area, for which the family of Young rather than Holland is to blame. Full of Victorian clutter, the main bar is split into two with a small service hatch in the partition for glass collectors to duck between public and saloon bars. Original snob screens provide a fine opportunity to see how they operated as most examples in other London pubs have been relocated or otherwise incorrectly incorporated into later fittings. A fine selection of mirrors having such inscriptions as 'Lacons Famous Yarmouth Ales' have survived several near misses during the blitz. Hollands may be in the heart of the East End, but it is the undoubted aristocrat of London Pubs.

London Hospital Tavern

176 Whitechapel Road

Allied Domecq
ML ME SL
Opening Hours: 11-11m-f 11-1s 12-3, 7-10.30su
Station: Whitechapel
Buses: 25, 253
Adnams Bitter, Tetley Bitter, Ridleys ESX, Marston's Pedigree + Guest Beers

Large, imposing, tavern style pub on the busy Whitechapel Road, which benefits from its association with the next door London Hospital (that's the one with the helicopter on the roof). The pub is notable as a lively fun place rather than for character, much of which has been 'refurbished' out of existence. Pictures on the ceiling and booth and settle seating impart some atmosphere but the piped music and games machines seem to be pulling in another direction. Across the road from the famous Whitechapel street market, the pub is definitely in the thick of London street life as it has always been. It is a handy place to stop in when exploring that vibrant immigrant quarter between Brick Lane and the Whitechapel road, famous for successive waves of immigrants, right back to the Hugenots in the seventeenth century, each of which has brought dynamism and new prosperity to London's East End.

Lord Rodneys Head

285 Whitechapel Road

Free House
Opening Hours: normal
Station: Whitechapel
Buses: 25, 253
Banks & Taylor Shefford Bitter, Banks & Taylor Shefford Old Dark, Banks & Taylor Shefford Strong + Guest Beers; Cider

Long, narrow and fine real ale pub right on the bustling Whitechapel Road Market. Wooden slat walls are topped by a bizarre wooden slat ceiling with panels of timber running in all directions. The long bar runs down the right of the pub, with a seating area in front. At rear is a bar billiards table. The walls are covered with pictures and old photographs whilst a shelf running at picture rail level is covered with old clocks, seemingly from the mantelpieces of 201 East End homes. A sign on the wall says 'Clocks Always Wanted'. The pub is an ideal port to drop in from the market, rest awhile with a fine beer and watch the fascinating street life that passes perpetually outside. Live music takes place on Thursday and Saturday evenings and the pub must be one of only a few outlets for Australian 'Razorback Wheat Beer' from the Matilda Bay Brewery.

Princess of Prussia

15 Prescott Street

S&N

ML ME SL SE

Opening Hours: 11-11m-f closed s-su

Station: Tower Gateway DLR

Buses: 15, 25, 42, 78, 100, B1, D1, D11

Theakston's Best, Theakston's XB, Courage Directors

The Princess could possibly be described as a games pub. There is a pool room to the rear; on the other side is a pair of darts boards. Two electronic racing machines nest under the stairs which lead up to an extra seating area where the bar billiards table can be found – all of which fits perfectly into the ethos of this pub. The central walk round bar and stillion are highly distinctive, as is the upstairs seating area which covers only half the upper floor space, leaving a high ceiling over the bar itself which, this being the 1990s, the brewery has managed to adorn with books, stone jugs etc. A vast map of Prussia adorns one wall. Very handy for the Tower of London and its attendant attributes and is just far enough off the tourist route to escape the hoards.

Town of Ramsgate

62 Wapping High Street

Bass

G ML ME SL SE

Opening Hours: normal

Station: Wapping

Buses: 100

Worthington Best Bitter, Fuller's London Pride, Draught Bass + Guest Beers

It was at Wapping Old Stairs, next to the pub where the bloodthirsty drunken tyrant Judge Jeffreys tried to flee the country in 1688 after the Glorious Revolution, dressed as a woman. He was recognised by one of the few people to have been in his dock and subsequently lived. The pub, which has a superb view of the river takes its name from Ramsgate fishermen who used to land their catch at Wapping Old Steps. Wapping is a much neglected corner of London but the Rotherhithe end near the Town of Ramsgate is a surprisingly attractive quarter of the capital. Beautiful houses, converted warehouses and a number of exceptional pubs make it an ideal place for a genteel pub crawl.

E2

Conqueror

1 Boundary Street

Free House
SL SE
Opening Hours: 11-2.30m-s 12-2, 7-10.30su
Station: Liverpool Street
Buses: 5, 22a, 26, 35, 43, 47, 48, 67, 78, 149, 243, 505, B1
Fuller's London Pride + Guest Beers

Small mock Tudor pub behind Hawksmoor's famous Shoreditch St Leonard's church, the "When I am Rich" of the Oranges and Lemons nursery rhyme. A two roomed pub with a dark wood panelled and red leather upholstered bench and stool saloon, decorated with prints of old regimental uniforms, while the ceiling is covered with a fine collection of copper pots and kettles. A small side room contains a pool table and darts board. A pub has been on the site since at least 1840 but the current building dates from 1927 when it was rebuilt in typical 'improved' public house style. The pub is, however, much smaller than the 'improvers' liked and so there are probably some other compelling reasons why the pub was rebuilt at all.

Marksman

254 Hackney Road

Free House
SL SE
Opening Hours: normal
Station: Shoreditch
Buses: 26, 48, 55
Courage Best Bitter, Courage Directors, Ruddles County, Morland's Old Speckled Hen

A lively locals pub, handy for the Columbia Road Sunday flower market. The pub caters for the local community rather than for visitors to the market and at the weekends is crowded with East Enders. On Sundays the bar is spread with a wide selection of seafood, cheese and pickles. The pub has been in the Good Beer Guide on many occasions and the beer quality is very good, the Ruddles County is possibly the best you can find. The wood panelled walls are hung with framed local histories, explaining the origins and history of the flower market, nearby Petticoat Lane, Shoreditch and Haggerston and Jack the Ripper. A spiral staircase in the middle of the pub provides unusual access to the landlord's premises upstairs. Darts and pool are played in the rear of the pub.

Pub on the Park

Martello Road, London Fields

Free House
G ML SL
Opening Hours: normal
Station: London Fields BR
London Pride, Ruddles County

A hidden gem close to a station but the station is London Fields BR which only has about three trains a day. The pub is part of that hidden London village of London Fields. Simultaneously part of that East End which produces treasures like Victoria Park and that East End which ignores them. This pub has its own cricket club but also a ground for that old Cockney game of Petanque. Right on London Fields, the park and the pub garden are one. The single room pub is bistroesque with plenty of foliage plus flowers and candles on each table but the gilt mirror advertising Truman, Hanbury & Buxton's Imperial Stout is the dominant feature of the place. The side of the pub is decorated with a mural/sculpture of two men on a ladder hoisting a piano onto the roof. A pleasant reminder that this part of Hackney has developed into a little Montmartre. The Fuller's London Pride is another reminder that this pub is more reminiscent of Fulham than Hackney.

Royal Oak

Columbia Road

G SL SE
Opening Hours: normal 8am-1.30su
Station: Shoreditch
Buses: 5, 22a, 22b, 26, 35, 43, 47, 48, 55, 67, 78, 149, 243, 505
Ruddles Best

Forget the Changing of the Guards and the Crown Jewels, visitors to London should not leave without a visit to the Columbia Road flower market, held every Sunday. A real taste of the East End, with real horticultural bargains to boot. Many plants are several times cheaper than can be bought elsewhere. The only pub actually on Columbia Road is the Royal Oak. The beer garden is given over to a stall on market days. The single island bar forms the focus of this busy pub, the clientele of which consists of market traders, visitors and a section of the local gay community. Quizzes are on Thursdays, Karaoke on Wednesdays and live acts on Sunday evenings. On market days the pub opens at 8 am and offers a cooked breakfast. A very lively pub.

Sebright Arms
31-35 Coate Street

Free House
ML SL
Opening Hours: 11.30-12m-s 12-10.3su
Station: Cambridge Heath BR
Buses: 26, 48, 55
Marston's Pedigree

Thursday nights are Old Time Music Hall nights at the Sebright, and are packed out, and, indeed, the pub is named after the old Hackney music hall from where Marie Lloyd started out to be the superstar of London of her day. The Sebright acts are the stalwarts of Panto and the end of the pier summer seasons, and tend towards the lewd, rude and very, very funny. Also packed out are Sunday lunches. If you do not book you will not be able to get a table and if you do not book early you will be in the overspill room downstairs, which is also used for the numerous functions and private parties the Sebright has got a name for putting on. Until about seven years ago the pub was a semi-derelict strippers' pub but it has been revamped by the current landlord. The recession has put an end to live music five nights a week but Country and Western nights are still held on a Saturday.

Ship & Blue Ball
13 Boundary Street

Free House
ML ME SL SE
Opening Hours: normal
Station: Shoreditch
Buses: 5, 22a, 22b, 26, 35, 43, 47, 48, 78, 149, 243
Boddingtons Bitter

A small one-room pub, recently reopened, with pavement seating in the summer. Plainly furnished, the ambience is provided by the staff and clientele rather than the decor. During the week it caters for office workers, with an appropriate menu; at weekends and Sunday lunchtimes it attracts a gay crew. Sunday's at 2pm there is a live act. When surveyed there was a stripper due but your surveyor unfortunately had too many pubs to visit to ascertain what gender the stripper would be. Tucked behind Shoreditch High Street the pub takes its name from the ensign of a ship of the blue and is a fun visit.

E3

Beehive

104 Empson Street

Free House
G ML SL
Opening Hours: 11.30-11m-f 11.30-5, 7-1s 12-1.30su
Station: Bromley By Bow
Buses: D8
Brains SA, Morland's Old Speckled Hen + Guest Beers

Spic and span back street local in Bromley by Bow, just a few yards from the Bow Creek stretch of the River Lea. A Free House, the pub is divided into a saloon area and a walk through to a public bar with a pool table. The bar is fringed with a collection of key rings – each pub has got its own little eccentricity after all. And speaking of which there is a photograph of Screaming Lord Sutch standing behind the bar. A good real ale house, with two permanently changing guests, the overall impression is one of tidiness. There's not a speck of dust anywhere, but the pub is cosy not clinical. A worthy holder of the 'hidden gem' accolade.

Bow Bells

116 Bow Road

Allied Domecq
ML SL
Opening Hours: normal
Station: Bow Road
Buses: 25, N76, N98
Tetley Bitter, Fuller's London Pride, Ind Coope Burton Ale + Guest Beers; Cider

Fine Victorian boozer with an impressive, though sooty exterior. A popular stopping place for tourist coaches on the 'London: The Sinister Side' tour because of the pub's bizarre ghost. Given to flushing the ladies toilet (it takes all sorts to make a – spectral – world), it is also responsible for mist rising from the floor. The L-shaped pub has a number of surviving Victorian artefacts. A function room is upstairs. The pub serves real cider as well as an unusual range of real ales.

Imperial Crown

50 St Leonards St

Allied Domecq
ML SL SE

Opening Hours: normal
Station: Bromley-by-Bow
Buses: 108, S2
Tetley Bitter, Ind Coope Burton Ale

There cannot be many Irish pubs called the Imperial Crown but it is that sort of pub. To try to describe the decor and atmosphere of the pub would tax the powers of the most eminent wordsmiths. Tucked in between the roaring Blackwall Tunnel approach road and the semi-derelict Jefferson Estate, the atmosphere inside the pub is cheery in direct proportion to the degree to which the view outside is depressing. Over the door it says 'a hundred thousand welcomes', in Gaelic and it is sincerely meant. To describe the interior as eclectic would be an understatement and it is probably better not to try. Down the left of the pub is a dining area and to the right is a pool table. The piped music is a confection of Irish Country favourites. Sunday lunchtimes a roast is available and Saturday nights sees live acts and occasional charity nights.

Widow's Son

75 Devons Road

Allied Domecq
G CP ML SL
Opening Hours: 12-3, 4.30-11m-th 12-11f-s 12-4, 7-30-10.30su
Station: Devons Road
Buses: D8
Tetley Bitter

One of the most famous pubs in the East End, also known as the Bun House. The story goes that c1848, a baker's son went off to sea and asked his mother to bake a hot cross bun for when he came home – he never did. Every year she hung up a bun each Good Friday. As everyone knows a hot cross bun baked on Good Friday never goes off, so each year, around midday on Good Friday, a Royal Navy sailor calls in to hang up a new bun. The bunch of buns hangs over the middle of the pub. The black ones in the middle are over 100 years old. On Good Friday the pub opens at 9am, is packed all day long and they hold a service in the pub. The pub, recently refurbished, is on the outside very much in the alehouse style that was popular at the start of the last century but which did not tend to survive the 'gin palace' refurbishments of the century's end. On the inside are famous mirrors and fittings which are original and priceless. The stone floor in the cellar used to be a skittle ally in which players taller than 4' 8" had a handicap. The pub also has a ghost, locally referred to as Albert, who has rung bells and opened doors. The landlady thinks

Albert is a Jewish ghost but there's only one way to hear the end of that story.

E5

Prince of Wales

Lea Bridge Rd, Clapham

Young's
G CP ML ME
Opening Hours: normal
Station: Clapton BR
Buses: 48, 56
Young's Bitter, Young's Special, Young's Winter Warmer

Large two-bar pub beside the river Lea, where the East London and City Branch of CAMRA was formed in 1974. A rare outpost of Young's in the east of London.

E7

Old Spotted Dog

212 Upton Lane

Inntrepreneur
FR G CP R ML ME SL SE
Opening Hours: 11-3, 5.30-11m-f, 11-3, 7-11s, 12-5, 7-10.30su
Station: Plaistow
Buses: 325
Marston's Pedigree, Ruddles County

A massive split-level pub with numerous drinking areas and two bars, back to back but on different levels. The weatherboard frontage of the pub dominates the bend of the road in Upton Lane. The timber framed lower area with its stone flagstone floor was once an old country alehouse. A massive fireplace, with a spotted dog painted on the chimney piece, dominates and is true to the alehouse tradition of drinking in the landlord's kitchen. The pub was an ordinary farm house before becoming a pub and the ovens in the fireplace date from that time. To the rear is the Dalmatian Bar, with a life-size wooden statue of Henry VIII with two spotted dogs at his feet. Further still to the rear is an extension, forming a conservatory drinking area, opening onto the beer garden, and children are welcome in this area. Above the bar is a restaurant, whilst on the bottom level is a further dining area in a parlour setting. When packed the pub could hold several hundred people.

E8

Dove

24-26 Broadway Market

Free House
ML ME SL SE
Opening Hours: 12-11m-s 12-10.30su
Station: London Fields
Buses: 26, 48, 55, 106, 253, D6
Flowers IPA, Boddingtons Bitter, Morland's Old Speckled Hen + Guest Beers

An oasis surrounded by boozers that are either closed or highly uninviting. The pub specialises in food and the table cloths and candles in bottles give it a bistro feel. The back room is opened in the evening but if you do not want to sit and eat, there are olives on the bar to nibble on. The menu changes everyday; there are always an equal number of vegetarian and meat dishes and a seafood course. The pub also serves a wide range of flavoured vodkas, vintage scotches and speciality beers such as Qwak with its distinctive glass. In fact, all the foreign beers are served in the correct glass and the staff are extra vigilant to make sure that all fancy glasses are returned. They have music on weekend evenings, which, due to some bizarre licensing condition, usually takes the form of duets. Other events include poetry nights and mystic nights with a resident medium and tarot reader.

E11

Birkbeck Tavern

45 Langthorne Rd

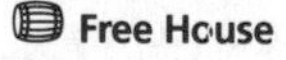

Free House
G
Opening Hours: normal
Station: Leyton
Buses: 69, 97, W16N26
Tetley Bitter, Courage Best Bitter, Draught Bass + Guest Beers

Large locals' pub, home to East London & City CAMRA Branch darts team. Rita's Special is a beer named after the landlord's wife. A really friendly back street local, with no frills but a first rate pint.

Duke of Edinburgh

79 Nightingale Lane

Allied Domecq
G ML ME SL SE
Opening Hours: 12-11m-s 12-10.30su
Station: Snaresbrook Br
Buses: W13, W14
Tetley Bitter, Young's Bitter + Guest Beers

Handsome mock Tudor, 'improved' public house, very much a suburban local. The marquetry in the wood panels, which reach up to picture rail height, is unmistakably late 1920s early 1930s. The local pub game is shove-ha'penny. A board is screwed, ironing board style, to the wall, whilst a second board is also available for those moments of peak demand. The horseshoe shaped pub has a larger limb to the left, leading to a beer garden at the rear, whilst the right hand limb is foreshortened by the kitchens and houses the darts board. Wednesdays are quiz nights and the pub has its own team which visits other pubs, so the standard must be pretty high.

Sir Alfred Hitchcock Hotel

145 Whipps Cross, Leytonstone

Free House
G ML ME SL SE
Opening Hours: normal
Station: Snaresbrook BR
Buses: 230, 257
Flowers IPA, Boddingtons Bitter, Whitbread Castle Eden, Flowers Original, Marston's Pedigree + Guest Beers

Established in 1980, the hotel bar looks much older. Taking its name from the most famous film director ever, the walls are decorated with prints of Hitch and some of his stars, as the great man was born on Leytonstone High Street. Other decorations include European street signs. There is a real fire in the grate and on the side of the chimney is a bellows for getting the fires going. Everything is bare wood, brick or plain plaster. The feel is very much that of an old style coaching inn. The usual collection of yards of ale, Toby jugs and case clocks is as it should be, the lobster pot requires a bit of additional explanation, however. The pub is exceptionally good value for money, most beers being a good sixty pence cheaper than in most other pubs. If only all hotels had bars like the Sir Alfred.

E13

Black Lion

59-61 High Street, Plaistow

Inntrepreneur

G CP ML ME SL SE

Opening Hours: 11-3, 5-11m-th 11-11f-s 12-10.30su

Station: Plaistow

Buses: 241, 262, 325, 473

Courage Best Bitter, Courage Directors + Guest Beers

Plaistow may no longer be in the countryside but the Black Lion still thinks it is. Around 450 years old many parts of the building are original. The frontage was rebuilt in 1875 but to the rear, the rambling nature of the pub is still visible. Many rooms are on different levels but still on the same storey. A secret staircase leads from a former bedroom to another house, once a hiding place for smugglers and highwaymen. Plaistow was once a village on the Thames' marshes, where watermen could smuggle in relative safety amongst the complex streams. The cellars under the pub are larger than may have been expected, a common clue to an old inn's smuggling past. Famous guests include the Earl of Essex (beheaded by Elizabeth I), the preacher John Wesley and prison reformer Elizabeth Fry. The stables in the courtyard are home to the West Ham Boys and Amateur Boxing Club, alumni of which include Terry Spinks, the flyweight, who was the first Briton to win an Olympic boxing gold in 1956. Other famous boxers to have trained there include George Walker and Michael Watson, just prior to the bout which tragically crippled him.

Lord Stanley

15 St Mary's Road

Shepherd Neame

G ML SL

Opening Hours: 11-11m-s 12-3, 7-10.30su

Station: Plaistow

Buses: 69, 241, 262, 473

Shepherd Neame Masterbrew, Shepherd Neame Best

A large suburban pub not far from West Ham football ground. The two bar pub is very much in the 1930s 'improved' style in the interior, with large rooms and plenty of seating space. The original decor would have been quite art deco and vestiges remain, though subsequent refurbishments have lost sight of the original style. A stage in the corner of the lounge is used for occasional discos but booze cruises have killed off the regular Friday and Saturday night entertainment. The public bar contains pool tables and the open plan bar offers a clear view of both drinking areas. The walls are wood panelled in an art deco style. The pub is busiest on match days when West Ham are at home.

E14

Blacksmiths Arms
25 West Ferry Road

Inntrepreneur
ML ME SL SE
Opening Hours: normal
Station: South Quay DLR
Buses: D7, D8, D9, N8
Webster's Yorkshire Bitter, John Smith's Bitter

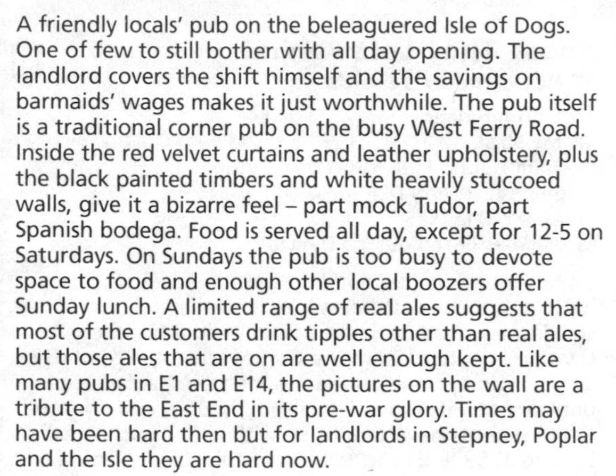

A friendly locals' pub on the beleaguered Isle of Dogs. One of few to still bother with all day opening. The landlord covers the shift himself and the savings on barmaids' wages makes it just worthwhile. The pub itself is a traditional corner pub on the busy West Ferry Road. Inside the red velvet curtains and leather upholstery, plus the black painted timbers and white heavily stuccoed walls, give it a bizarre feel – part mock Tudor, part Spanish bodega. Food is served all day, except for 12-5 on Saturdays. On Sundays the pub is too busy to devote space to food and enough other local boozers offer Sunday lunch. A limited range of real ales suggests that most of the customers drink tipples other than real ales, but those ales that are on are well enough kept. Like many pubs in E1 and E14, the pictures on the wall are a tribute to the East End in its pre-war glory. Times may have been hard then but for landlords in Stepney, Poplar and the Isle they are hard now.

Grapes

76 Narrow Street

Allied Domecq
G R ML ME SL SE
Opening Hours: 12-3, 5.30-11m-f 7-11s 12-3, 7-10.30su
Station: West Ferry DLR
Buses: D1, D11, X15
Tetley Bitter, Friary Meux Best Bitter, Ind Coope Burton Ale + Guest Beers

This long narrow boozer, with its superb prospect of the river, has a famous seafood restaurant upstairs, which has a well deserved reputation. All the fish served is landed at either Hull or Grimsby the same morning. The pub dates back to at least 1583, but a fire demolished the row around 1718-20 and the present building dates from 1720. The pub is most famous for its Dickensian connections. As a young boy Dickens was placed on a table in the pub and urged to sing for the assembled company by his Godfather who used to live nearby. The pub was refurbished at the end of 1994 and a new landlady took over in 1995, committed to keeping this famous house very much on an even keel. Trade has doubtless suffered by the closure of the western approach to Narrow Street as a result of the Limehouse tunnel construction, and in the landlady's own words the pub is 'London's best kept secret – find us if you can!' It's certainly worth persevering to find this superb pub, not just for the beer and the view either. According to the *Independent* newspaper, their hand cut chips are the best in London.

House They Left Behind
27 Ropemaker's Fields

Inntrepreneur
ML ME SL SE
Opening Hours: 11-3, 5.30-11m-s 12-3su
Station: West Ferry DLR
Buses: D1, D11, X15
Ruddles Best, Courage Directors

Do not mention liver and bacon to the landlady. She hates it, but the customers love it, so she ends up cooking a fair bit. It is also popular with Max, the German Shepherd from the Grapes across the road. The long, single bar pub takes its name from the fact that until recently it stood all by itself, though recent yuppie developments have caught up with it. The pub dates back to 1759 and used to be called the Black Horse and was next door to the old Taylor Walker brewery, which was taken over by Ind Coope in 1960. The whole area was flattened but as the pub was listed it was left standing. The pub's hours lengthen in the summer, when it is possible to play boules out front.

E17

College Arms
807 Forest Road, Walthamstow

Greenalls
ML ME SL SE
Opening Hours: normal

Station: Blackhorse Road
Buses: 123
Boddingtons Bitter, Courage Best Bitter + Guest Beers

A most interesting ex-Wetherspoon pub. It was originally a wine bar, then a Wetherspoon and is now part of the Greenalls group. It has a large lively bar with a separate eating and non-smoking area. There is lots to hold the interest on the walls, with a heavy sporting theme. Once the walls have been digested the two televisions showing the MTV channel will hold the attention. With a changing range of at least five guests in addition to the regular beers, it has probably the largest range of beer in the area, all in superb condition. Well worth a visit or three. The pub is just after the town hall coming from the Blackhorse Road tube and is located beside Waltham Forest College. The bus stop is just outside the pub.

Flowerpot

128 Wood Street

Bass
SL SE
Opening Hours: 11-11m-s 12-4, 7-10.30su
Station: Wood Street BR
Draught Bass

The mirror on the wall, advertising *Wenlock: Famous Ales and Stout*, is a reassuring sign of continuity in this traditional London boozer. At one time the pub was clearly divided into several rooms but has been a one bar pub now for quite some time. The fact that the only real ale is Bass has not stopped them from being frequent Good Beer Guide entrants. Indeed there is a school of thought that says the fewer the beers the better. Certainly with an ale like Bass, which needs a fair time in the cellar if it is not to be too green, it benefits from careful tending by cellar staff who know the beer intimately. The pub regularly turns over a dozen 18s of Bass a week so they are clearly doing something right. Decked out in traditional warming colours, the pub has recently undergone a refurbishment and may now be serving more extensive food than was previously possible. They also sell White Shield.

Lord Brooke

47 Shernhall Street, Walthamstow

Bass
FR G DA ML SL
Opening Hours: normal
Station: Wood Street BR

Buses: W12, W16
Worthington Best Bitter + Guest Beers

Walthamstow in old English means 'the Welcoming Place' and the Lord Brooke, as the original manor house, exudes a warm welcome. Interesting architecturally, it has three separate areas; a lounge, bar and games room which houses numerous trophies won by the young darts team. Saturday nights are live music nights and there are quizzes throughout the week, when the landlord delights in giving beer away. There is a strong local community feeling, putting all at ease, as absolutely everyone is welcome. The Lord Brooke is reached from Walthamstow Central, down St Mary Road and Church Lane (10-15 min walk) and the pub is on the corner of Valentine Road and Shernall St.

Ilford – IG1

Prince of Wales
63 Green Lane, Ilford

Allied Domecq
G CP ML SL
Opening Hours: 11-3, 5.30-11m-th 11-11f-s 12-3, 7-10.30su
Station: Seven Kings
Buses: 128, 129, 145
Tetley Bitter, Ind Coope Burton Ale

An excellent little pub on the main road (A1083) about three quarters of a mile east of Ilford town centre. Unlike most pubs owned by national brewers, this one has been more or less left alone. The main entrance leads to a snug bar with limited seating. Left takes you into a fairly basic public bar with darts board and to the right, a cosy saloon bar with a small serving area. Usually busy, it has a loyal local crowd, though it is popular with office workers at lunchtimes. The food is basic but superb value. There is also a split level beer garden, which is a small but pleasant place to spend a summer lunchtime. A good turnover of real ale ensures that this pub is frequently in the Good Beer Guide.

Rose & Crown

Ilford Hill, Ilford

Allied Domecq
G ML SL
Opening Hours: normal
Station: Ilford BR
Buses: B6, 128, 169, 551

Tetley Bitter + Guest Beers

Very pleasant pub situated only a few minutes from Ilford town centre. Wood panelling throughout, a variety of drinking areas surround a horseshoe shaped bar. Popular with office workers at lunchtimes and a friendly local crowd in the evenings, which is swelled on Thursday's quiz nights to give a real community atmosphere. A number of historic wine certificates adorn the walls although nowadays the pub is better known for having a variety of well kept beers, and is a regular entry in the Good Beer Guide. Normally at least four guest ales are on, taken from the Carlsberg-Tetley 'Tapster's Choice list.

Woodford Green – IG8

Cricketers

299-301 High Road, Woodford Green

McMullen
CP ML SL
Opening Hours: 11-3, 5.30-11m-f 11-11s 12-10.30su
Station: South Woodford
Buses: 179, W13
McMullen's AK, Draught Bass, McMullen's Country, McMullen Stronghart

Excellent two-bar pub just south of Woodford Green. A good example of a traditional split house with contrasting bars, basic public bar with darts etc and a comfortable saloon. Locals predominate in both areas, although the friendly crowd is very welcoming to visitors, especially those who display a fondness for McMullen's beers. Occasional food theme evenings are held, but at other times food is just available at lunchtimes.

Travellers Friend

496-498 High Road, Woodford Green

Grosvenor Inns
G CP DA ML SL
Opening Hours: 11-11m-s 12-3, 7-10.30su
Station: Woodford
Buses: 20, 179, W13
Ridleys IPA, Courage Best Bitter, Courage Directors + Guest Beers

Small detached pub situated very close to Woodford Green and a short distance from Epping Forest. Once inside this relatively unspoilt Victorian pub, conversation rules. Admire the wood panelled walls and snob screens;

and savour the atmosphere of the genuine English pub. The beer quality is excellent and the pub has been in the Good Beer Guide for many years - Ridley's IPA (which is rare for the area) is permanent but guest beers do make appearances. There is no public bar but the pub has various drinking areas set around a U-shaped bar. Parking is difficult so park in adjacent side roads, or better still walk from Woodford tube. It's downhill on the way back!

Barking – IG11

Britannia

1 Church Road, Barking

Young's

G ML ME SL

Opening Hours: 11-3, 5-11m-f 11-11s 12-3, 7-10.30su

Station: Barking

Buses: 179, 369

Young's Bitter, Young's Special, Young's Winter Warmer

Young's most eastern tied pub. Originally constructed in the mid-nineteenth century, but redeveloped in 1889 by a famous Victorian architect, Frederick Ashton. A comfortable saloon bar and a traditional style public bar provide a good contrast. One of the best features are the caryatids adorning the exterior; a reminder of Barking's days as an important Thames-side fishing port. Darts and other pub games are played in the public bar which is mainly frequented by a loyal local crowd. The beer quality means that it is a regular Good Beer Guide entry.

Romford – RM1

Golden Lion

2 High Street, Romford

S&N

G ML ME SL SE

Opening Hours: normal

Station: Romford BR

Buses: 174, 175, 87

John Smith's Bitter, Theakston's Best, Theakston's XB, Courage Directors, Theakston's OP + Guest Beers

A classic, rambling old pub which was extensively refurbished in 1995 but not spoilt. Located on the crossroads of Romford's busy marketplace and thus easy to find, the pub is often busy. Food is available at most times and is good value and varied. Plenty of seating in various areas throughout the pub, some a bit isolated from the main bar. An enterprising range of beers from small independent brewers is always available, some of which are rare for the area, and indeed for London generally. A blackboard informs drinkers of the beers that are expected in the forthcoming weeks.

Hornchurch – RM11

Pit Bar

2

Queen's Theatre, Hornchurch

Free House

ML SL

Opening Hours: 12-2.30, 6-11m-f 11-2.30, 6-11s 12-3, 7-10.30su

Station: Hornchurch

Buses: 246, 252, 256, 370, 373

Greene King IPA, Rayment's Special Bitter + Guest Beers

A bar situated on the lower ground floor of a popular and well established theatre, close to Hornchurch town centre, although the underground station is quite a walk. Not surprisingly the walls are covered with theatrical memorabilia – seating is available on two levels and the bar is open to the public irrespective of whether or not they are going to see a performance. Occasional live music in the bar is an attraction, though it can get fairly busy at weekends. The regular Greene King beers are augmented by up to five guests, some of which are served on gravity and all of which tend to come from smaller regionals and independent breweries.

NW1

Dingwalls

Camden Lock, Camden

Regent Inns
G ML SL
Opening Hours: normal
Station: Camden Town
Buses: 24, 31, 168, N5, N31, N93
Brakspear Bitter, Adnams Bitter, Theakston's Best, Wadworth 6X, Young's Special, Greene King Abbot

Famous former music venue and pub right in the centre of Camden Lock market and with a fine view of the lock itself. A split level pub under a large vaulted roof, upstairs an extra drinking area extends over half the lower level, whilst downstairs is a further room used for events. Sadly the Sunday lunchtime Jazz is now a thing of the past but on Friday and Saturday nights there is a comedy club. Dingwalls is probably the only pub in Britain where you can buy silk sunflowers: small, medium, or large – but this *is* Camden.

Engine Room

79 Chalk Farm Road, Chalk Farm

Free House
ML ME SL SE Opening Hours: 12-11m-su
Station: Chalk Farm
Buses: 24, 31, 168, N5, N31, N93
Guest Beers

The Engine Room could only be in Camden, for Camden is London's alternative quarter. The pub is a shrine to pop/trash culture. Acid head painted windows on the outside and a collage of film and music posters on the inside. Everything from Rocky Horror to the Marx Brothers is covered, with the Ramones, Batman, Bogey, Hendrix and the Munsters taken in on route. A Free House that owes no loyalty to any brewery, the pub has a varying range of up to seven guest beers, all of which are constantly changing. The pub has a quiz on Tuesday nights and, this being Camden, it is a pop quiz. On Wednesday nights the pub replaces its regular piped music with a DJ.

Enterprise

2 Chalk Farm Road, Camden

Inntrepreneur

ML ME SL SE
Opening Hours: normal
Station: Chalk Farm
Buses: 24, 31, 168, N5, N31, N93
Courage Best Bitter, Courage Directors, Morland's Old Speckled Hen

A bar, a bistro and a music venue, this lively pub has walls covered in posters with a mixture of church pew seating and stools. The Enterprise is dominated by the U-shaped bar in the centre from which staff dispense beer and bonhomie in roughly equal measure. The back wall is a bookshelf covered with those long out of print volumes that look like they would reward a quick look. For once a bookshelf does not look out of place in a pub, for if there is a theme to this pub (though the word theme is a little strong) it is Samuel Beckett. His craggy face stares impassively from a number of pictures and other Irish wordsmiths from Jonathan Swift to Denis Kavanagh back him up. Yet more Irish writers' faces are painted on the windows. The pub has an upstairs function room and occasional live music.

Feathers

Linhope St, Marylebone

Free House
ML SL FR
Opening Hours: normal
Station: Marylebone
Buses: 2, 13, 30, 74, 82, 113, 139, 159, 274
Wethereds, Flowers Original

A tiny pub with a loyal enough local following for size not to matter. Small is beautiful, or so the saying goes, and in the case of the Feathers it is certainly true. The small bar protrudes into one quarter of the twenty-foot square room. Take away the gentlemen's toilet, the chimney piece, and the stairs up to the ladies' on the first floor and the standing room in the pub is small enough indeed. Even the television in the corner is tiny. However, when the early evening office trade drifts away the locals wander in, so what the pub lacks in size, it makes up for in steady turnover. The windows are almost obscured from outside by the dense foliage descending from hanging baskets out front. From the street, stepping into the pub is like ducking under an arbour. Tucked away around the back of Marylebone station, the pub is both a hidden gem and yet convenient for mainstream transport.

Head of Steam

Euston Station

Free House

ML ME SL

Opening Hours: 11-11m-s, 12-3, 7-10.30su

Station: Euston

Buses: 10, 18, 30, 68, 73, 77a, 91, 168, 253, 188

Shepherd Neame Masterbrew, Draught Bass, Hop Back Summer Lightning, Biddenden Cider

This pub is eligible for the hidden gem accolade even though it is right on the forecourt of the busy London mainline Euston Station. The split level pub with a raised no-smoking area is stiff with memorabilia from the days when Britain's rolling stock was not a laughing stock. Just behind an old BR style food counter is a souvenir shop where mugs, sweatshirts and model trains can be purchased. This is also a first class (no pun intended) real ale pub, with up to six guest ales, including a real cider, and all these from highly respected micros and regionals. A snug in one alcove offers an intimate corner, whilst the bare floored and dark wood bar leads up to the carpeted raised area with a view of the Euston Road. Thousands of people pass daily and do not even know the pub is there. Considering several beers are 99p on Sunday lunchtimes one can only say, more fool them.

Perseverance

Shroton St

Bass

ML ME SL

Opening Hours: normal

Station: Marylebone

Buses: 139

Highgate Dark, Fuller's London Pride, Draught Bass

Friendly one-room pub, three minutes walk from Marylebone station. The wooden frontage presents a nautical air to the street and within, all surfaces are faced in wood, with a pale green decor on floor and ceiling; burgundy elsewhere. Recently refurbished with a new food and wine bar to the rear, this is a traditional local for this part of London, not quite residential area, but not quite in office-land either. The publican has been here for 21 years – and a pub comes with no higher recommendation than that. Decor wise it is spic-and-span, comfortable, without resorting to untidy posters, gimmicks etc.. An after work watering hole for a band of loyal regulars who like good beer. There is a function room upstairs, which is frequently used. The Perseverance is the sort of pub that is quite unpretentious, but is only noticed when it is has gone – as so many have.

Queens

49 Regents Park Rd

Young's

ML ME

Opening Hours: 11-3, 5-11m-f 11-11s, 12-10 su

Station: Chalk Farm

Buses: 274, C2

Young's Bitter, Young's Special

Luscious is one word that springs to mind when first entering the Queens. The green-based William Morris-inspired wallpaper (and blue-based William Morris-inspired carpet) and soft light filtered through stained glass windows accentuate the narrowness of the pub but the clever use of panelled mirrors covering the end wall prevents the pub from being pokey or claustrophobic. Just off Primrose Hill, the pub has a curved frontage facing the park and inside this provides a little alcove, raised three steps above the rest of the pub. A collection of photos of actors and actresses adorns the walls, most well known but one or two tax the brain. Upstairs is the Balcony Bar, a function room with an attractive view, so named for its small balcony.

Quinn's

65 Kentish Town Rd

Free House

ML ME SL SE

Opening Hours: 11-11m-th 11-1am f-s 12-10.30su

Station: Camden Town

Buses: 46, 134, 135, 214, C2, N1, N2, N93

Greene King IPA, Rayment's Special Bitter, Marston's Pedigree, Greene King Abbot

The lettering on the doors still says The Dutch Inn, but five years on they're still waiting for the chap to come over from Dublin to change the glass. The beautifully painted windows, depicting scenes of Edwardian genteel relaxation, were also shipped in. Quinn's is a fine conversion to an Irish pub, and an example of how it should be done to all those brewers who think bogus Irish is what the customer wants. Run by, no prizes for guessing, the Quinn family, it is, therefore, an authentic Irish pub. Irish style beer fonts alternate with real ale handpumps and tall fountains for draught foreign beers (there is an impressive range of imported foreign beers too, including Helles, Bocks and wheat beers). There is also a more than serviceable range of Irish whiskies on offer. The piped music varies greatly, it usually has a Gaelic influence to it and the back bar is also very much in the Irish style but if you want to know what that is you will have to visit Quinn's.

NW3

Duke of Hamilton

23-5 New End

Free House

G SL

Opening Hours: normal

Station: Hampstead

Buses: 268, N5

Fuller's London Pride, Fuller's ESB + Guest Beers

A friendly single-room pub, with the focus very much on fine ales, just of busy Heath Street. An attractive bar in an art nouveau style faces a bright frontage of spun glass windows. To the front is a seating area, raised some six feet above the street, giving drinkers a lofty view of passing life. Plenty of sunshine comes through the windows, giving the pub a lazy, balmy feel during the day. A first rate retreat for those who want to forget Hampstead for a few minutes.

Flask

Flask Walk Hampstead

Young's

DA ML ME SL SE

Opening Hours: normal

Station: Hampstead

Buses: 46, 268, N5

Young's Bitter, Young's Special, Young's Winter Warmer

The Flask and the Holly Bush are probably Hampstead's most famous pubs and certainly both are worth a visit. The Flask is divided into four areas. The public bar is a small corner separated from the rest of the pub by a panel and glass screen which contains five painted panels from the 1880s. The public and saloon bars date back to 1873 whilst the rear of the pub was refurbished in 1990, opening up a conservatory dining area. The pub dates back to the days when Hampstead was a spa (early eighteenth century) and spa waters were bottled at the Lower Flask Tavern. At the time Hampstead was quite a seedy place and Richardson in 'Clarissa Harlowe' described nearby Heath Street as a 'place where second rate characters are to be found, occasionally in a swinish condition'. The area started to go upmarket around 1746 and the respectability of the Flask rose along with the area, to become the highly respectable, fine alehouse it is today.

Freemasons

Downshire Hill, Hampstead

Bass
G ML ME SL SE
Opening Hours: normal
Station: Hampstead Heath BR
Buses: 46, 268, N5
Adnams Bitter, Hancocks HB, Fuller's London Pride, Draught Bass

Big Regency-style pub, with imposing whitewashed frontage set back from exclusive Downshire Hill. The interior has a 1930s look if anything. The rear lounge with its clipped-cornered chairs and pastel shades would be an appropriate location for a Poirot denouncement. The bare wood panels rise singly from skirting to picture rail and are a further '30s touch, which lends the pub an atmosphere of a country hotel. To the right is a public bar with bare floor, pool table and dart board, quite different in character from the lounge. At the rear of the pub is a massive garden with a central well, fountain, pergola and patio.

Holly Bush

Holly Mount Hampstead

Nicholsons
ML SL
Opening Hours: 12-3, 5-11m-f 12-4, 6-11s 12-3, 7-10.30su
Station: Hampstead
Buses: 268, N5
Benskins Best Bitter, Tetley Bitter, Ind Coope Burton Ale + Guest Beers

Hampstead's other famous pub is largely unspoilt and its three rooms are regularly full in the evenings with Hampstead locals, the occasional celebrity and visitors wishing to soak up the much loved ambience. Decorated throughout in various shades of brown, the aura is of solid permanence tempered by hedonism. In the room to the left of the bar is a real fire, whilst the pub is illuminated with authentic Victorian gas lamps, that flicker and dim occasionally as the gas pressure fluctuates. They tend to make the pub a trifle warm even on a winter evening but cast an unmistakable light that adds to the pub's essential cosiness. Addicts of 'cosy' can try to grab the snug but are advised to do so early. Once taken, it stays taken and is jealously guarded. The site of the pub was originally owned by the painter George Romney and was the stables of the adjacent house and studio he purchased in 1796. On his death in 1802 the stables were leased to a victualler who converted them into the pub that stands today.

Magdala
South Hill Park Hampstead

Bass
Opening Hours: 11-11m-s 12-3, 7-10.30su
Station: Hampstead Heath BR
Buses: 24, 168, N93
Worthington Best Bitter, Draught Bass

A notorious, rather than a famous pub with bullet holes still visible on the front of the pub (helpfully indicated by a plaque). These were made by the shots that ended the life of David Blakely, the errant lover of Ruth Ellis, who shot him in 1954 and so earned her place in history by being the last woman to be hanged in Britain. A photo of her, facsimiles of her last letter from prison, notice of execution and death certificate hold pride of place on the pub walls. The rest of the saloon bar walls are covered with pictures of famous British stars of stage and screen (plus Bette Davis). The choice seems fairly eccentric, Sir John Gielgud shares space with Harry H Corbett! Above are paintings of playwrights: Shaw, Wilde, Coward, Lawrence, to name but a few. The L-shaped public bar is larger than the saloon but is nowhere as interesting or intimate. Right next to Hampstead Heath BR, the pub is a very popular local.

Spaniards
Spaniards Road Hampstead

G CP ML ME SL
Opening Hours: normal
Station: Hampstead
Buses: 210
Hancocks HB, Fuller's London Pride, Adnams Extra, Draught Bass + Guest Beers

The Spaniards is probably the most historic pub in London. It was built in 1585 as a residence for the Spanish Ambassador but takes its name not from this connection but from its first landlords, a pair of Spanish brothers. Legend says they fought a duel over a woman, who then deserted them both soon after. Needless to say a pub this famous was visited by Dickens, who used the rose garden as the location of Mrs Bardell's taking of tea, before her arrest in the breach of promise case against Pickwick. Other literary figures who frequented the Spaniards included Goldsmith, Byron, Lamb and the painter Sir Joshua Reynolds. Dick Turpin was also a customer and used the pub as a hideout and base from which to prey upon travellers across Hampstead Heath. The pub is ideal for visiting the Heath, Kenwood and the catacombs of Highgate Cemetery, London's most famous burial ground.

Washington

Englands Lane, Belsize Park

Allied Domecq

ML SL SE

Opening Hours: 10-11m-s 12-10.30su

Station: Belsize Park

Buses: C11, C12

Tetley Bitter, Young's Bitter, Marston's Pedigree, Ind Coope Burton Ale

A magnificent gin palace of a pub, with original features in spades. Originally the Washington Hotel, it was, like so many early Victorian pubs, once divided into many more bars. Half of one dividing partition remains in situ, to form a small public bar complete with dart board. The pub has a wide collection of mirrors dating from several periods; those over the bar which match the cut lights above the doors are the oldest. There are some particularly fine painted mirrors in a belle epoch style set into the walls around the small raised seating area in the midst of which is a curiously sunken fire, left at the original floor level. The ceiling is covered in original lyncrysta or anaglypta mouldings and the etched glass in the doors is also original, as is the glaze tiling in what was once the hotel entrance. On Saturday nights the pub hosts a comedy club in its upstairs room, whilst the pub opens an hour earlier than most, at 10am, to serve exceptionally large breakfasts.

NW4

Greyhound

Church End, Hendon

Richardson Inns

G CP DA ML ME SL SE

Opening Hours: normal

Station: Hendon Central

Buses: 113, 143, 183, 240, 326

Brakspear Bitter, Flowers IPA, Fuller's London Pride, Hook Norton Old Hooky, Greene King Abbot + Guest Beers

Popular with students from nearby Middlesex University Business School this site was first mentioned as an inn in 1655, the current building dates from 1896. Refurbished in 1995, this music-free, single bar pub serves three distinct areas, each decorated in a different period style.

The 'upper' area, known as 'Happy's Bar', features a large drop-down television screen which is used mainly for sports events. Monday is quiz night and there is an 'open-the-box' style raffle on Sunday lunchtimes. Adjacent is the church farm house museum, dating from the reign of Charles II, which contains the London Borough of Barnet Collection (free admission). Also adjacent is the picturesque St Mary's Church which has featured in several television programmes. The RAF museum at Hendon is a fifteen minute walk away.

Hungry Horse

29 Station Rd, Hendon

Magic Pub Co.
G CP DA ML ME SL SE
Opening Hours: normal
Station: Hendon BR
Buses: 83, 183
Boddingtons Bitter, Theakston's Best, Courage Best Bitter, Draught Bass, Newcastle Exhibition + Guest Beers

A welcoming and comfortable two-bar pub. The rear bar caters mostly for diners. Typical Magic Pub Co decor, ie red wall lamps and fisherman's keep nets abound. The 1960s background music is just that – in the background. Sports equipment adorns the walls together with a large number of sporting prints and photographs. See how many different sports you can count as you enjoy your pint, or try to identify the stars as yesterday in the photos. Very good value for money meals with frequent special offers at off-peak times. There is an outside floodlit drinking area where you can listen to the constant roar of the traffic on the M1 which runs through the cutting adjacent to the pub. All in all a definite improvement to choice and value in the area.

White Bear

56 The Burrows, Hendon

Allied Domecq
G DA ML ME SL SE
Opening Hours: normal
Station: Hendon Central
Buses: 113, 143, 183, 186, 326
Greene King IPA, Tetley Bitter, Ind Coope Burton Ale, Young's Special

A big, 1930s roadhouse style pub in a residential area, containing a comfortable, single bar with lively music 'for all ages', ie rock and roll, with Trad Jazz at the weekends. Separate conservatory.

NW5

Pineapple

51 Leverton St

Free House

CP

Opening Hours: 12.30-11m-f 11-11s 12-10.30su

Station: Kentish Town

Buses: 134, 135, N1, N2

Benskins Best Bitter, Brakspear Bitter, Marston's Pedigree

Small but well appointed mid-Victorian local pub. Facing the door is the bar counter, the back of which contains beautiful mirrors and well illuminated adverts for whiskies, brandies and wines. The pub itself is U-shaped with seating areas down each side. A small room for darts down one side is balanced by the toilets on the other. The pub enjoys a near but not exact symmetry, with a fireplace underneath large mirrors advertising Bass & Co Pale Ale on either side, a gas fake-coal fire burns in each grate. Dark red velvet drapes and dark pink walls give the pub a very cosy atmosphere. Definitely worthy of the hidden gem accolade.

NW6

Arkwright's Wheel

283-285 West End Lane, West Hampstead

Allied Domecq

G ML SL

Opening Hours: 12-11m-s

Station: West Hampstead

Buses: 28, 159, C11

Tetley Bitter, Young's Bitter, Wadworth 6X, Ind Coope Burton Ale

The first in Allied Domecq's Arkwright's Wheel chain of alehouses. Converted from a Chinese restaurant to a single bar in the bare floorboard genre. Large front doors open up in summer, with alcoves and snugs situated to the rear.

NW7

Railway Tavern

129 Hale Lane

S&N

FR G CP DA ML SL
Opening Hours: normal
Station: Edgware
Buses: 221, 240, 292, 305
Theakston's Best, Theakston's XB

A friendly single bar in an otherwise beer desert, it was formerly a Mitchell and Aldous house, later coming under the control of Trumans, and now part of S&N. The pub was converted from what was once two cottages. The steel pole rising through the bar is the only remnant of the dividing wall between them. The rear conservatory welcomes children, whilst the background music stays just that, leaving drinkers free to concentrate on their darts. However, this lively and popular locals' pub, can be noisy on occasions, for example on the Tuesday quiz nights. Other features include a small, pleasant garden with facilities for children. All in all this pub has everything one needs for an enjoyable visit.

NW8

Crockers

22 Aberdeen Place, Maida Vale
Regent Inns
ML ME SL SE
Opening Hours: normal
Station: Maida Vale
Buses: 16, 16a, 98, 139, N16, N99, N139
Brakspear Bitter, Adnams Bitter, Young's Bitter, Hancocks HB, Theakston's Best, Draught Bass, Shepherd Neame Spitfire, Gales HSB + Guest Beers

A symphony in marble, Crockers was built towards the end of the last century, by a property speculator, named Crocker, who has taken a gamble on the siting of the terminus of what was to be the Great Central railway. For some strange reason he thought it a certainty that the railway was going to end between Maida Vale and St John's Wood, and so he built a magnificent pub, with carved mahogany fittings, broad hunting lodge style fireplaces and over 50 different types of marble. Soon after this railway hotel was completed it was announced that the Great Central Railway was going to terminate at Marylebone. Crocker threw himself out of a window and the pub became universally known as Crocker's folly. There are three separate bar areas and food is served in the large drawing room all day. A wide range of real ales is always available. This is one of the finest pubs in Britain.

Star

38, St Johns Wood Terrace

Bass

ML ME SL SE

Opening Hours: normal

Station: St Johns Wood

Worthington Best Bitter, Draught Bass

A traditional street-corner locals' bar, a short walk from St John's Wood station. A hidden gem for a visit to Lords. Busy at lunchtimes.

N1

Albion

10 Thornhill Rd, Barnsbury

S&N

G DA ML ME SL SE

Opening Hours: normal

Station: Caledonian Rd BR

Buses: 4, 19, 30, 43, 279, N19, N92

Brakspear Bitter, John Smith's Bitter, Theakston's Best, Theakston's XB

Very large pub with a country theme. One central bar serves several rooms, each with a distinct feel to it. The main bar area is covered in horse brasses and horse collar yokes and carriage lamps and has the feel of a converted tack room. In front of French windows that open onto a large garden, there is a lounge area with settees and armchair seating, a more brightly lit ambience; beyond is a dining area with a country kitchen feel and more equine equipment. A second occasional bar is hidden behind pull-down glass shutters. An unexpected find for the back streets of Islington.

Crown

Cloudsley Square

Fuller's

G ML

Opening Hours: normal

Station: Angel

Buses: 4, 19, 30, 38, 43, X43, 56, 73, 171a, 279

Fuller's Chiswick Bitter, Fuller's London Pride, Fuller's IPA, Fuller's ESB

A hugely impressive interior in a modest building, hidden away in a quiet quarter of Islington. An oblong island bar stands in the centre of the pub. Genuine snob screens at front and glass partitions at rear allow even untrained eyes a good guess at visualising where the original divisions of the pub into smaller snugs would have been. The door to what would have been the publican's office is still in place. The original anaglypta ceiling tiles would at the time have been regarded as quite inferior but the value of them today is an example of how the system worked. There is plenty of original glasswork. An interesting enamelled, old fashioned radiator makes an original feature. The rest of the pub is done in tasteful green with red velvet upholstery. A more modern room at rear acts as a dining area for lunchtime meals. Bar billiards is played in the corner of the pub, which is tucked just off Liverpool Road, five minutes walk from Angel Tube. The beer is moderately priced by comparison with many other local pubs and is very well kept.

Eagle

Shepherdess Walk, Near City Road

Bass
ML ME SL SE
Opening Hours: normal
Station: Old Street
Buses: 43
Wells Eagle, Draught Bass + Guest Beers

"Half-a-pound of tuppeny rice, Half a pound of treacle. That's the way the money goes, Pop goes the weasel." The Eagle Tavern was London's mid-Victorian upper class pub par excellence. Its famous pleasure gardens were a major attraction and by today's standards would be on a par with any major tourist site. The licence was bought by the Salvation Army but to their dismay they were prevented from completely destroying the site and in one of those delicious ironies beloved of history, were forced to maintain a licensed premises on the site. The Eagle is thus the only pub to have been run by a temperance organisation. The building as it stands today is the one the Sally Anny left, and is a fraction of the size of the great Eagle Tavern. A small bare-floored public bar with pool table and pin table is separated by frosted glass doors from a warm and cosy saloon, dominated by two central pillars. A good real ale pub with well kept beer, and guests chosen from Bass's regularly changing approved list.

George & Vulture

63 Pitfield St, Hoxton

Fuller's
ML SL

Opening Hours: normal
Station: Old Street
Buses: 5, 243, 505
Fuller's London Pride, Fuller's ESB

From the outside, the George and Vulture is a huge pile of a pub. In the nineteenth century, Hoxton was a notorious neighbourhood, so the size of the pub illustrates the importance of the pub to the community as well as the potential money to be made from it, even in a poor area like Victorian Hoxton. The residents of Pitfield Street are knowledgeable about beer as the Pitfield Brewery was once, and will be again, at the Old Street end of the road. One of London's premier beer shops and home brewing suppliers is also located there. The pub is nominally divided into public and a saloon by a glass proscenium style partition so it is quite possible to see from one to the other. The public bar consists of pool table and piano, whilst the larger carpeted saloon, with its high ceiling, is very much in the London style. Food is served from 12-3 Monday to Friday, snacks are available at other times.

Island Queen

87 Noel Road

Bass
G R ML ME SL SE
Opening Hours: 12-3, 5.30-11m-s 12-3; 5.30-1.30su
Station: Angel
Buses: 4, 19, 30, 43, 279, X43
Greene King IPA, Fuller's London Pride, Draught Bass

A fine old Victorian 'gin palace' style one-room pub, converted to a pirate theme, with a tongue firmly planted in a cheek and which actually works well. Unique enamelled mirrors with raised green foliage motifs along one wall, a ship's figurehead, a fully furled sail and pirate mannequins do not harm the Victorian lushness of the original fittings. An island bar stands in the centre of the pub and the large windows in the bowed front project a warm glow onto Noel Road. There is a feel of pirates on the Spanish Main which may explain why the attached restaurant specialises in Mexican food. The Island Queen is a good example of how an old pub can be revamped without destroying its original features and be good fun to boot.

Kings Head

115 Upper St

Allied Domecq

ML ME SL SEN
Opening Hours: normal
Station: Angel
Buses: 4, 19, 30, 38, 43, X43, 279
Benskins Best Bitter, Adnams Bitter, Ind Coope Burton Ale

Possibly London's most famous theatre pub, which uses its fame to ensure that its productions are generally of the highest standard. The pub is, in effect, a large theatre foyer. Performances often take place at lunchtimes, though not always the same as the evening's production. Food in the evening is available for theatre goers only. Booking for popular productions is advisable (0171 226 1916). The pub is also notorious for its refusal to become decimalised and the till still rings up pounds, shillings and pence, ie proper money. The decor is suitably motley in keeping with the Bohemian/theatrical tastes of the clientele. The lighting is provided by theatre spotlamps and the walls are decorated with old playbills. Hardly a table or chair match and some of the old theatre sets along the walls go some way to explaining why old music hall audiences often threw things.

Marquess Tavern

Canonbury St

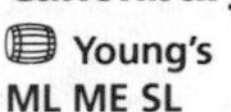

ML ME SL
Opening Hours: normal
Station: Essex Rd BR
Buses: 38, 56, 73, 171a, N73, N96
Young's Bitter, Young's Special, Young's Winter Warmer

The monthly quiz at the Marquess (first Monday of the month) is possibly one of the most fiendishly difficult pub quizzes in London. That fact seems only to act as an attraction for the pub is always packed on quiz nights. The pub can appear deceptively empty but in reality everyone is sitting in the back room, with its fine mirrors, arched ceiling and protruding raised lamps, giving it a music hall feel. To the right of the main bar is a small games room with darts and bar billiards. Notable for the generosity of its portions, this stately looking public house is very much a favourite with Islington locals.

Narrow Boat

St Peters St

G ML ME SL Opening Hours: normal
Station: Angel

Buses: 4, 19, 30, 38, 43, 56, 73, 171a, 214, 279
Fuller's London Pride

The Narrow Boat lives up to its name in that a modern style spit and sawdust front bar opens onto a long, narrow lounge with a wood lined ceiling and walls which slope inwards giving the impression of being on a barge. The balcony overlooks the Grand Union Canal and narrow boat moorings at Wenlock Basin. The walls are covered in photographs of the canal in its working days and the pub is a pleasant retreat, idyllic on a sunny evening. Bar billiards is played in the front bar as is piped music. The back room is quieter. The pub has a lovely cat which does not mind dogs at all, unless there is competition for your food.

Old Red Lion

St John Street, Islington

Bass
G ML
Opening Hours: normal
Station: Angel
Fuller's London Pride, Draught Bass

Pretty scruffy as theatre pubs go, but always crowded nonetheless, the Old Red Lion is less of a theatre pub than a pub with a theatre in it. A hotchpotch pub which has mercifully never had a proper refit, is one room, yet is two; its old partitions no longer quite going far enough to fulfil their original functions. The effect is to convert the bulk of the room into the public bar and leave the smaller, secluded area between bar and frosted glass partition as the saloon area. The bulk of the seating is down the long north wall, whilst the south side of this tapering pub is taken up by the bar and the pool table. In many ways, it is one of those odd London pubs that seem to do well despite having no real defining quality, other than doing well. The box office is open a half hour before the performance but tickets are available from the bar at other times.

Waterside Inn

Crinan St

Whitbread
G ML ME SL
Opening Hours: normal
Station: Kings Cross
Buses: 10, C12
Boddingtons Bitter, Flowers Original, Marston's Pedigree + Guest Beers

If there was a prize for 'most stupid insertion of a fake interior into a brand new building', this would be a good candidate. There is a millstone in the middle of the floor, and fake beams all over. However, the fact that the decor is clichéd does not mean it is necessarily a bad pub. The pub works because its customers, who include office workers and dancers, want it to succeed. It has a very lively atmosphere at lunchtimes but the view from the canal side is soothing and has the merit of rendering the pub interior invisible. A Berni Inn with a low food counter, suggesting food is a significant portion of the pub's trade. When visited Adnams Bitter was served on a swan neck and sparkler, exactly how it should not be served.

Wenlock Arms

Wenlock Rd

Free House
SL SE
Opening Hours: normal
Station: Old Street
Buses: 76, 141, 271
Tetley Bitter + Guest Beers; Ciders

North London's premier real ale pub, the Wenlock is a small single-roomed house with a U-shaped bar, cornered with handsome uplights and surrounded with pump clips from a hundred guest ales gone by. The landlords are CAMRA stalwarts and the pub is a good beer guide regular, which hosts its own festivals. Apart from a regular beer there is always at least one mild ale for sale, plus no fewer than four guests, which are all kept exceptionally well. There are always real ciders on sale and a perry, more often than not. Ale is very much the focus of the pub. The hot salt beef sandwiches are the non-ale house speciality. The juke box is inside a wooden cabinet, takes muscle power rather than money and only plays 78s. Thursday night is quiz night, and on Sunday lunchtimes 'Maestro' Johnny Parker sits himself behind the Union Flag draped 'Joanna'. Definitely a hidden gem.

York

82, Islington High St

Allied Domecq
ML SL
Opening Hours: normal
Station: Angel
Buses: 4, 19, 3, 0, 38, 43, 56, 73, 153, 171a, 279
Tetley Bitter, Eldridge Pope Hardy Country, Ind Coope Burton Ale + Guest Beers

A fun and permanently busy pub, well placed for Camden's antiques quarter, just a minute's walk away from Angel tube. There is a fine, original bar back and otherwise it is furnished very much in the modern style of 'traditional', if that is not a contradiction in terms. Background music adds to the atmosphere, but is not obtrusive. Decor gives a good impression of Victorian clutter. Set back from Islington High Street by a wide pavement, the squat corner location of the York is a fine example of London pub architecture. The pub is quite typically Allied Domecq, but no less good for all that.

N2

Old White Lion

121 Great North Road, East Finchley

Bass
G DA ML ME SL SE
Opening Hours: normal
Station: East Finchley
Buses: 102, 143, 263, N1, N92
Fuller's London Pride, Draught Bass

Large comfortable former Wenlock Brewery house. Single large bar serving three distinct areas. Adjacent to East Finchley tube station, the building is a fine example of 'Brewers Tudor'. It dates from 1938 and was rebuilt by the Wenlock Brewery (1893-1961) when the station was relocated. The former pub on the site was known as the 'Dirt House', being a favourite port of call for carriers who took produce up to London and returned with loads of soot and manure. The pub features a large and lively public bar and a vast saloon/lounge serving a good selection of food lunchtimes and evenings. A walled garden leads off the main lounge area.

Welch's Ale House

130 High Road, East Finchley

ree House
ML ME
Opening Hours: normal
Station: East Finchley
Buses: 143, 263, N92
Webster's Yorkshire Bitter, Fuller's London Pride, Timothy Taylor's Landlord, Wadworth 6X, Greene King Abbot + Guest Beers; Ciders

One of the earliest shop conversions, this former ice cream parlour now specialises in a more potent range of flavours. Usually 12 real ales are available, many of them unusual for London,. together with a selection of real cider and English country wines. A single bar serves the narrow front and wider rear drinking areas. A large, easy to read, chalk board price list displays the current range of beers. The pub is handily situated only a five minute walk from one of London's oldest independent cinemas, The Phoenix, which is well worth a visit.

N3

Catcher in the Rye

315-9 Regents Park Rd, Hendon

Regent Inns
ML ME
Opening Hours: normal
Station: Finchley Central
Buses: 82, 143, 260, 326
Brakspear Bitter, Draught Bass, Theakston's XB + Guest Beers

A brand new pub split onto and into an existing building. It is named after J D Salinger's novel which gained notoriety when a copy was found in the possession of John Lennon's assassin when he was arrested. One large bar is divided into three split level areas with exposed brickwork and much wood panelling. There are some comfortable armchairs in stark contrast with the bare floorboards. The beer range is complemented by a constantly changing guest beer and a house beer called 'Catcher Bitter'. Popular with all ages, this is a. very welcome addition to local real ale outlets.

N6

Flask

77 Highgate West Hill, Highgate

Allied Domecq
G ML ME SL SEO
Opening Hours: normal
Station: Highgate
Buses: 46, 268, N5
Tetley Bitter, Young's Bitter, Ind Coope Burton Ale, Young's Special + Guest Beers

The pub dates from 1716 when Highgate was growing as a fashionable community, more upmarket than neighbouring Hampstead. It was a popular stopping point for people going to take the waters at Hampstead Wells. People stopped to pick up a 'flask' to carry the waters away with them, hence the name of the pub. Dick Turpin is believed to have evaded capture by hiding in the cellars of the Flask and the Painter William Hogarth used to repair to drink with fellow painters Morland and Cruickshank (Morland was such a drinker and painter of tavern life that he had a brewery named after him). The Flask is also one of the Highgate pubs where the 'Swearing on the Horns' takes place. The initiate kisses a pair of antlers tied to a pole and is required to swear an oath to the effect that he shall avoid small beer when strong ale is to hand, nor kiss the maid when the mistress is about but sooner than miss the chance kiss them both. He then kisses the prettiest girl in the room. Another excellent reason to visit this fine old pub.

N7

Admiral Mann

9 Hargrave Place, Holloway

3

McMullen
ML ME SL SE
Opening Hours: normal
Station: Kentish Town
Buses: 10, 29, 253, C12, N29, N90, N253
McMullen's AK, McMullen's Country, McMullen's Gladstone

Small, neatly appointed two bar in hidden back street tucked behind the corner of busy Camden Road and Brecknock Road. One of a handful of McMullen's pubs in London, it is well worth sniffing out for their beers alone. In keeping with the name of the pub the theme is nautical but in an understated fashion; no anchors hanging from the ceiling, merely prints of square riggers and nineteenth century ships on the walls. In the saloon the seating is in the form of a number of settles that extend into the centre of the room to form a small number of corners. The public bar has a darts board and a large montage of photos taken in the pub of all those embarrassing moments everyone would rather forget. You know the kind.

N9

Lamb

52-54 Church St, Lower Edmonton

Wetherspoon

G DA ML ME SL SE

Opening Hours: normal

Station: Edmonton Green BR

Buses: 102, 144, 149, 191, 192, 259, 279, W6, W8, N90

Younger's Scotch, Theakston's Best, Marston's Pedigree, Theakston's XB, Courage Directors + Guest Beers; Weston's Old Rosie

Opened in February 1993 in the premises of the former Blue Cat restaurant. This pub offers a welcome haven of peace and calm in contrast to most neighbouring pubs. The name is taken from the nineteenth century romantic poet and essayist Charles Lamb, who lived in the area who wrote the verse "If ever I marry a wife/ I'll marry a landlord's daughter, / For then I may sit in the bar, and drink cold brandy and water". His work, and that of poets John Keats and William Cower, who also lived in the area, is featured on the walls. The pub has a typical Wetherspoon decor with wood panelling much in evidence. A single bar serves an open area with tables and chairs on the left and at the rear of the pub the ever popular alcoves can be found in the no-smoking area. There is level access to the disabled toilet but not to the no-smoking area. The pub has several beer festivals during the year.

N13

Fox

413 Green Lanes, Palmers Green

S&N

G CP ML ME SL SE

Opening Hours: normal

Station: Palmers Green BR

Buses: 329, W2, W6, N29

John Smith's Bitter, Theakston's Best, Theakston's XB, Courage Directors

Large multi-room corner pub on main road. Built in 1904 and still has some of the original etched windows. The decor is very much in keeping with this style of pub with a very large split-level lounge and several brightly lit, comfortable seating areas. There is also a rather tatty public bar with two pool tables, a dart board and juke box which attracts a younger, noisier clientele. In the rear there is a function room for weddings, which is also home to the 'Bound & Gagged' comedy club, monthly acoustic evenings (Thurs). The pub also houses a small 56-seater theatre which puts on monthly plays. The pub is rather pricey for the area.

Whole Hog

430-434 Green Lanes, Palmers Green

Wetherspoon
DA ML ME SL SE
Opening Hours: normal
Station: Palmers Green BR
Buses: 329, W2, W6, N29
Younger's Scotch, Theakston's Best, Marston's Pedigree, Theakston's XB, Courage Directors + Guest Beers; Cider

Typical Wetherspoon pub with all the usual Wetherspoon features, which was opened in October 1990 in a former hardware shop. Refurbished and enlarged in Spring 1995 into a split level-bar with the lower level mostly a no-smoking area. Disabled toilets are on the lower level with a wheelchair lift for easy access. The pub has a friendly atmosphere with a regular clientele which spans all ages. The pub puts on several beer festivals during the year.

Woodman

128 Bourne Hill, Palmers Green

Whitbread
G CP SL
Opening Hours: normal
Station: Southgate
Buses: W9
Wethereds, Boddington's Bitter, Flowers Original, Marston's Pedigree

Small local built as a cottage in 1727. It remained so until 1868 when a retired police sergeant Henry Wale was granted a licence to sell ale from his front room. He was landlord until 1893 when Henry Reed and his wife Caroline took over. Henry died in 1924 and Caroline carried on as landlady until her death, aged 94. Nearby is a small green where there is an old wooden pound, once used to restrain stray horses and livestock. The owner would have to pay the Pinder (pound keeper) a fee for their release. The last Pinder was landlord Henry Reed from 1897 until the pound closed in 1904. The Woodman still retains its small friendly, country cottage pub atmosphere.

N14

Olde Cherry Tree

22 The Green, Southgate

Allied Domecq
G CP ME SL SE
Opening Hours: 11.30-11m-s
Station: Southgate
Buses: 121, W6, 299
Tetley Bitter, Young's Bitter, Ind Coope Burton Ale + Guest Beers

Ye Olde Cherry Tree enjoys a reputation for good service and hospitality dating back to 1624 when Valentine Pool, gentleman, gave the site to the poor of Barnet. The trustees kept The Cherry until 1920 when it was sold outright to Allied Domecq. At the turn of the century a front porch was added as the walls were bulging and the porch was added by the landlord at the time to save the pub from being pulled down. The pub overlooks the village green, complete with village stocks and horse trough. Inside, the single bar serves three distinct areas, a recently opened 'library' room, a front saloon and a split-level area to the right with a few armchairs. The restaurant to the rear has a good reputation. There are two function rooms. The Selbourne Suite can seat 250 and is ideal for weddings whilst the Saddle Room, overlooking the bowling green, can seat around 40.

N16

Steptoes

Stoke Newington Church St

Charles Wells
FR G CP ML SL
Opening Hours: normal
Station: Stoke Newington BR
Buses: 73, N73
Wells Eagle, Boddington's Bitter, Wells Bombardier, Adnams Broadside, Young's Special + Guest Beers

Once the boring old Clarence, now one of many lively alehouses in swinging Church Street . There is lots of bric-a-brac including stuffed birds and advertising signs. The bar has a raised seating area. A small family room behind leads to a sunny and secluded courtyard.

N18

Phoenix

56 Upper Fore St, Upper Edmonton

Whitbread
ML SL
Opening Hours: 11-3, 5.30-11m-f, 11-4, 7-11s
Station: Silver Street BR
Buses: 149, 259, 279, N90
Boddington's Mild, Fuller's London Pride

A small traditional pub which is a welcome recent convert to real ale. This pleasant friendly locals' pub offers traditional home cooked meals, served lunchtimes Monday to Saturday and free bar snacks at Sunday lunchtime. Beer prices are discounted between 11am and 3pm, as are pensioners' lunches. This quiet pub is a good venue for darts, cribbage and pool players and viewers of Sky TV. Other features include charity raffles and occasional live cabaret or music hall type entertainment. Very much an oasis in this area.

N21

Dog & Duck

74 Hoppers Road, Winchmore Hill

Whitbread
G SL
Opening Hours: 12-11m-s
Station: Winchmore Hill BR
Buses: W9
Boddington's Bitter + Guest Beers

Small tucked away local voted CAMRA Enfield & Barnet branch Pub of the Year, 1995. Very much a regulars' pub, but worth seeking out for the excellent quality of the beer. There are always four beers available from the Whitbread portfolio and guest beers which are served in tip-top condition. This is a single bar pub located in a terraced cottage dating from the turn of the century. It was built on the site of an ale house also named the Dog & Duck which dates back to at least 1880. There is a small secluded garden and a shove ha'penny board. The pub is known locally as the 'woof and quack.' Worth seeking out.

Half Moon

The Broadway, 749 Green Lane, Winchmore Hill

Wetherspoon
ML ME SL SE
Opening Hours: normal
Station: Winchmore Hill BR
Buses: 125, 329, W2, N29
Greene King IPA, Younger's Scotch, Theakston's Best, Theakston's XB, Courage Directors, Greene King Abbot + Guest Beers; Westons Old Rosie Cider

Typical Wetherspoon pub with all the Wetherspoon features. The building was once an old Sainsbury's store and the wall tiles opposite the bar date from that time. The decor in this very friendly pub is enhanced by many surreal depictions of the moon in its various phases, carved wooden moons hang from the ceiling and many moon-themed prints and quotes adorn the walls. There is always a jovial atmosphere in this well run pub which achieved its first entry in the Good Beer Guide in 1996. The pub has several beer festivals throughout the year.

Orange Tree

18 Highfield Road, Winchmore Hill

Allied Domecq
G ML ME SL SE
Opening Hours: 11.30-11m-s
Station: Winchmore Hill BR
Buses: 125, 329, W2, N29
Adnams Bitter, Greene King IPA + Guest Beers

Back street local which features a variety of pub entertainment on Saturday nights. These vary from live acts, 60s nights and theme nights. Midweek there is a quiz night. Barbecues are held in the garden (weather permitting), which has a children's play area. The building boasts a splendid ornate exterior and inside it is a busy and popular locals' pub which seems to have lost none of its character since the public and saloon bars were integrated in the 1980s. Dominoes and cribbage are played. Evening meals finish at 7pm. Please note that there is no access by car into Highfield Road from Green Lanes.

Salisbury Arms

Hoppers Road, Winchmore Hill

Bass
G CP R ML ME SL SE

Opening Hours: normal
Station: Winchmore Hill BR
Buses: W9
Fuller's London Pride, Draught Bass + Guest Beers

This pleasant, popular, well run, early 1930s pub is situated in leafy suburbia close to Winchmore Hill Green with its many antique shops. The well designed interior layout has a dining area to the right, a narrow bar and wider area with tables and chairs to the left. It has an excellent restaurant and bar meals, though snacks are served all day. The pub also hosts occasional mini-beer festivals with a regional theme as well as other special events. A function room is available.

N22

Phoenix Bar

Alexandra Palace

ML SL SE
Opening Hours: normal
Station: Alexandra Palace BR
Buses: W3
Tetley Bitter + Guest Beers; Cider

The view from the patio of the Phoenix Bar is undoubtedly the finest in London, well, of London, to be exact. On a clear day the whole city is laid out below you; the horizon only appearing at Alexandra's matching South London hillside palace, Crystal Palace. Situated in the south-west corner of the Alexandra Palace, the original home of British television broadcasting, the name refers to the fire which destroyed the Palace in the early 1980s. The bar opens onto the Palm Court atrium foyer, with its pyramid fountains and attendant palm trees, and a further seating area allows people to sit under the glass canopy and enjoy the fountains' soothing gushing. There is a wide range of real ales, up to 10 guest beers, as well as an impressive range of Belgian and German beers and real cider

---

Starting Gate

Station Road, Wood Green

Allied Domecq
G ML SL
Opening Hours: 12-11m-s 12-10.30su
Station: Alexandra Palace BR
Buses: 84a, W3

Adnams Bitter, Tetley Bitter, Young's Bitter, Eldridge Pope Hardy Country, Draught Bass + Guest Beers

An amiable mix of old and new greets visitors to the Starting Gate. Twenty yards from Alexandra Palace BR, the large simple bar consists of a central oblong shaped island bar, around which is the drinking area. The presence of snob screens and vestigial glass partitions indicates that this was a mid-Victorian pub once divided into numerous drinking areas, each of which would have corresponded to a social class present in the local community. Domestic servants would have drunk out of sight of their employers; apprentices, away from their masters. The pub's walls are decorated with large, three feet by five feet, painted panels depicting a number of rural or seaside scenes as well as landscapes of Alexandra Palace and Windsor Castle. A number of pot plants add life to the shelves and window sills, including aspidistras, to provide a genuine Victorian feel. All in all a sympathetic and realistic preservation of the Victorian Gin Palace. Monday nights are quiz nights.

Enfield – EN2

Jolly Farmers

2 Enfield Road, Enfield

McMullen

G CP R ML ME SL SE

Opening Hours: 11-3;5.30-11m-s

Station: Oakwood

Buses: 121, 307, 517

McMullen's AK, McMullen's Country, McMullen's Gladstone, McMullen's Stronghart

Large two bar pub with function room, situated between Enfield Town and Oakwood. The pub is a winner of the 'Enfield in Bloom' competition and there is always a riot of colour in the flower beds and window boxes. Good bar snacks and a restaurant (booking advisable: 0181 363 1917). No food is available on Sunday evenings when every seat in the house is occupied by participants in the popular quiz. Regular live music/sing-a-long on Tuesdays in the public bar. There are frequent special events such as 'theme' menus in the restaurant. Darts are played in the public bar but the pub can become rather smoky when busy. McMullen Special Reserve beers are served in addition to the usual range, when available.

King & Tinker
Whitewebbs Lane

Allied Domecq
G CP ML SL SE
Opening Hours: 11-3, 5.30-11m-f, 12-3, 7-10.30su
Benskins Best Bitter, Adnams Bitter, Tetley Bitter, Ind Coope Burton Ale

Winner of the 1992 Enfield & Barnet CAMRA Pub of the Year Award, it is a gem of a country pub, parts of which date back some 400 years, although an alehouse is said to have stood here for almost 1000 years. This is supposedly the ale house referred to in the ballad of 'King James and the Tinker.' Cosy interior with low ceilings and very solid beams (duck or grouse always on the menu!) An inglenook fireplace complements a perfect setting for an evening's enjoyment. Always busy with a good mix of clientele on two and four legs! The pub is well run by a keen manager who has scooped numerous accolades for his colourful floral displays, high quality food and beers. Runner up in the Burton Guild of Master Cellarmen Awards in 1989 and Winner in 1990 – no small achievement. Fish dishes are a speciality on the menu. The pub features a large fenced garden with a play area; try and spot the converted beer cask now used as a bird house. Part of the charm is its remote location, but this can make it a bit hard to get to.

King's Head
Market Place, Enfield

Allied Domecq
G ML SL
Opening Hours: normal
Station: Enfield Town BR
Buses: 121, 191, 231, 307, 310, 311, 313, 316, 317, 329, W2, W9
Benskins Best Bitter, Tetley Bitter, Ind Coope Burton Ale + Guest Beers

This fine Victorian pub built in 1899, stands at back of the small but popular and colourful Enfield market place (market days: Thurs to Sat). You will find no keg bitter, but you will find etched windows, an upstairs games room with pool and darts and a popular quiz every Tuesday evening. First impression on entry is that the bar itself takes up too much space but there is plenty of room including an area to the rear used mainly by diners at midday. There is also a small 'snug' with comfortable armchairs and a television for sports events. A pub has stood on this site since the market was granted its charter by James I whose portrait is on the pub signs –

not a common choice of monarch. The market place can be used as a car park from Sunday to Wednesday afternoon.

Moon Under Water

115/117 Chase Side, Enfield

Wetherspoon
G CP ML ME SL SE
Opening Hours: normal
Station: Enfield Chase BR
Buses: 191, 231, W9
Greene King IPA, Younger's Scotch, Theakston's Best, Theakston's XB, Courage Directors + Guest Beers

Large, typical Wetherspoon house opened in September 1988 and which maintains the high standards of quality, service and value for money which are the hallmarks of this company. The cavernous, barn like smoking area with alcoves around the sides is decorated to give the impression that customers are under water. Smaller, very welcome, no-smoking area to the rear. Despite a complete lack of music, this pub is very popular with a younger clientele in the evenings, particularly weekends Other features include reasonably priced food served all day every day – including 'flavour of the month' and the Sunday roast is good value. The pub puts on several beer festivals during the course of the year. The outside drinking area is rather limited.

Old Wheatsheaf

3 Windmill Hill, Enfield

Allied Domecq
G CP ML SL
Opening Hours: normal
Station: Enfield Chase BR
Buses: 121, 307, 313, 517
Benskins Best Bitter, Tetley Bitter, Ind Coope Burton Ale + Guest Beers

Fine, ivy clad, two bar pub, situated just one minute from Enfield Chase BR station. The present building, replacing a much earlier structure, dates from the turn of the century and features a salt-glazed tiled frontage, together with some fine etched glass and ornate woodwork. The saloon 'upper' bar extension added in the 1930s does not detract from overall appeal. The 'lower' bar has been refurbished including the fitting of period fireplaces, one with a fine overmantel. This smart, clean, well run pub is host to a well established, popular weight lifting club which meets most evenings in rear building. A former London CAMRA Pub of the Year under the previous licensee, it continues to maintain high standards, including impressive exterior floral displays in summer. Convenient for historic Gentleman's Row.

Pied Bull

Bulls Cross, Enfield

Whitbread
G ML ME SL SE
Opening Hours: normal
Station: Turkey Street BR
Buses: 217, 310, 311, 317
Boddington's Bitter, Fuller's London Pride, Flowers Original, Marston's Pedigree + Guest Beers

Attractive historic seventeenth-century pub which was formerly the hunting stables and kennels of James I, with plenty of low beams to avoid. Situated a quarter of a mile off the A10 and within sound of the M25. A conservatory style rear extension has been added in recent years which provides a no-smoking and family area. Monday night is quiz night and Tuesdays sees live Jazz; other features include an extensive menu and a pleasant outdoor drinking area. The pub is very convenient for visitors to Capel Manor Gardens or nearby Myddleton House.

Rose & Crown

Clay Hill, Enfield

S&N
FR G CP SL ME SE
Opening Hours: normal
Station: Enfield Town BR
Buses: 191, 231, W10
Webster's Yorkshire Bitter, Theakston's Best, Courage Directors

This is one of the oldest pubs in Enfield, dating back to the seventeenth century. It proudly displays its oak beams, with many nooks and crannies to hide away in and enjoy your beer. An upstairs galley provides extra seating and a dart board. Located on the edge of Whitewebbs Park, where urban area meets countryside and a half mile walk from nearest buses. Unfortunate fruit machines should not allow you to become distracted as low beams can cause severe headaches. A small children's play area has recently been constructed. The pub is extremely popular, particularly in the summer.

Stag

Little Park Gardens, Enfield

Bass

ML ME SL SEO

Opening Hours: 11-3m-th, 11-11f-s closed su

Station: Enfield Chase

Buses: 121, 191, 231, 307, 310, 311, 317, W2, N29

Tetley Bitter, Draught Bass + Guest Beers

Small, pleasant and comfortable single bar pub situated directly opposite Enfield Town Bus terminus. Very good home cooked food is served lunchtimes and until 8pm evenings and is complemented by good real ale. Background music plays quietly unless someone feeds the juke box. Located very close to historic Gentleman's Row and Enfield Registry Office and so is ideal for a quick nerve calmer before taking the marriage vows. Monday nights – July to September is cribbage night. Upstairs is a small function room with it own bar facilities.

EN4

Builders' Arms

3 Albert Road, New Barnet

Greene King

G ML SL

Opening Hours: 11-3, 5.30-11m-f 11-3, 6-11s

Station: New Barnet BR

Buses: 84a, 307, 326, 384

Greene King IPA, Greene King Abbot

Hidden away in a side street, this pub is only three minutes away from New Barnet BR station. Despite being renovated in the 1980s, it still retains its character as well as a public bar. In the saloon the only sound you will hear is that of conversation as it is free of music and the noises and flashing lights of fruit machines. The public bar is a traditional drinking room with a dart board. Both bars were originally centred on what is now the saloon bar and the pub was known locally as 'The Little House'. There is a paved garden at rear.

Cock & Dragon

14 Chalk Farm, Cockfosters

Allied Domecq

G CP DA R ML ME SL SE

Opening Hours: normal

Station: Cockfosters

Buses: 298, 299, 384

Tetley Bitter, Wadworth 6X, Ind Coope Burton Ale + Guest Beers

East meets West in this impressive pub with its excellent Thai Restaurant and decor to match. A weathercock astride a clock tower on a copper roof, tops this large single bar now run by Dragon Inns and Restaurants. The pub has an oriental saloon and bare floor-boarded, but comfortable, former public bar area. The aroma of exotic oriental herbs and spices wafts through the bar to start your mouth watering in anticipation of the delights to be enjoyed in the restaurant (booking recommended: 0181 449 7160) or as bar snacks. The garden features an ornamental pond with Koi Carp, children's climbing frame and a barbecue. Situated eight minutes from the M25 (J24), set back to the right of the main road (A111) as you head south.

Barnet – EN5

Mitre Inn (Ye Olde)

58 High St, Barnet

Allied Domecq

CP ML SL

Opening Hours: 11-11m-f, 11-3, 7-11, s

Station: High Barnet

Buses: 34, 84, 84a, 263, 307, 326, 384

Benskins Best Bitter, Tetley Bitter, Ind Coope Burton Ale + Guest Beers

Historic, old coaching inn in prominent high street location. Themed as an 'ale house' by Allied Domecq which allows pubs to choose from a wide range of unusual guest beers, the pub is a haven of tranquillity in contrast to its neighbouring young persons' venues. The archway to one side betrays the former coaching inn status of this seventeenth-century Grade II listed building. A restful split level watering hole, ideal to go to after watching Barnet FC. The pub features an old fireplace discovered during recent major restoration. Consistently good real ale has made this pub a regular entry in the Good Beer Guide and it can be very crowded, especially at weekends – despite no food on Sundays.

Moon Under Water

148 High St, Barnet

Wetherspoon

CP ML ME SL SE

Opening Hours: normal
Station: High Barnet
Buses: 34, 84, 84a, 263, 307, 326, 384
Greene King IPA, Younger's Scotch, Theakston's XB, Greene King Abbot, Morland's Old Speckled Hen + Guest Beers; Weston's Old Rosie Cider

The narrow street frontage opens out into a larger rear drinking area in this Wetherspoon pub located opposite 'Spires' shopping centre. Often crowded at weekends, local CAMRA members voted this their pub of the year 1994. Opened in January 1989 in what was formerly a carpet shop, this is a welcome improvement in choice and value for the area. Typical Wetherspoon's panelling prevails throughout with a no-smoking area to the front. The long narrow bar has an unusual, curved perspex roof. Other features include good value food served all day, every day and a Sunday roast. The pub has several beer festivals during the year.

Old Red Lion

Underhill, Barnet

McMullen
G CP ML ME SL SE
Opening Hours: 11-3, 5.30-11m-s
Station: High Barnet
Buses: 34, 234, 263, 307
McMullen's AK, McMullen's Country, McMullen's Gladstone

A two-bar pub on a busy street corner close to High Barnet tube (Northern Line). It is also the nearest pub to Barnet Football Club and therefore can get very busy on match days when the public bar remains open all day long. The pleasant saloon bar is typical McMullen's with genuine 'ye olde' plastic beams and bare brick, though the walls are difficult to see as they are so covered with artefacts such as pictures of local scenes and horse brasses etc. The traditional public bar is small and cosy with no frills attached. It can be busy on Tuesday evenings if the ladies' darts team is at home. There is live music on alternate Fridays.

Watford – WD1

Wellington Arms

2 Woodford Road, Watford

Free House
ML ME SL SE

Opening Hours: normal
Station: Watford Junction BR
Buses: W2
Adnams Bitter, Tetley Bitter, Fuller's London Pride + Guest Beers

A pub with accommodation, the Wellington is only five minutes walk from the BR station. The regular beers are from the Allied Domecq stable. The two guest beers often include interesting choices not usually seen in the area. Visitors to Watford will find this pub conveniently on their way to most parts of Watford, including the Harlequin Centre (shopping) and the museum, which has a brewing section, found near Watford High Street Station. The pub has regular discos weekly.

White Lion

79 St Albans Road, Watford

Inntrepreneur
ML SL
Opening Hours: 11-11m-s, 12-4, 7-10.30su
Station: Watford Junction BR
Buses: W2
Courage Best Bitter, Wadworth 6X, Courage Directors

A busy locals' pub with two bars. The public bar is basic and favoured by games players, the saloon is comfortable. Many of the staff have worked at the pub for quite a time, which is always a good sign. The food consists of rolls made on the premises and cooked meals with daily specials of standard pub fare. The bus stop outside is for the W2 from Watford Town Centre, a local circular route. However, all routes that go to Watford Junction will leave visitors with a short walk. This pub is close to the Town Hall and its attached concert hall.

WD2

Black Boy

19 Windmill Street, Bushey Heath

Allied Domecq
G CP ML ME SL
Opening Hours: 11-3, 5.30-11m-th 11-11f-s
Buses: 142, 258
Benskins Best Bitter, Adnams Bitter, Chiltern Beechwood, Ind Coope Burton Ale + Guest Beers; Occasional Ciders

Tucked away in the back streets of Bushey Heath, the Black Boy is ideal for tourists and business people alike. Popular for food at lunchtimes and justifiably so, the single L-shaped bar is not large, so you are advised to get there early in order to get a seat if you wish to eat.

Compasses
95 Tibbs Hill Road, Abbots Langley

Inntrepreneur
G CP DA ML ME SL
Opening Hours: normal
Buses: W4, 344
Courage Best Bitter, Fuller's London Pride, Courage Directors, Ruddles County

The large saloon bar has a 'public bar' section with a regular local clientele. Some people prefer to eat in this area. The menu is supplemented by home cooked specials at lunch time. Popular with disabled people, the pub is a trifle hard to find for those not in the know. It also has a selection of over 100 whiskies.

Swan

25 Park Road, Bushey

Pubmaster
Opening Hours: normal
Buses: 142, 258
Benskins Best Bitter, Ind Coope Burton Ale

The first CAMRA Good Beer Guide described the Swan as a 'basic pub mostly used by locals; friendly'. Nothing has changed in twenty-two years. This one-bar pub draws its customers from all walks of life. In winter there is a real fire and ladies must go outside to find the toilet. This pub is in a back street off Bushey High Street. To find it, get off the bus at the Red Lion or the White Hart. Park Road is on the left going up the High Street.

WD3

Black Horse

Dog Kennel Lane, Chorleywood

Greenalls
G CP ML ME SL SE
Opening Hours: normal
Station: Chorleywood BR
Adnams Bitter, Greenalls Bitter, Greenalls Original + Guest Beers

Attractive pub on Chorleywood Common, much used by walkers and locals. The pub sports a stone floor and one bar split into three distinctly separate areas. Good home cooked food as well as real fires in winter provide a suitably comfortable ambience in this deceptively large pub. There's a welcome for dogs.

Fox & Hounds

183 High Street, Rickmansworth

Inntrepreneur
G CP ML SL
Opening Hours: normal
Station: Rickmansworth BR
Courage Best Bitter, Courage Directors + Occasional Guest Beers

This two-bar pub in Rickmansworth High Street, a stone's throw from the station, has a rather unusual inn sign. The pub is handy for those wishing to scratch below Rickmansworth's surface. The town is older than people tend to think and has an interesting church and a canal museum. There is no food on Sunday but during the week it is very good, with a home cooked special each day. Guest beers are not a permanent feature but those they do have are interesting and unusual choices.

Land of Liberty, Peace & Plenty

Long Lane, Heronsgate

Free House
Opening Hours: 12-11m-s 12-10.30su
Station: Rickmansworth
Buses: R4
Courage Best Bitter, Young's Special + Guest Beers; Ciders

A handy pub for those desperate to get off the M25 (J17). Heronsgate was originally a Chartist co-operative community set up by Fergus O'Connor in 1846. It is still unspoilt but could no longer be called a co-operative. The pub takes its name from the community. Food is available all day and vegetarian options are on the menu. Up to six Belgian beers are available on draught, as well as several bottled brands. There are also four guest British ales, which are usually from the smaller breweries. The pub used to belong to Harmans of Uckridge and evidence of this can still be seen. If you are not in your car, the infrequent R4 bus will get you there, but alternatively it is a good walk across the fields from Rickmansworth Station or from Chorleywood Station.

WD4

King's Head

Bridge Road, Hunton Bridge, Kings Langley

Allied Domecq
FR G CP ML ME SL SE
Opening Hours: 11-3, 5.30-11
Benskins Best Bitter, Tetley Bitter, Ind Coope Burton Ale + Guest Beers

Large garden with children's facilities backing onto the Grand Union Canal, which makes it ideal for canal users, whether fishing, boating or walking. The old canal stables have been converted into a skittles alley and children's room in the summer. An interesting curved door opens onto the main road. The pub is on many different levels having been a post office in a previous existence and gradually expanded into neighbouring cottages. Guest beers are from the Tapster's Choice List. The pub is used by a wheelchair bound regular but the toilets are upstairs so would not be suitable for most disabled people. Convenient for M25 users – come off at junction 22 and head south. Turn left at traffic lights.

SE1

Abbey

94 Webber St,

Free House
ML SL SE:
Opening Hours: 11-11m-f closed s 12-3.30, 7-10.30su
Station: Borough
Buses: 45, 63, 172
Shepherd Neame Masterbrew, Shepherd Neame Spitfire

There are an awful lot of wine bottles in the Abbey, which is odd considering it's a Free House, serving good beer. This slatted wood panelled pub is very much a locals' venue, picking up lucrative trade from the more discerning office workers at the nearby business centre. The unusually shaped corner pub is split into two with the public bar doubling as a pool room. The front corner of the pub provides a nook for the food serving area with shelves covered in wine bottles, giving it a Victorian pantry feel. Dark wood, neat blue upholstery and subdued lighting as well as quiet background music provides a genial and unpretentious atmosphere.

Anchor

1 Bankside, Southwark

Greenalls
G ML SL
Opening Hours: normal
Station: London Bridge
Buses: 17, 21, 22a, 35, 40, 43, 47, 48, 133, 501, 521, D1, X43
Courage Best Bitter, Courage Directors, Ruddles County + Guest Beers

Over 300 years old in parts, the pub stands on the site of the notorious Southwark 'stews' (brothels) of the Tudor age. It was built in the seventeenth century to replace an earlier inn that had burnt down. We know the Anchor itself was not a stew, for it falls inside the boundary of what was the Bishop of Winchester's garden (the Bishops had a role in regulating the stews). The Anchor would have been a popular watering hole for visitors to the notorious Bear Garden – the traditional site of animal baiting. The pub is supposed to have its own ghost as well as secret passages for the use of smugglers. Dr Johnson is commemorated in a room there and would certainly have been familiar with the Anchor. Downstairs there is a huge model of the Globe Theatre, which has just been rebuilt a hundred yards or so away. Upstairs, the bar celebrates the Financial Times because the world's leading financial paper has had a long association with the pub and is published nearby. The pub is at the start of a riverside walk that now runs right down to County Hall.

Anchor Tap

28 Horsleydown Lane, Borough

Sam Smith's
FR G ML ME SL SE
Opening Hours: normal
Station: London Bridge
Buses: 42, 78
Sam Smith's OBB

Historic and nautical looking wood-fronted pub that takes its name from the now defunct but still standing Anchor Brewery (Courage's original site). This was for many years, one of the major breweries of London, occupying a site that was popular with brewers since early Tudor days. John Courage's first pub is a multi-roomed house with half panelled walls throughout and a combination of settle and table seating. The bar extends through a low doorway (low enough to have a padded lintel) into a second room. Off the front room is a games room with table football, a family room with a table with a chess board set into it and a further room containing only a pool table. At the rear is a beer garden that opens onto Gainsford Street. The pub has a very authentic feel to it and it would not stretch the imagination to roughen up some of the furnishings, fill it with pipe smoke and replace the office and tourist customers with canvas clad sailors and Thames watermen. Handy for Tower Bridge and the Design Museum.

Doggetts Coat & Badge

1 Blackfriars Bridge, Southwark

Nicholsons
G R ML ME SL SE
Opening Hours: 11-11m-f s-su closed
Station: Blackfriars
Buses: 45, 63, 172
Tetley Bitter, Wadworth 6X + Guest Beers

Doggetts Coat & Badge is an annual race on the Thames for sculls, the winner of which becomes one of the Queen's watermen. The pub is of modern design with a pleasingly complicated interior. There are two bars on two different floors. The lower is an authentic looking, City wine cellar 'office'. In summer, this bar offers an entry to a patio area with tables and chairs with a view of the Thames. There is a restaurant on the first floor and the top floor hosts a function room with a panorama encompassing the Thames and St Paul's. Access has recently been improved by the opening of a new path under Blackfriars Bridge in October 1995, which takes riverside walkers from the Anchor at Bankside, past the Founders Arms to the Doggett.

Founders Arms

52 Hopton St, Southwark

Young's

G R ML ME SL SE

Opening Hours: normal

Station: Blackfriars

Buses: 45, 63, 172

Young's Bitter, Young's Special, Young's Winter Warmer

The Founders makes no pretensions to be anything other than a viewing platform from which to relax and enjoy the ebb and flow of the Thames, though for a tourist pub it has a strong local following. Sandwiched between Blackfriars Bridge on the left and Southwark Bridge on the right it affords an ideal view of St Paul's (as far as such a thing is possible in modern London), the City of London School and the ever changing City skyline. It is a certainty that whenever you use this guide there will be at least one crane visible to you from the Founders Arms. From here you will also hear snatches of commentary as sightseeing boats ply up and down the river. If you are tempted to listen to a potted history on a pleasure boat, be warned. There is no real ale on board and you can soak up more atmosphere and history in a pub.

George Inn

77 Borough High St, Southwark

G ML ME SL SE

Opening Hours: normal

Station: London Bridge

Buses: 21, 35, 40, 133, P3

Bishop's Cathedral, Boddington's Bitter, Flowers Original

Owned by the National Trust, the George is London's most historically important pub, as well as one of its most enjoyable. Known to be on the site in the sixteenth century, the present building dates from 1677, its predecessor having been destroyed in the fire of Southwark. The last of Southwark's galleried inns, only a small fragment of the original gallery remains. Galleries were a feature of London's great coaching inns, the aristocrats of the pub world, allowing accommodation to be lifted above the busy stabling activities of the ground floor, as well as allowing light into rooms that would have backed onto other properties. Shakespeare was familiar with the original George, whilst Dickens was familiar with the current building, mentioning it in *Little Dorrit*. A long narrow building with a restaurant on the first floor, it is divided into several rooms each with a feel of antiquity, but each with a slightly different ambience. The George is a favourite stop for the tourist coaches, so it is best to visit it in the evening when the coach tours are over and the tourists have gone. Jazz is played on Wednesday evenings.

Horniman at Hays

Hays Galleria, Tooley St

Nicholsons
G ML ME
Opening Hours: 11-11m-f 11-4.3 s 11-3.30su
Station: London Bridge
Buses: 47, P11
Tetley Bitter, Wadworth 6X, Ind Coope Burton Ale + Guest Beers

Perpetually busy riverside pub attached to South Bank boutique, crafts and office development. The view of the river is rather restricted by having HMS Belfast moored just outside. On the other hand it has the best possible view of HMS Belfast. In a large open plan style with a 1930s feel that does not really come with any particularly Thirties piece of decor, a large number of pillars and a tiled floor give the impression of an old City banking hall. The pub sports the usual range of the Nicholson's ales plus a variety of guests that is a little wider than is often found, though there is no doubt that the real ales are all 20 pence too expensive and the beers are not always served at their best. A busy lunchtime trade is made up by office workers whilst in the evenings tourists tend to make up the numbers. Apart from the obvious presence of HMS Belfast, the pub is only one minute away from 'The London Dungeon' and Tower Bridge is two minutes walk in the other direction.

Kings Arms

25 Roupell St, Waterloo

Allied Domecq
ML SL
Opening Hours: 11-11m-s, 12-3, 8-10.30su
Station: Waterloo

Buses: 149, D1, P11
Adnams Bitter, Tetley Bitter, Ruddles Best, Ind Coope Burton Ale

Busy corner local in a residential area and in the shadow of Waterloo East Station and which benefits greatly from being on the route back to the station of many office workers. This modest, neat and tidy one bar pub is divided into a saloon and public by a three-quarter length, leaded glass partition which gives a 1930s feel. Space in the pub is maximised by means of an island bar, the central stillion of which must be one of the smallest in any pub anywhere. There is a large function/sports TV room in a conservatory style extension to the rear. Trade is very local at weekends and the street itself consists of Victorian terraced houses of the style that were once demolished to make way for high rise towers but are now very desirable. The pub, which has been a frequent entry in the Good Beer Guide is just a few minutes walk from both the Old and Young Vic Theatres.

Leather Exchange

15 Leathermarket St

3

Fuller's
ML ME SL SE
Opening Hours: 11.30-11m-s 12-3, 7-10.30su
Station: London Bridge
Buses: 42, 47, 78, 188, P11
Fuller's Chiswick Bitter, Fuller's London Pride, Fuller's ESB

The pub was leased by the More Balls Than Most juggling and circus co-operative before it went bust at the end of 1995, whereupon it reverted to Fuller's who have decided that it should drop its name (the Juggler's Arms) and revert to its old identity as the Leather Exchange. The old leather exchange building is just around the corner on Weston Street. Being on Leathermarket Street, just off Tanner Street, we may make an informed guess as to the nature of the historic local industry. Locals and taxi drivers always still referred to it as 'the Leather' even during its short incarnation as the Juggler's Arms. Very much in the modern minimalist style, with bare walls and floor, high ceiling, unvarnished wooden tables and chairs with plain wood framed black and white prints of the local industry. One of few pubs in the vicinity with a function room, it concentrates on good ale and good and reasonably priced pub grub. Handsome rather than elegant, the pub offers a wide range of games of the quiet pub variety, ie chess, draughts, cribbage, dominoes etc.

Market Porter

9 Stoney St, Borough

Free House
ML SL
Opening Hours: normal
Station: London Bridge
Spinnaker Buzz, Bishop's Cathedral, Young's Bitter, Harvey's Sussex Bitter, Wadworth 6X + Guest Beers

Busy and bustling, this ex-brew pub now takes real ale from the Bishop's micro brewery next door. It is a cosy 'nook and cranny' pub with a bar on each floor, open fires and stained glass. The upstairs bar is mostly used by diners at lunchtimes and doubles as a function room in the evenings. The ground floor is unusual with four different areas including a snug like room to the right of the entrance with internal glass windows. To the left is a television area which is very popular when football and other sport is on. Opposite Borough Market.

Trinity Arms

29 Swan St

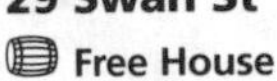

Free House
G ML SL
Opening Hours: normal
Station: Borough
Buses: 133
Marlow's Rebellion + Guest Beers

A Free House since 1994, the pub is made by the landlord and his beer-loving staff. A large range of ales is always on offer, Marlow's Rebellion is the only permanent feature, as the staff like it, whilst there is always at least one beer from the Crouch Vale brewery at Chelmsford. Thursday nights are Jazz. The walls of the pub are festooned with posters and beer mats of real ales that have been served. The pub is divided into public and saloon with bottle-bottom glass windows, and bare brick chimneys. The pub is truly a hidden gem, if it were not for the beer the friendliness of the bar staff alone would warrant a visit.

Wheatsheaf

6 Stoney St

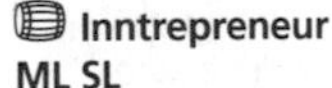

Inntrepreneur
ML SL
Opening Hours: 11-11m-s 12-3, 7-10.30su
Station: London Bridge
Buses: 45, 63, 172, 344, D1, P11

Shepherd Neame Masterbrew, Bishop's Cathedral, Courage Best Bitter + Guest Beers

One of London's dwindling band of true market pubs, though no longer with an early licence. Directly opposite the Borough fruit and vegetable wholesale market, the Wheatsheaf is also a first rate real ale pub. Unusually one of the guest beers will always be a mild or a dark beer. The long pub is split into two by a partition which does not quite make it all the way to the ceiling. The main distinction between the public and saloon is a carpet. This is a functional pub in the way so few are these days; it is designed for working people to drop in to have a beer and be away again. Pay the pub a visit and you will gain a sight of a slice of London life that has vanished from other London market sites like Covent Garden and Spitalfields.

SE3

British Oak

Old Dover Road, Blackheath

S&N
G ML SL
Opening Hours: normal
Station:
Buses: 53, 54, 108, 202, 286, 306, 380, 386
Theakston's Best, Courage Best Bitter, Marston's Pedigree, Theakston's XB, Courage Directors, Morland Old Speckled Hen

Good 'old fashioned' local which has retained a public bar in spite of some recent cosmetic refurbishment, resulting in its acquiring a reputation overnight for its 'historic' sausages, much to the amusement of its solidly regular clientele. The attraction of this pub is that it has consistently sold real ale in excellent condition and still does. The Courage Best is the 'best' for miles around; the volume it is drunk in ensures this. Even in the dark days of the '70s this was one of the very few outlets in London for 'real' Courage, the much lamented mild in particular. There is a wide social mix and conversation is ever present. This is a traditional local of a type that is disappearing in the area and as such is a gem. The 386 bus stops outside.

Princess of Wales

1a Montpelier Road, Blackheath

Vintage Inns

Opening Hours: normal
Worthington Best Bitter, Harvey's Sussex Bitter, Fuller's London Pride, Draught Bass

Large 'Vintage Inn' opposite the pond on Blackheath, which is a popular meeting place, especially for the young professionals of the area. Very busy in the summer and in the evenings, it is the home of several sports teams. There is good quality food at lunchtimes. The 'Heath Bar', overlooking the heath, has some comfortable armchairs and 'open' gas fires in winter. Otherwise, the pub's main attraction for the ale drinker is the regular guest beers, usually from small independents. The pub hosts the occasional beer festival, usually on or around public holidays or important international sports fixtures.

SE5

Fox on the Hill

149 Denmark Hill, Camberwell

Wetherspoon
G ML ME SL SE
Opening Hours: normal
Station: Denmark Hill BR
Buses: 68, 68a, S13
Younger's Scotch, Theakston's Best, Theakston's XB, Courage Directors, Theakston's OP + Guest Beers

A large Wetherspoon's roadhouse decorated and fitted out in standard company style. Clean efficient and anonymous service; food is served until an hour before closing every day of the week; 'fresh' grills and steaks are available after 6pm. The guest beers come from the Wetherspoon's list of 30 which is updated every three months or so. Beer festivals take place in spring and autumn. Close to Denmark Hill station and a pleasant and comfortable venue for a meal and a drink if you require something a little less lively and noisy than the nearby 'Phoenix' (q.v.).

Phoenix & Firkin

5 Windsor Walk, Denmark Hill

Firkin
G ML ME SL SE
Opening Hours: normal
Station: Denmark Hill BR
Buses: 40, 68, 68a, 176, 185, 484, S13, N79
House beers + Guest Beers; Weston's Old Rosie Cider

One of the original and most characterful Firkin pubs, rebuilt by David Bruce from the gutted remains of the listed Denmark Hill station booking office. Initially there was some opposition, but eventually the Phoenix duly arose. The bar is open plan, with an upstairs gallery, and is fitted with railway memorabilia. There is a huge clock suspended from the ceiling and a model train shuttles back and forth above part of the bar. An obvious meeting place, especially for railway enthusiasts. The house brewed beers are generally kept under blanket pressure. Guest beers, including some imported from other Firkin breweries, generally are not. However the situation is unclear and if in doubt ask.

SE6

Black Horse & Harrow

167 Rushey Green, Catford

Allied Domecq
G DA ML ME SL SE
Opening Hours: normal
Station: Catford BR
Buses: 181, 185, 202, 208
Adnams Bitter, Tetley Bitter, Marston's Pedigree, Ind Coope Burton Ale + Guest Beers

A large, wide fronted pub which dominates the Catford Road. Built in 1897, it has been recently and tastefully refurbished in a manner sympathetic with its original Victorian style. The dining area has a fine domed ceiling with original plaster work and the decor gives a fair idea of the Victorians' fondness for 'plush'. Divided into three distinct areas, the pub has retained many fine features, notably a J Mills and Sons mirror over an original fireplace. The bar stillion is also original as are the embossed wall coverings below the dado rail, whilst modern etched glass work blends in well with original. The pub is directly across the road from Catford's Town Hall and its theatre, noted for its pantomimes.

Rutland Arms

55 Perry Hill, Catford

Free House
ML SL SE
Opening Hours: normal
Greene King IPA, Young's Bitter, Fuller's London Pride, Adnams Broadside, Draught Bass, Young's Special

Until a few years ago, this was a run-down disco pub. It is now a family local offering a range of excellently kept real ales, many unusual for the area, such as the bottled Worthington White Shield and a seasonal beer from the Pilgrim Brewery. It has gained a reputation for quality live music; jazz of all styles is played most evenings, except Thursdays when rock and roll or country invades. As such, it attracts musicians and fans from far and wide and is an excellent meeting place. Tasty home-cooked meals are available at lunchtimes, the Sunday roasts are a speciality. This pub is a superb example of what a little care and attention can do to turn round a run-down establishment.

SE8

Crystal Palace Tavern

105 Tanner's Hill, Deptford

Free House
SL SE
Opening Hours: 3-12m-th 3-1f 12-1s 3-10.30su
Station: New Cross BR
Buses: 21, 36, 53, 136, 177
Varying range of beers and ciders

A genuine side-street Free House which manages to get through a staggering number of beers, mostly from small independents, many of them rare, or unusual, on its eight handpumps. As such it is a must for the beer hunter and connoisseur. Basic and bare-boarded, it nevertheless extends a warm welcome to all. Live music is on many nights when there are also licence extensions. It opens at 3pm, when the Royal George, which used to sell real Sam Smith's just down the road, closes.

Dog & Bell

116 Prince St, Deptford

Free House
G SL SE
Opening Hours: normal
Station: Deptford BR
Fuller's London Pride, Fuller's ESB + Guest Beers

A back-street gem not far from Deptford station and High Street, which is well regarded for the quality of its interesting guest beers and warm friendly atmosphere, not to mention its wide range of malt whiskies. The pub has recently been extended to cater for its increasing popularity. In spite of the fact that the cellar is reputedly haunted, it still delivers excellent ale. Sunday night quizzes are becoming popular. The pub was voted South East London CAMRA Pub of the Year 1993.

SE10

Admiral Hardy
7 College Approach, Greenwich

Free House
ML SL
Opening Hours: normal
Station: Greenwich BR
Buses: 177, 180, 188, 199, 286, 386, N1
Shepherd Neame Masterbrew, Tetley Bitter, Shepherd Neame Best, Ind Coope Burton Ale + Guest Beers

Single bar with one entrance directly onto Greenwich Market, a popular meeting place at weekends. There is a nautical theme to the pub which is popular with locals, tourists and market traders. The atmosphere is friendly, lively and smoky. Live music Sundays, quiz nights Mondays.

Cutty Sark
6 Ballast Quay, Greenwich

Free House
FR G ML SL SE
Opening Hours: normal
Station: Greenwich
Buses: 177, 180, 188, 199, 286, 386, N1
Worthington Best Bitter, Draught Bass

A large 400-year old Grade II listed building on the South Bank of the Thames, with wooden panelling and a nautical feel. The upper floor is divided into galleries at different levels around a central staircase and maybe used by families at lunchtime. In one direction, the pub is dwarfed by the old Greenwich power station. Directly across the Thames is Canary Wharf. In between, however, there are panoramic views of the river, both from the pub and an outside patio. Food is of excellent quality. The pub may be reached from Greenwich via a riverside walk, otherwise head for the power station chimneys and you will not be far away. Well worth a visit.

Gipsy Moth
60 Greenwich Church St, Greenwich

Allied Domecq

FR DA ML ME SL SE
Opening Hours: normal
Station: Greenwich BR
Buses: 177, 180, 188, 199, 286, 386, N1
Adnams Bitter, Tetley Bitter + Guest Beers

Large single bar pub within the shadow of the Cutty Sark, that was once called the Wheatsheaf but has now been renamed and dedicated to Sir Francis Chichester. His widow re-opened the pub in 1974. Meals at lunchtime are popular with tourists. The evenings are largely dominated by local students. As with most pubs in Greenwich there is a sizeable collection of nautical bric-a-brac.

Mitre

291 Greenwich High Road, Greenwich

Free House
G
Opening Hours: normal
Station: Greenwich BR
Buses: 177, 180, 199, N1
John Smith's Bitter, Courage Best Bitter, Fuller's London Pride, Draught Bass

A long single-roomed pub with a rear conservatory and enclosed garden, just around the corner from Greenwich BR station. Recently refurbished with the kind of mottled maroon wallpaper that is currently much in vogue in pubs and fine, matching upholstered armchairs, much in an 'Admiralty' style. A mitre motif runs through the glasswork in the windows and in stained glass partitions. Raised areas at either end of the pub break up the floor. Overall the Mitre is a sunny, modern example of the traditional style pub in central Greenwich, just that extra 50 yards off the main drag to avoid the tourist crush.

Richard I

52 Royal Hill, Greenwich

Young's
G ML SL
Opening Hours: normal
Station: Greenwich BR
Buses: 177, N1
Young's Bitter, Young's Special, Young's Winter Warmer

Quiet local with two attractive bowed windows, directly adjacent to another pub, The Fox & Hounds. It has a slight nautical feel, like most Greenwich pubs, due to the nature of the wood settle seating and low, slatted wood ceiling, which gives it a 'tween deck atmosphere.

Wooden seating extends into the bowed windows in the public and saloon areas, whilst a single bar serves both. There is a patio at the front and a garden at the rear, where barbecues are held in Summer. Well worth walking up Royal Hill for.

Trafalgar Tavern

6 Park Row, Greenwich

Inntrepreneur
G R ML ME SL SE
Opening Hours: normal
Station: Maze Hill
Buses: 177, 180, 188, 199, 286, 386, N1
Courage Best Bitter, Courage Directors, Ruddles County, Morland's Old Speckled Hen

A fascinating and historic riverside inn, dating back to the eighteenth century. The present building, in Regency style, was built in the early years of Queen Victoria's reign. It was the haunt of Dickens and Thackeray, as well as Stanfield the seascape artist who regularly dined there. Dickens used the Trafalgar as a setting for the wedding breakfast in *Our Mutual Friend*. It was also one of the famous venues for the Ministerial Whitebait dinners of the late nineteenth century. The pub was actually closed in 1915 for a number of years before being rescued and reopened. Today it is a lively pub, popular with tourists and locals. There is live jazz two or three nights a week. Superb views of the Thames are to be had from its many rooms, and the menu is imaginative and well regarded.

SE11

Greyhound

336 Kennington Park Road, Kennington

Inntrepreneur
ML ME SL SE
Opening Hours: normal
Station: Oval
Buses: 3, 36, 109, 133, 159, 185, 355
courage Best Bitter, Wadworth 6X, Courage Directors + Guest Beers

People travel to drink the Guinness at the Greyhound, which is first rate and the pub is not bad either, especially on a Sunday, when instead of the usual pub bar fare of cheese and biscuits, half Billingsgate market is spread over the tables. Unlike many pubs where the Guinness is good, the ale is not neglected and customers are encouraged to complain if things are not right. The long narrow mock-Tudor pub is always busy and its quality of service and beer is what keeps them coming in. Nearby pubs are not nearly as full. Your Editor surveyed this pub and ordered a pint of Bateman's (that week's guest ale), he then sat down to commence the above description but before pint was even put to lips, an efficient, aproned, Irish barman snatched his pint away saying, 'Don't have that one, it's the end of the barrel, this will be much better.' The number of pubs where that will happen is small indeed. Next door but one to Oval tube (there's another pub in between), it is convenient for the ale desert of the Oval Cricket Ground and historic Kennington Park.

SE12

Ashburnham Arms

3

25 Ashburnham Grove, Greenwich

Shepherd Neame
FR G ML ME
Opening Hours: 12-3, 6-11m-s 12-3, 7-10.30su
Buses: 53, 180, 199, 177
Shepherd Neame Masterbrew, Shepherd Neame Spitfire, Shepherd Neame Porter, Shepherd Neame Bishop's Finger

Quality 'local', popular with professional classes, in a back-street between Lewisham and Greenwich. It has a friendly welcoming atmosphere and the beers are invariably in superb condition – the best Shep's for miles around! Pasta dishes are home cooked with numerous options, including vegetarian, available lunchtimes and Tuesday and Friday evenings until 8.30pm. There are regular quizzes and occasional 'unplugged' music in the new extension, which can be used as a family room. This eases the crush at weekends but does not detract from the overall ambience and allows people to get to the bar billiards table.

SE13

Hogshead

354 Lewisham High St

Whitbread
SL
Opening Hours: normal
Station: Ladywell BR

Flowers IPA, Boddington's Bitter + Guest Beers

Until a couple of years ago this local, then called the Elephant, was one of the few Fremlins badged pubs in London. Now a Whitbread 'Hogshead Ale House', it has however retained some of its character. The popular manager produces his own magazine for the regulars, many of whom are in the 25-35 age bracket. The guest beers (usually around six, two of which are on gravity) come from independents from all over the country, as well as the specials for the chain. Close to Ladywell Station, it is also handy for Lewisham Hospital.

SE14

Rose Inn

272 New Cross Road, New Cross

Inntrepreneur

SL SE

Opening Hours: 11-4, 5.30-11m-s 12-10.30su

Station: New Cross Gate BR

Buses: 21, 36, 53, 136, 171, 172, 177, N21, N36, N53, N71, N81

Courage Best Bitter, Courage Directors, Young's Special

A good 'honest' local in a relative desert for cask conditioned ale. The open plan design is divided into discreet alcoves by wooden partitions. The locals are active in collecting for charity and there are several sports teams. The pub is situated directly opposite New Cross Gate station and a new Sainsbury's Superstore and offers, arguably, the most pleasant environment for a meeting and a 'real' drink in the area. There is a strong 'boxing' theme associated with the pub and photographs of such are much in evidence.

SE15

Goat House

2 Penge Road, South Norwood

Fuller's

G DA CP ML ME SL SE

Opening Hours: normal

Station: Norwood Junction BR

Fuller's Chiswick Bitter, Fuller's London Pride, Fuller's ESB

Large multi-roomed ex-Charrington's pub; now a Fuller's tied house. The name apparently derives from the days when the site was a clearing in the 'North Wood' where a goatherd lived, and is marked 'Goat House' on an enclosure map of 1797. There is emphasis on food and social activities, excellent beer and service. The pub does fine Sunday lunches, a rare thing in South East London and it is an easy five minutes from Norwood Junction.

SE16

Angel

101 Bermondsey Wall East, Rotherhithe

Greenalls
G R ML ME SL SE
Opening Hours: 11-3, 5.30-11m-s 12-3, 7-10.30su
Station: Rotherhithe
Buses: 47, 188, P11
Young's Bitter, Courage Directors

One of the last galleried pubs overlooking the Thames. The present building dates from the nineteenth century although there has been an inn on the site for much longer. The Angel is at the meeting of the Rotherhithe and Riverside walks and there are superb views of the Thames and Tower Bridge. Walk along the river to find 'Dr Salter's Daydream'. Opposite are the remains of a moated manor house of Edward III (mid-fourteenth century), one of the many royal dwellings along the Thames. Apart from Samuel Pepys and Judge Jeffreys, Laurel and Hardy are also numbered amongst the celebrity customers. The restaurant has an excellent reputation and is open 12-1.45pm Sundays to Fridays and 7-9.45pm Monday to Saturday; booking is recommended. Combine a visit to the Angel with one to the Mayflower (q.v.) using the Rotherhithe Walk.

Mayflower

117 Rotherhithe St, Rotherhithe

Greene King
G ML ME SL SE
Opening Hours: 11.30-11m-s 12-0.30su
Station: Rotherhithe
Buses: 47, 188, 225, P11, P13, P14, N47, N70
Greene King IPA, Greene King Abbot

The Mayflower, carrying the Pilgrim Fathers, is supposed to have sailed from the steps alongside the riverside pub back in 1620, when the inn was known as the 'Spread Eagle'. Part of the pub dates back to the sixteenth century and it has been skilfully restored. At one time, it was also licensed to sell both British and American postage stamps; this was for the convenience of sailors arriving on odd tides. An extremely well regarded restaurant is open at lunchtimes and evenings (until 9pm) except Mondays. Sunday lunch from 12-2.15pm can be enjoyed on the patio in summer, giving a fine view overlooking the Thames. Whilst in the area, visit nearby St Mary's Church, designed by John James, an associate of Sir Christopher Wren and the pumping house for Brunel's tunnel under the Thames, or, better still, travel from nearby Rotherhithe station and see the listed tunnel itself. The well kept Greene King beers are unusual for the area. All in all, a must.

SE17

Beehive

60 Carter St, Walworth

Free House
G ML ME SL
Opening Hours: normal
Station: Elephant & Castle
Buses: 12, 35, 40, 45, 68, 171, 176, P5
Courage Best Bitter, Fuller's London Pride, Wadworth 6X, Courage Directors

There has been a pub on this site for over 200 years but it is definitely still a hidden gem amidst the back streets, off the Walworth Road. The large horse-shoe shaped bar is surrounded by candle-lit tables and a wreath of interesting photographs, paintings and bric-a-brac. An extensive and imaginative bistro style menu is available everyday until 10pm; vegetarian options included. There is also a large range of malt whiskies, and whiskeys, including some rare ones. The pub has an association with Surrey cricket. This is an excellent place for a meal and a drink in a very pleasant atmosphere. Well worth a visit.

Crown

116 Brandon St, Walworth

Bass
SL SE
Opening Hours: normal
Station: Elephant & Castle
Buses: P3
Worthington Best Bitter, Draught Bass, Young's Special

Unfortunately, the interior of this friendly back-street one bar local does not match up to the magnificent tiled Wenlock Brewery facade on the outside. However, in a somewhat run down area, this is something of an oasis, with a definite community feel. The Guinness handpump is, however, only a dummy but the others dispense some excellent quality ale. Not many facilities but a genuine warm welcome makes up for this. The pub may be found a short walk from the Walworth Road.

SE18

Bull

151 Shooters Hill Road, Woolwich

S&N
FR G SL SE
Opening Hours: 11-3, 5.30-11m-s 12-3, 7-10.30su
Station: Welling BR
Buses: 89, 122, 161, 178
Courage Best Bitter, Courage Directors

Homely pub near the top of Shooters Hill, not far from the famed Oxleas Wood, now apparently reprieved from planning blight. The building itself is typical of those from the old Beasley's Brewery of Plumstead (founded 1845, registered as a private company in 1943, taken over by Courage in 1963). There is a pool table in the public bar and occasional live music. A combination of a stroll in the nearby woods and a few pints outside in the garden would make a very pleasant sunny afternoon.

Prince Albert (Rose's)

49 Hare St, Woolwich

Bass
Opening Hours: 11-11m-s 12-3su
Station: Woolwich Arsenal
Buses: 54, 161, 177, 178, 180, N77
Varying beer range

Popular one bar, wooden panelled, town centre pub with an ever changing range of guest ales. This is an excellent place to stop and have a drink whilst enjoying shopping; facilities are limited but it's busy and lively. Not far from Woolwich Arsenal station and a plenitude of bus routes, the pub is a regular Good Beer Guide entrant.

SE19

Royal Albert

42 Westow Hill, Upper Norwood

Bass
G ML
Opening Hours: normal
Station: Crystal Palace
Buses: 2, 3, 63, 122, 137a, 157, 202, 227, 249, 306, 322, 450
Charrington IPA, Hancocks HB, Fuller's London Pride, Draught Bass

Set back behind the building line in the main shopping centre of Crystal Palace's 'triangle', the Royal Albert is a friendly two-bar pub local whose front door serves a small public bar, whilst the side serves a much larger wood-panelled lounge at the rear. An impressive collection of jugs adorns the ceiling beams in the lounge. Close to Crystal Palace Park with its concert bowl, athletics stadium and camp site.

SE20

Moon & Stars
164-166 High Street, Penge

Wetherspoon
G CP DA ML ME SL SE
Opening Hours: normal
Station: Kent House BR
Buses: 176, 194, 227, 312, 351, 358,
Younger's Scotch, Theakston's Best, Marston's Pedigree, Theakston's XB, Theakston's OP + Guest Beers; Weston's Old Rosie Cider

A fairly large Wetherspoon's house built on the site of a former cinema, and through good design still manages to maintain an intimate atmosphere. The large no smoking area and multitude of small alcoves all contain descriptions of Penge history. The pub is the best meeting place in the area and the only outlet for consistently good real ale. It is notable for a large number and range of guest ales from independent brewers.

SE21

Crown & Greyhound
73 Dulwich Village, Dulwich

Allied Domecq
G R ML ME SL SE
Opening Hours: normal
Station: West Dulwich BR

Buses: 37, P4, P13, S11, S13
Tetley Bitter, Young's Bitter, Ind Coope Burton Ale + Guest Beers

A fine imposing Victorian pub divided into a number of areas. The pub retains plenty of original features including wood panelling, glasswork, its embossed ceiling, fireplaces, carved settles and the bar stillion. The pub is especially popular on Sundays when the restaurant's roast dinners are very popular. It benefits from being the only pub in the area. The pub is a handy place to rest after a walk on Dulwich Common, or to contemplate the fine collection of painting at the famous Dulwich Picture Gallery, the Bourgeois Mausoleum which inspired Gilbert Scott's design for the old red London phone box.

SE22

Clockhouse

196a Peckham Rye Common, Peckham

Young's
ML ME SL SE
Opening Hours: normal
Buses: 12, 312, 63
Young's Bitter, Young's Special

An attractive pub, originally an off-licence, that features a large collection of unusual clocks and jugs. Note the original stained glass window as a clock in the front right-hand bar. There is also a large collection of bottled beer labels. The outstanding feature of this pub, apart from the excellent Young's beers, is the wonderful floral displays in and outside, The pub is three times winner of the Young's 'Garden Display' competition. The pub also has a pleasant view out onto Peckham Rye.

SE23

Bird in Hand

25 Dartmouth Road, Forest Hill

Wetherspoon
G ML ME SL SE
Opening Hours: normal
Station: Forest Hill
Buses: 122, 176, 312, N71
Younger's Scotch, Theakston's Best, Marston's Pedigree, Theakston's XB, Courage Directors + Guest Beers

One of the smallest Wetherspoon's outlets, the 'Bird' was refurbished from a rather run down Charrington's pub, and as such, has brought a much needed fillip to the area. Certainly the average price of a pint of ordinary bitter has gone down in Forest Hill as other pubs in the neighbourhood have had to respond to the challenge. A succession of good managers has given the pub a reputation for serving high quality ale, with many interesting guest beers. Being small, however, the Bird does not hang onto its managers long and a period of stability would be welcome. Very close to Forest Hill station, this is a good place for meeting. The pub has retained its locals and community feel in spite of corporate ownership and is definitely one of the more characterful 'Wetherspoons'.

Railway Telegraph

112 Stanstead Road, Forest Hill

Shepherd Neame
FR G ML SL SE
Opening Hours: normal
Station: Forest Hill BR
Buses: 122, 185
Shepherd Neame Masterbrew, Shepherd Neame Spitfire, Shepherd Neame Porter, Shepherd Neame Bishop's Finger

Two-roomed local decorated with memorabilia and often frequented by anglers and bikers. A family room was added a few years ago and a small garden enables you to study the traffic on the busy South Circular outside. The pub became tied to Shep's in the 1970s and there is a faithful local following. Known by some as the 'Torygraph' as it is very close to the Lewisham Labour Party HQ, it numbers Councillors and even MPs amongst its frequent customers but do not let that put you off.

SE24

Lord Stanley

31 Hinton Road, Herne Hill

Free House
ML ME SL SE
Opening Hours: 12-11m-s 12-10.30su
Hancocks HB + Guest Beers

Although on first entering, this one-bar, side-street local may appear a little run-down, rather like the area in which it is situated, a few minutes stay should convince the drinker that here is a pub that is intent on providing quality beer, good wholesome food, and a warm welcome, all at very competitive prices. Pot plants and American number plates provide an interesting backdrop; the CDs on the juke box are hand chosen and the pool table is large. This is a genuine Free House, ex-Charrington's and an example of the disappearing breed of honest, old-fashioned community locals. As such it is a gem. It is also handy for Loughborough Junction, though unfortunately the trains do not stop there very often (Mon-Fri peak hours only, last train 7pm). The pub is named after Lord Stanley, fourteenth Earl of Derby and one time prime minister in the last century.

SE25

Alliance

91 High St, South Norwood

Inntrepreneur
SL SE
Opening Hours: normal
Station: Norwood Junction BR
Courage Best Bitter, Wadworth 6X, Courage Directors, Morland's Old Speckled Hen

Good old-fashioned local very close to the main entrance of Norwood Junction station. Large collection of plates and brass ornaments but they do not detract from the cosy atmosphere which is mainly due to the buzz of local conversation, especially in the evenings. A previous landlord started an enlightened and interesting guest beer policy, which has been maintained; the beers invariably come from small independents. The pub even stocks Imperial Russian Stout, so it knows how to look after people. The meals are only available at lunchtimes but are good quality and value; O'Hagan's famous speciality sausages were sold at the time of the visit.

Portmanor

1 Portland Road, South Norwood

Free House
ML ME SL SE
Opening Hours: normal
Station: Norwood Junction BR
Buses: 197, 312
Fuller's London Pride, Young's Special, Greene King Abbot + Guest Beers

A good ale house for the area, which specialises in beers from small independent brewers. Otherwise very much a sporting house with a large satellite TV screen on permanently.

SE26

Dulwich Wood House

39 Sydenham Hill, Sydenham

Young's
G ML SL SE
Opening Hours: normal
Station: Sydenham Hill BR
Buses: 63, 202
Young's Bitter, Young's Special, Young's Winter Warmer

Large pub, originally designed by Joseph Paxton, set on top of Sydenham Hill overlooking Dulwich College estate. There are magnificent views across London to be had nearby and many local walks through the surrounding woods, as well as a nature reserve. The pub itself is a popular meeting place for a varied clientele. In summer, the large garden is extremely popular with families. There is a children's play area, space for Petanque and a barbecue and garden bar (no real ale). Inside there are many rare photographs of the old Crystal Palace racing circuit which now forms part of the nearby sports complex. You may reach the pub via a steep uphill footpath from Sydenham Hill Station.

Greyhound

315 Kirkdale, Sydenham

Allied Domecq
G CP DA ML ME SL SE
Opening Hours: normal
Station: Sydenham BR
Buses: 2, 306, 312, N71
Adnams Bitter, Tetley Bitter, Young's Bitter

This is the oldest surviving inn in Sydenham and was once a well respected hotel, next to the Croydon Canal, now the main London Bridge to Croydon railway line that was built over it. The pub has been refurbished recently in a style similar to Wetherspoons. However, the two notable architectural features have been retained. What was once a magnificent tiled, mosaic entrance with a glass roof is now inside the pub. The bar itself, not dissimilar to a large Welsh dresser with etched glass, has been rotated through 180° and now forms the centre-piece of the pub. Both of these are worthy of inspection. Food is available most of the day. There is regular live music in a separate room; mostly blues/indie.

SE27

Hope

49 Norwood High St, West Norwood

Young's
G ML SL
Opening Hours: normal
Station: West Norwood BR
Buses: 2, 68, 68a, X68, 196, 315, 322, N2, S11
Young's Bitter, Young's Special, Young's Winter Warmer

A typical South London locals' pub. On a Sunday the world and his wife are in and very jolly it is too. A modest horseshoe style single bar pub, with the front of the bar facing the front windows of the house, and additional seating down each flank. Unusual lampshades adorn the simple bar top shelf, and the colour scheme is traditional Young's cream, nicotine and pale wood throughout. In many respects this is an archetypal Young's house with all ages represented and the gossip is local. The notice board posts up the results of the weekly raffles. The Hope, which was a beer house until after the last war, would seem to take its name from sailors' Hope, as a number of nautical prints all manage to depict the uncertainty of life at sea. It is instantly recognisable as a South West London pub. East End boozers have a slightly different feel. This is the public house as it has always been, and, God willing, as it will always be.

Bromley – BR1

Arkwrights Wheel

12 Widmore Road, Bromley

Allied Domecq
ML SL
Opening Hours: normal
Station: Bromley South
Buses: 208, 227, 351, 358, 361, 726
Adnams Bitter, Tetley Bitter, Ind Coope Burton Ale + Guest Beers

Small U-shaped corner pub with nicotine coloured decor. One limb hides a pool table, the other a quieter, coloured wallpapered drinking room. Very much a drinking pub, just off Bromley Market Square, it is a stop off on the way home and popular at weekends with shoppers. Fine original fireplaces compensate for the ugly bar mounted tills and the one or two slightly inferior repro fittings detract slightly from what is otherwise a fine example of a small, town centre, 'drop in for a quick one' pub. The guest beers are from the Carlsberg-Tetley list and the exterior is decorated with mottoes from Dr Johnson and Plato. Who can argue with the logic of: *'There are two reasons for drinking, One is when you are thirsty, to cure it. The other when you are not thirsty, to prevent it.'*

Pamphilion

High Street, Bromley

Regent Inns

G DA ML SL

Opening Hours: normal

Station: Bromley South BR

Buses: 61, 119, 126, 138, 146, 162, 208, 261, 314, 320, 336

Brakspear Bitter, Courage Best Bitter, Wadworth 6X, Theakston's XB

Cleverly refurbished large single-room corner pub, with an impressively understated Regency frontage, reminiscent of an old fashioned wine merchants. The pub is divided into a number of seating areas. A wood panelled front area, with upholstered sofa and free newspapers, gives way to a bare brick walled, pine tabled, raised drinking area, which in turn opens onto a lighter rear conservatory area and finally, a large sheltered enclosed garden with palm tree motifs. The floors match the areas, varying from herringbone parquet, carpet to small flagstones.

Beckenham – BR3

Coach & Horses

Burnhill Road, Beckenham

S&N

G ML SL

Opening Hours: normal

Station: Beckenham Junction BR

Buses: 54, 162, 227, 351, 367, N3

Theakston's Best, Courage Best Bitter, Theakston's XB, Courage Directors, Theakston's OP

Small one-bar pub, with front seating area just off the main High Street. A small saloon at the rear is little more than a snug separated by velvet curtains. The pub's broad, fully windowed frontage makes the pub a bright airy place. A pleasant little locals' pub.

George

111 High Street, Beckenham

Bass
G CP ML ME SL SE
Opening Hours: normal
Station: Beckenham Junction BR
Buses: 54, 162, 194, 227, 367, 726, N3
Hancocks HB, Fuller's London Pride, Draught Bass + Guest Beers

The George is a large imposing weatherboard building on Beckenham High Street. There has been a pub on the site since 1662 and the current building is the last original building on the High Street and was the first to be lit with gas lighting. The Grade II listed building has led an interesting and charmed life. It narrowly missed being flattened by a V1 in 1945. A century or so previously Pitt the Younger was known to ride out of London to The George for romantic assignations. In 1715, a coaching run to the Star Inn, Fish Street, London was set up, which returned the same day. In 1886 the pub hosted the petty sessions.

Jolly Woodman

9 Chancery Lane, Beckenham

Bass
G ML SL
Opening Hours: normal
Station: Beckenham BR
Buses: 227, 726
Joules Crown Ale, Charrington IPA, Draught Bass

Small intimate L-shaped local with a bar at front and a small drinking area at the side leading to a rear garden. The whitewashed outside walls are broken only by the colour of hanging baskets, while inside there are the plain and simple fittings that have been accumulated over the course of the years, which is as it should be. The light reflected from the lino floor is filtered through the frosted glass windows by geraniums in window boxes. Very much a back-street local and a find for those who like to sit quietly in a corner and eavesdrop on life. The pub is hidden away just off the main Bromley Road.

Orpington – BR6

Cricketers

93 Chislehurst Road, Orpington

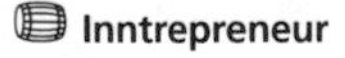

G CP ML SL
Opening Hours: normal
Station: Orpington
Buses: 61
Courage Best Bitter + Guest Beers

An old carriers' pub dating back to before the 1860s, the Cricketers has always been a tenanted house. Standing just at one corner of Broomhill Common, it saw good business in the days when the common operated as a horse market but has survived as suburban Orpington has grown up around it. An unassuming decor with fragments of wood panelling and real ceiling beams give the pub much of that 'Kentish Courage' look of years ago. A good locals' pub tucked a few streets back from Orpington High Street, it has a modesty that lends charm. Not opening Sunday afternoons for the time being.

Harvest Moon

High St, Orpington
Wetherspoon
ML ME SL SE
Opening Hours: normal
Station: Orpington
Buses: 51, 61, 208, R1, R2, R3, R4, R7, R8, R11
Younger's Scotch, Theakston's Best, Theakston's XB, Courage Directors, Greene King Abbot + Guest Beers

Busy pub in Orpington High Street, seemingly popular with pensioners. There is a dining area of partitioned seating, with a no-smoking area at rear. A dark interior with the usual line in Wetherspoon decor, lightens towards the front of the pub with the also usual Wetherspoon feature of the front full height windows opening, café style, onto the street. A large semi-nude alabaster statue forms an interesting conversation piece in the middle of the frontage. Perhaps she represents the spirit of the harvest?

Old White Lion

Farnborough Common, Locksbottom
Free House
G CP ML SL
Opening Hours: normal closed su
Station: Orpington
Buses: 61, 208, 358, 402, R1, R11
Greene King IPA, Shepherd Neame Masterbrew, Courage Best Bitter, Wadworth 6X, Draught Bass, Shepherd Neame Spitfire + Guest Beers

A Free House since 1626, this attractive whitewashed and timber framed pub is immediately obvious as a carriers' inn. It is situated on the old London to Hastings road and is of unusual construction in that the interior is built of largely non-local stone, with one or two knapped flint walls, which are rather more typical of East Kent. Modern fittings are of a mock Tudor nature and the garden is now in what was the old wagoners' yard. There is a wide range of well kept beers, barbecues on Sunday lunchtimes and Jazz on alternate Sundays. Customers are mainly locals but the pub is also convenient for Down House (Charles Darwin's birthplace), Chartwell, Westerham, and the old Roman sites at Lullington Castle and Orpington Villa.

SW1

Albert

52 Victoria Street

S&N

R ML ME SL SE

Opening Hours: normal

Station: St James Park

Buses: 11, 24, 211

John Smith's Bitter, Theakston's Best, Wadworth 6X, Theakston's XB, Courage Directors, Ruddles County, Greene King Abbot, Theakston's OP

The Grade II-listed pub is one of the few nineteenth-century buildings to escape the mass rebuilding of Victoria Street in the late 1960s. First licensed in 1831 as the Blue Coat Boy, it was rebuilt and renamed in 1864 by architect J Carter Woods of the Artillery Brewery, for which it served as the brewery tap. The brewery was taken over by James Watney's Stag brewery in 1899, which was only a few hundred yards away in what is still named Stag Place. Large and very busy at lunchtimes and evenings with office workers, it is a favourite stop for coach parties on the tourist trail and is also popular with Chelsea Pensioners, who are not slow to let the tourists stand them a drink. There is a restaurant on the first floor, which is reached by the kind of staircase debutantes favour for making dramatic entrances. The staircase is lined with prints of British prime ministers, the incumbent having pride of place at the top.

Antelope

22 Eaton Terrace

Allied Domecq

R ML SL

Opening Hours: normal

Station: Sloane Square

Buses: C1

Adnams Bitter, Tetley Bitter, Everards Tiger, Wadworth 6X, Ind Coope Burton Ale

Small unspoilt haven built in 1830 mainly for use by the servants of the nearby gentry. A wood-panelled bar with island servery, small side room and a wine bar and restaurant on the first floor. The pub has a slightly upmarket clientele but one that is nowhere near as 'Sloaney' as might be expected, given the pub's close proximity to Sloane Square. Fortunately, it is slightly towards Victoria rather than the Kings Road, so escapes the worst excesses of *Sloaneism*. The pub has a strong rugby following and also runs its own cricket team.

Bag 'O' Nails

6 Buckingham Palace Road

T&J Bernard

ML ME SL SE

Opening Hours: normal

Station: Victoria

Buses: 11, 121, 239, C1, C10

Theakston's Best, Theakston's XB, Theakston's OP + Guest Beers

Bow-windowed corner pub with a wood-panelled interior and an additional bar upstairs. Not surprisingly it is usually filled with tourists as it is the nearest pub to Buckingham Palace; indeed it is next to the palace exit when Buck House is open to the great unwashed in summer. One of the first in the T&J Bernard chain of houses (in the classic style rather than their kitchen style). T&J Bernard established a brewery in Canongate, Edinburgh in 1840. They were taken over and closed down by Scottish Breweries in 1960, who later that year were merged with the Newcastle Brewery to form Scottish and Newcastle. The pub was licensed in 1774 as Satyre (Devil) and Bacchanals (pack of dogs) which, by the following decade, had been corrupted to the 'bag o'nails', which was the name of a play by Ben Johnson. The present pub was rebuilt in 1939 as part of the development of Belgravia and the surrounding area by the Grosvenor estate and is Grade II listed.

Buckingham Arms

62 Petty France

Young's

ML ME SL SE

Opening Hours: 11-11m-f, 11-3, 5.30-11s, 12-3, 7-10.30su

Station: St James Park

Young's Bitter, Young's Special, Young's Winter Warmer

Long-established popular office workers' pub, just opposite the rear of St James's Barracks. The pub has a long mirrored bar, a curved counter and a corridor drinking area, no doubt to make the many civil servants from the nearby Home Office feel at home. The licence dates from at least 1785 when it was known as the Black Horse. It was rebuilt in 1898 and renamed in 1901. The pub is handy for the Home Office, the Passport Office, the headquarters of London Underground and the Crown Prosecution Service and is therefore one for those with official business to conduct.

Cardinal

23 Francis Street, Westminster

Bass

G DA R ML

Opening Hours: 11-11m-f 11-3, 8-11s 12-3, 7-10.30su

Station: Victoria

Buses: 507

Charrington IPA, Worthington Best Bitter, Fuller's London Pride, Draught Bass

A large Charrington establishment (formerly tenanted to Finch's) with a wine bar food area at the rear and a restaurant on the first floor. Holds a number of real ale festivals throughout the year. Called the Windsor Castle until it underwent major refurbishment in 1962 (it won an American architectural award some eight years later). The present pub was rebuilt in 1896 by the New Westminster Brewery, at a cost of £4,450. The architect was H W Budd who did all that brewery's work at the period.

Cask and Glass

39 Palace Street

Shepherd Neame

SL

Opening Hours: 11-11m-f 11-3, 6-11s 12-3su

Station: Victoria

Buses: 11, 24, 211

Shepherd Neame Masterbrew, Shepherd Neame Spitfire

Tiny intimate pub, in fact the smallest in SW1, with a horticultural display on the frontage. The pub may be small but the welcome is big and it is the only Shepherd Neame outlet for quite a distance. At one time beer was served only in half pints but now this practice has happily ended, for as Dickens pointed out, 'It can't be tasted in a sip!'. The pub was licensed comparatively late in 1862 and was called the Duke of Cambridge until 1963.

Fox and Hounds

29 Passmore Street

Bass

ML SL

Opening Hours: 11-3, 5.30-11m-s 12-2, 7-10.30su

Station: Sloane Square

Buses: 11, 211, 239

Charrington IPA, Greene King IPA, Hancocks HB, Draught Bass

If ever a pub deserved the epithet 'hidden gem' this is it. Run by the same landlady for 25 years this tiny corner pub has a beer and wine licence only – probably the only one left in London – and has appeared in every edition of the Good Beer Guide. The pub, which has a very friendly atmosphere, can get a bit crowded before and after performances at the nearby Royal Court Theatre. It is also handy for Sloane Square and the Kings Road.

Golden Lion

25 King Street

Nicholsons

G ML SL

Opening Hours: 11.30-11m-f 12-4s closed su

Station: Green Park

Buses: 3, 6, 9, 12, 13, 15, 23, 53, 88, 94, 139, 159, X53

Brakspear Bitter, Greene King IPA, Tetley Bitter

Ornate bay-fronted pub facing Christie's auction rooms. The upstairs 'theatre' bar and dining area are furnished with memorabilia from the former St James Theatre which stood next door from 1835-1957. The pub's licence dates from 1685 and it has occupied the present site since at least 1732. The present pub was designed by the architects Eedle and Meyers and was rebuilt around 1899/1900. The ground floor bar can be hired for functions on Saturday. The pub is handy for the clubland, St James's Palace and the park.

Graftons

2 Strutton Ground

S&N
ML ME SL SE
Opening Hours: 11-11m-f 12-3s
Station: St James's Park
Buses: 11, 24, 211
Worthington Best Bitter, Fuller's London Pride, Draught Bass

Although built in 1850 as the 'Kings Arms' and bought by a member of the Grafton family two years later, it was not until 1899 that it took the name. In the 1950s another member of the family, Jimmy Grafton (the BBC comedy script writer), Spike Milligan and Michael Bentine wrote several episodes of the Goon Show in a room over the pub. The pub is very much a shrine to the Goons with a large number of pictures and prints on the walls. A huge photomontage on the wall contains a wide collection of British stars of post-war radio and TV. The pub's 'olde English' interior – exposed wood and brickwork – is a relic of its old Clifton Inn days. The pub is close to Victoria Street, the Department of Trade and Industry, Caxton Hall (the famous rich people's registry office) and New Scotland Yard.

Grenadier

18 Wilton Mews, Belgravia

S&N
G R ML ME SL SE
Opening Hours: 12-3, 5-11m-f
Station: Victoria
Buses: 2, 8, 16, 36, 38, 52, 73, 82
Theakston's Best, Courage Best Bitter, Theakston's XB + Guest Beers

Historic and expansive wood-panelled mews pub and restaurant hidden away in an exclusive private cul de sac off Wilton Crescent near Belgrave Square. A notice outside states that the licensee is only allowed to serve customers who have arrived by taxi or on foot. The pub was once the officers' mess for the Duke of Wellington's, and the walls are decorated with prints depicting the history of the Grenadier Guards. It is a popular venue for guards officers off duty from Buckingham Palace. The ghost of a disgraced officer caught cheating at cards reputedly haunts the pub every September. Part of the original pewter bar remains and is believed to be the oldest of its kind. On Sundays the pub opens a special Bloody Mary bar and many people come just to drink Bloody Marys. A sentry box stands at the foot of the stairs outside the pub. One of London's great pubs.

Horse and Groom

7 Groom Place

2

Inntrepreneur
ML SL
Opening Hours: 1-11m-f closed s-su
Station: Hyde Park Corner
Buses: 2, 8, 16, 36, 38, 52, 73, 82
Webster's Yorkshire Bitter, Ruddles County

Tiny pub still reminiscent of its beer house origins, which were in 1846. The pub is wood panelled and with a very cosy atmosphere. It can be a bit cramped at lunchtimes, which, given its size, is not surprising. The bar is available for private hire at the weekends.

Lord Burleigh

250 Vauxhall Bridge Road

2

Inntrepreneur
ML SL
Opening Hours: normal
Station: Victoria
Buses: 2, 36, 185
Webster's Yorkshire Bitter, Wadworth 6X, Courage Directors, Young's Special

Small pub with an attractive bow-fronted window and a split level mock-Tudor interior decor. Its friendly atmosphere is very popular with the local office workers and it is probably the cheapest pub around for beer and food. Built in 1852 as a beer shop, it was enlarged in 1890. It is handy for Victoria station and is an unlikely venue for karaoke singing on Friday nights.

Nags Head

53 Kinnerton Street

3

Free house
ML ME SL SE
Opening Hours: normal
Station: Knightsbridge
Buses: 9, 10, 14, 19, 22, 52, 74, 137, 137a
Adnams Bitter, Tetley Bitter

Tiny unspoilt historic pub off Wilton Place, Knightsbridge, which seems caught in a time warp. Staff serve from an authentic zinc topped nineteenth-century beer engine behind a low-level bar that connects to a basement room. The pub contains a number of amusement machines from bygone eras. Very much off the beaten track but a real pleasure. Very convenient for hotels and Knightsbridge shops.

Red Lion

48 Parliament Street

Allied Domecq

ML SL

Opening Hours: normal

Station: Westminster

Buses: 3, 11, 12, 24, 53, 77a, 88, 109, 159, X53

Tetley Bitter, Young's Bitter, Ind Coope Burton Ale

Ornate corner pub which still retains most of its original interior fittings, ie a hardwood bar counter and panelling. The ground floor bar is supplemented by a cellar bar and an upstairs restaurant. The pub contains a division bell, which summons imbibing MPs to a parliamentary vote in the House of Commons just around the corner. The Red Lion was rebuilt in 1900 and was designed by the architects Gardner and Theobland for the Cannon Brewery. The pub is an ideal watering hole for visitors to Whitehall, Downing Street, the Cenotaph, Parliament and Horse Guards.

Red Lion

2 Duke of York Street

Nicholsons

ML SL

Opening Hours: 11-11m-s

Station: Piccadilly Circus

Buses: 9, 14, 19, 22, 38

Greene King IPA, Tetley Bitter, Ind Coope Burton Ale + Guest Beers

Described by a former editor of the Architectural Revue as 'a perfect example of a Victorian Gin Palace at its best'. It was licensed in 1788 and rebuilt in 1821. The interior etched glass mirrors, polished woodwork and tiles probably date from the alterations by the architect W H Rawlings in 1871. Despite its small size, it used to have five bars grouped around its island shaped counter. This is a classic pub of the 1870s-1880s period, of a kind which took much inspiration from gin palaces but to say that such a small pub with so many snugs was a gin palace is to misunderstand what gin palaces were. The Red Lion is typical of the Victorian pub that specifically catered for domestic servants from grand houses. They frequently were the most ornate pubs as their clientele were used to being surrounded with finery and also had larger disposable incomes than many other working class trades. Such customers would not have been seen dead in a true Gin Palace, which were flash, showy premises for extracting money from the poorest sections of society. The Red Lion is, however, a great London pub.

Stage Door

13-15 Allington Street, Victoria

T&J Bernard
ML SL
Opening Hours: normal
Station: Victoria
Buses: 11, 16 24
John Smith's Bitter, Theakston's Best, Theakston's XB, Courage Directors, Theakston's OP; Bulmer's Trad Cider

Large pub by the side of the Victoria Palace Theatre and close to the Apollo Victoria as well as Victoria Station. Was originally a coffee house, then in 1860, it got a licence to become a beer shop, which was named the Victoria Stores until 1962. When it was granted a full licence, it was one of only two taverns in London bearing the name of a retail shop. It used to be sited at number 10 Allington Street, which is now a tower block, but it was rebuilt on the sites of numbers 13-15 in 1924. Now a T&J Bernard House, its interior is fairly typical of the chain. Can be a bit expensive for the area.

Star Tavern

6 Belgrave Mews West

Fuller's
ML ME SL SE
Opening Hours: 11.30-3, 5-11m-th 11.30-11f 11.30-3, 6.30-11s
Station: Knightsbridge
Guest Beers: No
Buses: 2, 8, 38, 52, 73, 82, 185, 239, 507, C1, C10
Fuller's Chiswick Bitter, Fuller's London Pride, Fuller's ESB

Attractive, unspoilt mews pub hidden off the west side of Belgrave Square. The side room has scrubbed tables and two real fires in the winter. Function room with its own bar upstairs. Liable to get so crowded that the customers overflow into the mews outside. Food during weekdays only. The Star has appeared in every edition of the Good Beer Guide.

Tom Cribb

36 Panton Street

Bass
ML SL
Opening Hours: normal
Station: Piccadilly Circus
Buses: 14, 19, 38
Hancocks HB, Fuller's London Pride, Draught Bass

Small popular corner pub off Leicester Square. The bar still retains its original matchwood ceiling from when it was rebuilt in 1878 at a cost of £1,660. Until 1960 called the Union Arms, it was renamed in honour of Tom Cribb (1781-1848) the Gloucestershire pugilist, who became champion of England for three years from 1808. He later became the landlord of the Union Arms, for at least a decade from 1825, when the pub was nicknamed 'Tom Cribb's Parlour'. It was a much-painted pub at the time and a famous print of a dog show being held in the upstairs room is occasionally reprinted. Tom himself is in the foreground, the dogs are all sitting on the tables around the walls, behind which are their male owners, each still wearing a top hat and many smoking pipes. The pub's original name commemorates the 1707 Act of Union between England and Scotland rather than the trades unions.

Two Chairmen

1 Warwick House Street, Trafalgar Square

Inntrepreneur
SL SE
Opening Hours: normal
Station: Charing Cross
Buses: 3, 6, 9, 11, 12, 13, 14, 15, 19, 22, 23, 29, 77a, 91
Courage Best Bitter, Wadworth 6X, Courage Directors, Morland's Old Speckled Hen

Unspoilt, small, narrow, wood-panelled bar that is more like a suburban local than a West End pub, yet Nelson's Column is visible from the doorway. It has been licensed since 1695 and anyone choosing to visit it would be well advised to hide their copy of this book, as the landlady prefers to keep the pub special for the regulars and does not want its existence too widely broadcast. It's well worth a surreptitious visit, however, to see how different parts of London cohabit, yet are completely invisible to each other, one of the great characteristics of this city.

Westminster Arms

9 Storey's Gate, Westminster

Regent Inns
ML SL SE
Opening Hours: normal closed su
Station: Westminster
Buses: 3, 11, 12, 24, 53, 77a, 88, 109, 159, 211, X53
Brakspear Bitter, Wadworth 6X, Draught Bass + Guest Beers

Situated near Westminster Abbey and the Houses of Parliament, this pleasant wood-panelled house offers a good centre for exploring the Westminster and St James's

Park area. Ideal for Horse Guards, Downing Street, Churchill's Bunker and Victoria Embankment. Downstairs houses a wine bar and restaurant. Within easy walking distance of both St James's and Westminster tubes.

SW2

Crown and Sceptre

2 Streatham Hill, Brixton

Wetherspoon
ML ME G
Opening Hours: normal
Station: Brixton
Buses: 45, 57, 109, 118, 133, 137, 159, 250, N109
Greene King IPA, Younger's Scotch, Theakston's Best, Courage Directors, Greene King Abbot + guests

Large Wetherspoon pub rescued from an appalling previous incarnation as a Grand Met 'Open House' young persons' pub, a happily defunct genre. The interior design has forced a slightly different decoration from the standard *Wetherspoonisation*, giving a rather bookish ambience. The marble-topped bar is often thronged at weekends. The pub hosts a chess club and regular charity events, as well as Wetherspoon beer festivals. Despite being rescued from an ignominious past, Wetherspoon decided to call the pub JJ Moons, a name more in line with its previous incarnation. Happily pressure from locals has persuaded the company to allow it to revert to its original name, Crown and Sceptre, an encouraging precedent for many other Wetherspoon's houses languishing under equally stupid names. Take a bus from Brixton tube (Victoria Line) and get off at the top of Brixton Hill.

Hope and Anchor

Brixton

Young's
G, ML, ME, SL, SE
Opening Hours: normal
Station: Clapham North
Buses: 35, 37
Young's Bitter, Young's Special, Young's Winter Warmer

South West London CAMRA's London Pub of the Year 1993 has a delightful garden with cooling fountain. A good traditional pub in the 'Tudor brick' style typical of the popular 'improved' pub movement of the 1930s (the present pub was opened in 1937, although a pub of the same name has been on the site since 1815). The pub's popularity rests fairly and squarely on the quality of its beer and food and has been fortunate in that successive landlords have been consistently determined to maintain high standards.

Trinity Arms

Trinity Gardens, Brixton

Young's

G ML SL

Opening Hours: normal

Station: Brixton

Buses: 2a, 45

Young's Bitter, Young's Special, Young's Winter Warmer

Brixton's hidden gem, in an elegant square, just off the main drag, gives an idea of what a chic area was like in the latter part of the last century. The pub was built in 1850 when the square was laid out, and takes its name from a nearby charitable establishment of alms houses. The house has been selling Young's beers since 1885.

SW3

Admiral Codrington

17 Mossop Street

Bass

G ML ME SL

Opening Hours: normal

Station: South Kensington

Buses: 14, 19, 345

Worthington Best Bitter, Fuller's London Pride, Draught Bass

Wood-panelled pub off Draycott Avenue, South Kensington. Was once a well-known haunt of Sloane Rangers, including the then future Princess of Wales. The pub is named after the Admiral who led the Allied Fleet which defeated the Turks at Navarino in 1827.

Australian

29 Milner Street

Nicholsons

G ML

Opening Hours: normal

Station: Sloane Square

Buses: 19, 22, 137, 137a, C1

Adnams Bitter, Tetley Bitter + Guest Beers

Large Victorian ivy-clad pub off Cadogan Square close to Sloane Street. It stands at what used to be the corner of Princes Cricket ground where the Australians first played in England, hence the name. The interior is plainly furnished and the wood-panelled walls are covered with Aussie Cricket memorabilia. The pub takes up to six guest beers at a time.

Builders Arms

13 Britten Street

Whitbread
G ML SL
Opening Hours: normal
Station: South Kensington
Buses: 49
Brakspear Bitter, Boddington's Bitter, Flowers Original + Guest Beers

Friendly and welcoming locals' pub close to St Luke's Church (built 1820-24). The walls of one bar have a painted frieze of the old Battersea Bridge (pulled down in 1890) and Britten Street in the nineteenth century; also, an 1830s map of old Chelsea. The other bar is split-level with a ramp up to the unisex, disabled toilet at the rear. The pub specialises in fish and chip suppers on Monday nights. Games include darts, crib, dominoes and other board games. It was built in 1840 and not as is commonly thought in the 1820s for the builders working on the construction of St Luke's Church. For many years it operated as the 'tap' for the then adjacent Anchor Brewery (Mathews and Canning), which was eventually taken over by Whitbread in 1899. Brewing continued until 1907 after which it became a bottling plant.

Bunch of Grapes

207 Old Brompton Street

S&N
ML ME SL SE
Opening Hours: normal
Station: South Kensington
Buses: C1
John Smith's Bitter, Theakston's Best, Courage Best Bitter, Theakston's XB, Courage Directors, Theakston's OP

A Grade II-listed building, rebuilt in 1845 and now dwarfed by its more modern surroundings. It still retains most of its fittings of carved woodwork, decorative glass divisions and fine coloured mirrors. The wooden snob screens on the bar were originally introduced in the days when rich and poor were more closely intermingled than today. They enabled the more well-to-do to get a drink without being recognised by the 'lower orders' in adjoining bars. Those who enjoy the historic feel of the Bunch of Grapes will also no doubt enjoy the nearby South Kensington museums.

Crown

153 Dovehouse Street

Whitbread
G ML ME SL SE
Opening Hours: normal
Station: South Kensington
Buses: 14, 345
Brakspear Bitter, Boddington's Bitter, Adnams Extra, Flowers Original

Small back-street local off the Fulham Road which has recently been refurbished and enlarged with the arrival of a new tenant. It is enjoying an increase in trade after suffering a decline in recent years. Originally licensed as a beer house from 1867-1953, it was one of the few remaining Whitbread houses to keep real ale in the 1960s and 1970s, due to the determination of the then landlord to retain his handpumps. If only more publicans has been as stubborn.

Moore Arms

61-63 Cadogan Street

Allied Domecq
ML ME SL SE
Opening Hours: normal
Station: Sloane Square
Buses: 19, 22, 137, C1
Adnams Bitter, Tetley Bitter, Marston's Pedigree

Not a Sloanie pub at all but a good honest working-class local, despite the postcode. As such, the single bar is comfortably furbished to 'front-parlour' standards and the atmosphere is quite decidedly homely. Wealthy business people in the day give way to locals from Guinness Trust dwellings in the evenings and weekends when there is not a Rupert or a Fiona in sight.

Phene Arms

9 Phene Street

Inntrepreneur
G R ML ME SL SE
Opening Hours: normal
Station: Sloane Square

Buses: 11, 19, 22
Webster's Yorkshire Bitter, Adnams Bitter, Ruddles County

Small, pleasant, cosy pub in a leafy Chelsea backwater. The bar has an island servery, three separate restaurant areas, a well-placed beer garden at the side and a patio on the first floor rear level. Dr John Samuel Phene (pronounced Feeny), who built the pub and street in 1853, was a wealthy eccentric and local landowner. He is credited with the idea of planting trees in the streets. As a result of his plantings in Chelsea, Queen Victoria followed his example outside the Natural History Museum in South Kensington.

SW4

Manor Arms

128 Clapham Manor Street, Clapham
Whitbread
G ML
Opening Hours: normal
Station: Clapham North
Buses: 45a, 88, 155, P5, N87
Flowers IPA, Boddington's Bitter, Marston's Pedigree, Morland's Old Speckled Hen + Guest Beers

Small very friendly local on a quiet corner site just off the busy Clapham High Street. Close to the local swimming baths, the pub is highly suited to those who have worked up a thirst as the beer is of a consistently high quality. The pub is well supported by the local community. Well worth seeking out.

Windmill

Clapham Common Southside, Clapham
Young's
G CP DA R ML ME SL SE
Opening Hours: normal
Station: Clapham South
Buses: 60, 155, 355, N87
Young's Bitter, Young's Special, Young's Winter Warmer

A large and very famous London pub with accommodation. Traditionally a stopping place for crowds returning to London from the Derby, the pub is in the background of the famous J F Herring print *Return from the Derby*. The Windmill has recently been expanded and the hotel facilities upgraded. Always busy, it can still be surprisingly local in the front bar area. In summer, the Common acts as the pub garden and the Windmill must rank as one of the busiest pubs in London. Taking its name from a long-gone nearby windmill, there has been a pub on the site since 1665 and Young's' beers have been served there since 1848.

SW5

Blackbird

209 Earls Court Road, Earls Court

Fuller's
ML ME SL SE
Opening Hours: normal
Station: Earls Court
Buses: 31, 74, C1
Fuller's Chiswick Bitter, Fuller's London Pride, Fuller's ESB

A Fuller's 'Ale and Pie' house located on a corner towards the lower end of the Earls Court Road near the tube station. The premises once belonged to the Midland Bank and this can be seen in some of the decor. Plenty of wood panelling and a central bar complete the picture. Handy for the Earls Court Exhibition Centre, or just for watching the busy street life in vibrant Earls Court.

SW6

Eight Bells

89 Fulham High Street

Inntrepreneur
G DA R ML SL
Opening Hours: normal
Station: Putney Bridge
Buses: 14, 22, 39, 74, 85, 93, 220, 265, 270, C4, N9, N14
Webster's Yorkshire Bitter, Boddington's Bitter, Ruddles County

Small and cosy wood-panelled bar with pew-style seating. A useful base on boat race days. The oldest surviving public house in Fulham, it was originally licensed in 1629 as the 'Blue Anchor'. It underwent several name changes over the following years from Blue Anchor to Anchor (by 1855), the Anchor and Eight Bells, ending as plain Eight Bells. It was during one of these name changes that it was rebuilt. This part of the High Street was called Bridge Street, as it led to the old Fulham Bridge built in 1729. The old bridge was pulled down shortly after the new Putney Bridge opened in 1886.

Jim Thompson's Oriental Bar

617 Kings Road

Allied Domecq
G R ML ME SL SE
Opening Hours: normal
Station: Fulham Broadway
Buses: 11
Tetley Bitter, Marston's Pedigree

Recently refurbished bar with a strong atmospheric decor and theme that seems to work well. The former rear bar area has been converted into a large Thai restaurant that sometimes has to be booked in advance. Jim Thompson was an American who expanded the silk industry in Thailand and disappeared in mysterious circumstances in 1969. The pub has been called the 'Horns' since the seventeenth century and renamed the 'Hand and Flower' when it was first rebuilt in 1784. The present pub, designed by architects Gardner and Theobald, was rebuilt by Meux and Co in 1897. The pub also has a garden restaurant and jazz on Sunday nights.

Jolly Brewer

308/310 North End Road

Inntrepreneur
Opening Hours: 11-11m-s 12-3, 7-10.30su
Station: Fulham Broadway
Buses: 28, 391
Webster's Yorkshire Bitter, Courage Best Bitter, Ruddles County

Popular two-bar local in a bustling street market, with a large chamber pot collection around the walls and over the bar (the landlord has a collection of over 3,000). Licensed from 1853-1953 as a 'Beerhouse', it was rebuilt in 1890 by the Royal Chelsea Brewery, who were taken over by the Welch Ale Brewery in 1898. Welch Ale were unusual in that their outlets were run in conjunction with Bass, Ratcliffe and Gretton of Burton until they were taken over in 1922, not by Bass but by Watneys.

White Horse

1 Parson's Green

Bass
G ML ME SL SE
Opening Hours: normal
Station: Parsons Green
Buses: 22
Highgate Dark, Draught Bass + Guest Beers

Large, popular, upmarket pub facing Parsons Green. The present pub was built in 1984 although a hostelry has been on the site since 1688. It has a pleasant paved drinking area at the front and an old carriage yard at back. Although large, it has a warm and welcoming feel. The pub hosts regular in-house festivals including the annual Old Ale Festival in November. Imaginative food includes hearty breakfasts, weekend lunchtimes as well as Sunday lunches. A large selection of speciality foreign beers always available as well as guest real ales. The pub is well known for its championing of beer styles.

SW7

Anglesea Arms

15, Selwood Terrace, South Kensington

Free House

ML SL

Opening Hours: 11-3, 5.30-11

Station: South Kensington

Buses: 14, 345

Brakspear Bitter, Adnams Bitter, Fuller's London Pride, Young's Special, Greene King Abbot

One of the first free houses in London to sell a range of real ales from independent brewers. Charles Dickens and D H Lawrence lived nearby. It has a large outside drinking area in front and is an extremely popular dining establishment which can be very busy. This pub has appeared in every edition of the Good Beer Guide.

Old Red House

133 Battersea Park Road, Battersea

G CP ML

Opening Hours: normal

Station: Battersea Park BR

Young's Bitter, Courage Best Bitter, Wells Bombardier, Wadworth 6X, Courage Directors

A single-room pub, named after its red roof, this traditional south London local is just opposite Battersea Dogs home. Karaoke is on Sunday lunchtimes. Its charm lies in its unpretentiousness. There are a number of pictures of the pub drawn over the years hanging on the walls. The dark walls and red upholstery give it a very lush feel.

Priory Arms

83 Lansdowne Way, Stockwell

Free House

G ML

Opening Hours: 11-11m-s 12-3, 7-10.30su

Station: Stockwell

Buses: 2, 45a, 77, 88, 155, 322, 355, N68

Young's Bitter, Young's Special + Guests; Thatcher's Cider

A good local brought back to life by enlightened management. The Priory is a classic example of what a free house should be, looking after its customers just as much as it looks after its beer. The wide range of real ales is always changing and real ciders and perries are popular with the students from nearby South Bank University. There is a wide range of foreign bottled beer as well as fruit beers and even fruit wine on offer. The pub was South West London CAMRA's Pub of the Year in 1992 and 1994. A terrific pub, well worth seeking out. The Grade II-listed corner building in a conservation area is on the London Cycle Network, as well as being easily accessible from Vauxhall tube and Wandsworth Road BR.

Roebuck

84 Ashmole Street, Vauxhall

Bass

G DA R ML ME SL SE

Opening Hours: normal

Station: Oval

Buses: 3, 36, 109, 133, 159, 185, 355

Worthington Best Bitter

A good, modern and comfortable pub built to replace the original which was badly damaged during the war but which nevertheless survived until the late 1980s with a corrugated iron roof. The pub is ideally suited for visitors to the Oval cricket ground. Those lucky enough to get into the Oval Pavilion will find Young's beers but other cricket fans should be aware that only keg bitter is served elsewhere in the ground, which is another good reason to visit the Roebuck.

Surprise

16 Southville, Stockwell

Young's

G ML SL

Opening Hours: normal

Station: Stockwell Buses: 77, 77a

Young's Bitter, Young's Special, Young's Winter Warmer

A gem of a pub, tucked away next to the local park with a large outside patio and pergola. Retaining something of its working class 1830s beer shop origins, it is now the only building in a row of streets that was converted into a park in war damaged Stockwell. This pub is very near to South Bank University and, with a traditional Pie and Mash shop just around the corner on bustling Wandsworth Road, gives the impression of the Surprise as a peaceful haven from the hurly burly. The back room walls are festooned with caricatures of the regulars and the pub sports its own boules team.

SW10

Fox and Pheasant

1 Billing Road, Chelsea

Greene King
G SL SE
Opening Hours: 12-3, 5.30-11
Station: Fulham Broadway
Buses: 14, 211, N14, N31
Greene King IPA, Rayment's Special Bitter, Greene King Abbot

Popular, small, low-beamed two bar local on a private road off the Fulham Road near Chelsea Football Ground. Built in 1848 and turned into a pub named the Bedford Arms two years later, it acquired its present name in the 1960s when the landlord bought a display case containing a stuffed fox and a pheasant. This is still in the cosy lounge bar. The basic public bar has a dartboard and leads out to a beer garden. The Fox and Pheasant has a very 'local' feel about it and is a good reminder of how much London is still just a large number of villages all run together.

SW11

Beehive

197 St John's Hill, Clapham Junction

Fuller's
G DA ML ME SL SE
Opening Hours: normal
Station: Clapham Junction
Buses: 37, 39, 77a, 170, 219, 295, 337, N68
Fuller's Chiswick Bitter, Fuller's London Pride, Fuller's ESB

A quiet, unpretentious and intimate locals' pub with

plenty of atmosphere. A Fuller's house in the heart of Young's country, it is actually leased from Charrington. A rare chance to try all the Fuller's beers in this part of London. The Beehive is a good example of a small high-street pub, with traditional red and nicotine-style interior and a few mock-Tudor features. Good home-cooked food.

Cornet

57 Lavender Gardens, Clapham Junction

Regent Inns
ML ME SL SE
Opening Hours: normal
Station: Clapham Junction BR
Buses: 45a, 77, 77a, 137, 137a
Brakspear Bitter, Courage Best Bitter, Wadworth 6X, Courage Directors

This rambling pub is quite an entertainment centre. Apart from the pub itself there is Jongleurs Comedy Club upstairs and Andersons bar with live music six nights a week and a late licence. Recently refurbished it has improved the quality of its food menu. The pub is very handy for the nearby Battersea Arts Centre, venue of CAMRA's Battersea Beer Festival each February.

Falcon

2 St John's Hill, Clapham Junction

Bass
ML ME SL SE
Opening Hours: normal
Station: Clapham Junction
Buses: 5, 37, 39, 45a, 49, 77, 156, 170, 219, 239, 249, 295
Worthington Best Bitter, Fuller's London Pride, Draught Bass + Guest Beers

Bustling, large Victorian pub retaining many original features at the centre of the Clapham Junction shopping area, just opposite the famous Arding and Hobbs department store. Very close to Clapham Junction, Britain's busiest railway station, the pub also hosts its own beer festivals.

Latchmere

503 Battersea Park Road

S&N
ML ME SL SE
Opening Hours: normal
Station: Clapham Junction

Buses: 44, 344, N88
Greene King IPA, John Smith's Bitter, Courage Directors

Large theatre pub that has become increasingly upwardly mobile in recent years. A fine, handsome mid-Victorian pub with very solid yet stately lines, the Latchmere dominates the approach down Battersea Bridge Road. The upstairs Grace Theatre is one of the most widely respected fringe venues south of the river and has a long pedigree. Plenty of easy chairs, fires and a daily range of newspapers make it a pub to linger in and, despite the background music (not too obtrusive), it is very much a conversation pub. Tuesday nights are quiz nights, which sees the pub packed and the standard is pretty high too. A long bar front extends into an L-shape on the right facing the stairs up to the theatre and the seating caters more for those who are coming to or leaving the performances. On the left, a set of fine mirrors lines the walls enclosing the old pub 'office'. Here the clientele are less theatre-minded. The pub is open to serve breakfasts.

Raven

140 Westbridge Road, Battersea
Phoenix Inns
FR G ML ME SL SE
Opening Hours: normal
Station: Clapham Junction
Buses: 239
Young's Bitter, Courage Best Bitter, Wadworth 6X, Draught Bass

The oldest pub in Battersea and the only one with accommodation. It is a fine cosy locals' pub, with a well in the cellar and a reputed smugglers' tunnel that extended down to the Thames.

River Rat

2 Lombard Road
Bass
G ML ME SL
Opening Hours: normal
Station: Clapham Junction
Buses: 239, 295, C3, N88
Hancocks HB, Draught Bass + Guest Beers

Very pleasant pub in a new development on the site of the White Hart. The river terrace looks across to Chelsea Harbour, where the ball on the top of the tower rises and falls with the Thames tide.

Unity

228 York Road, Battersea

Free House
ML ME SL
Opening Hours: normal
Station: Clapham Junction
Buses: 44, C3
Batemans XB, Fuller's London Pride + Guests; Thatchers Cider

A recently refurbished pub on the main road, with open fires, booth seating, elegant furniture and a nice line in bric-a-brac of the kind granny would have approved of. The decor in this Irish pub is based on a toned-down emerald green and this being the 1990s, the pot plants are yuccas but really aspidistras would look much better. The food is excellent. The Guinness is imported from Dublin, and is a rare opportunity to try the real stuff. Thursdays and Saturdays are Jazz nights. To get there, take the 44 bus from Wandsworth Town BR or the C3 from Earls Court Station or Clapham Junction BR.

SW12

Bedford

77 Bedford Hill, Balham

S&N
ML SL
Opening Hours: normal
Station: Balham
Buses: 155, 315, 355, N87
Webster's Yorkshire Bitter, John Smith's Bitter, Ruddles County

A 1930s improved pub, with a large public bar and even larger saloon. The function rooms that were a de rigeur feature of this type of pub, are now used for one of South London's best known comedy clubs, the Banana Cabaret, which takes place on Friday and Saturday. The Cabaret is one of the best comedy venues in the capital. When it gets busy, they open up an overspill room and each act does their turn in each room, but in a different order.

Duke of Devonshire

39 Balham High Road, Balham

Young's
FR G ML ME SL SE
Opening Hours: normal

Station: Balham
Buses: 155, 315, 355, N87
Young's Bitter, Young's Special, Young's Winter Warmer

Large, recently refurbished street corner pub. The pub was clearly not the large open-plan bar it is now but the bar and the wood- and mirror-lined walls give a good indication of the gin palace-type interior. Little imagination is needed to visualise the glass partitions that once divided the bar into 'snugs' so that drinkers' pleasures were not interrupted by the gaze of their social superiors or inferiors. Design your own pizzas from the menu at the rear of the pub.

Nightingale

97 Nightingale Lane, Clapham South

Young's
FR G DA ML ME SL SE
Opening Hours: normal
Station: Clapham South
Buses: G1
Young's Bitter, Young's Special, Young's Winter Warmer

Small, busy local with 1853 date mark on frontage. Renowned for its beer and its annual charity walk, organised by the regulars, which has collected £200,000 over the past 15 years. The pub was probably built in a deliberately unassuming style, in what was once a fairly rural part of town, which, when it became developed, clearly had pretensions to gentility. The pub has won several prizes. It has been the South West London CAMRA Pub of the Year and the Young's 135 Association pub of the year, twice. The 135 is a club for those drinkers who have visited every Young's pub – for years there were 135 of them. If you live near a pub like this, add 50 per cent to the value of your house.

SW13

Coach and Horses

27 Barnes High Street

Young's
G ML ME SL SE
Opening Hours: 11-11m-s 12-3, 7-10.30su
Station: Barnes Bridge BR
Buses: 9, 9a, R61
Young's Bitter, Young's Special, Young's Winter Warmer

The small frontage and cosy single bar of this old coaching inn hide the large rear function room (the

Paddock Room) and an attractive garden and patio. The bar area is dark wood-panelled and has some stained glass in its windows. The tables are a rustic style and brass and copper bric-a-brac abounds. Note the hogshead incorporated into the bar. The large garden has children's play equipment and a barbecue which sees heavy use in the summer, especially on Sunday lunchtimes. At the river end of Barnes High Street, this is a predominantly quiet pub, the only noise intrusion being the TV. It is a regular Good Beer Guide entry.

Sun

7 Church Road, Barnes

Allied Domecq
G CP ML SL
Opening Hours: normal
Station: Barnes Bridge BR
Buses: 9, 9a, R61
Allsopps Stout, Tetley Bitter, Eldridge Pope Best Bitter, Marston's Pedigree, Ind Coope Burton Ale

Well known and well loved pub in upmarket Barnes with pretty prospect of Barnes Pond. Full of nooks and corners, a large walk-round bar forms the focus of the front bar, with a number of small rooms off it. The largest one at the back serves as a dining area. Food is served 12-2.15 daily, making the pub a popular venue for Sunday lunches. The features are very traditional, with bare boards, a low ceiling, original mantelpieces and plain wooden furniture. The walls are a treasury of local history, and an impressive collection of old bottles is generously dispersed throughout the pub. Very popular as a weekend pub and as an attractive spot to sit outside on sunny days and balmy evenings. It has a wide selection of real ales as well as a guest which changes every six weeks or so. The dark walls and low ceilings give the pub an old alehouse feel and its higgledy-piggledy layout makes it very distinctive. Everyone in South West London has heard of the Sun, even if they have never visited it.

SW14

Railway

11 Sheen Lane

Hall and Woodhouse
G CP ML ME SL SE
Opening Hours: normal
Station: Mortlake

Buses: R61, R69
H & W Badger Best Bitter, Wadworth 6X, H & W Tanglefoot, H & W Hard Tackle + Guests

A change of management early in 1995 won back a lot of custom and restored much of the Railway's former glory. There are well-kept ales and continuously available food plus customer involvement in novelty competitions and local charities. The decor is railway orientated, consisting of pictures, prints, memorabilia and a model train which runs around part of the bar area, just below ceiling level. Quizzes are held on Wednesdays (trivia) and Fridays (music) and attract custom, as do the occasional Tuesday night live bands. Fridays in particular can be very busy. Close to Mortlake Station (turn left on leaving the station), the pub attracts homeward-bound commuters as well as 'all-evening' regulars. The Railway has table football as well as darts and board games, and children are welcome until 8pm. There is a small outside patio and a few car parking spaces.

Ship Tavern

10 Thames Back, Mortlake

S&N
G ML ME
Opening Hours: normal
Station: Mortlake
Buses: R61
John Smith's Bitter, Courage Best Bitter, Wadworth 6X, Theakston's XB

Fine pub in a smart residential area boasting impressive views of the Thames. It can be awkward to find if one is not travelling by river, in which case it is hard to miss, as it is tucked directly behind the Stag Brewery (which unfortunately now only brews inferior lager brands). Noted for its Shakespearean connections, the large single bar enjoys a real fireplace and much wooden adornment. Ideally suited as a vantage point for the finishing line of the annual University Boat Race. It is a very popular pub in good weather, when the outside tables, in particular, can be in great demand.

SW15

Duke's Head

8 Lower Richmond Road, Putney

Young's
ML ME SL SE

Opening Hours: 11.30-3, 5-11m-f 11-11s
Station: Putney BR
Young's Bitter, Young's Special, Young's Winter Warmer

Nineteenth-century pub with ornate glasswork inside and out. The pub overlooks the University stone, the starting point for the annual University boat race and the finishing point for the Head of the River boat race. A Young's pub since 1832, it was rebuilt in 1894. The pub currently refuses admission to anyone under 21.

Green Man

Putney Heath, Putney

Young's
G ML ME SL SE
Opening Hours: normal
Station: Putney
Buses: 14, 85
Young's Bitter, Young's Special, Young's Winter Warmer

The present building can be traced to around 1700. At the front is a drinking area with a large garden suitable for barbecues. Inside, there is a small comfortable saloon with an interesting engraved mirror and a good public bar with a game of Ring the Bull. Previously the haunt of highwaymen, the pub is also associated with the poet Swinburne. The pub lies at the edge of Putney Heath which was a notorious spot for duelling. Prime Ministers and Lords fought with swords or took pot shots at each other on the Heath and many a shaking hand will have been steadied at the Green Man.

Half Moon

93 Lower Richmond Road, Putney

Young's
G SL
Opening Hours: normal
Station: Putney BR
Buses: 22, 265, N9
Young's Bitter, Young's Special, Young's Winter Warmer

This pub is famous for having music every night, including top names. Fans of rock, blues, folk and jazz are catered for in a separate back room. Music usually starts around 8.30pm (ring 0181 780 9383). The musical theme of the pub is continued in the decor of the saloon bar, the walls of which are adorned with numerous photographs, many signed, of the bands both famous and not so famous, unforgettable and best forgotten, who have played in the Half Moon.

Railway

202 Upper Richmond Road, Putney

Wetherspoon
DA ML ME SL SE
Opening Hours: normal
Station: East Putney
Buses: 14, 37, 39, 74, 85, 93, 270, 337, N14
Younger's Scotch, Theakston's Best, Marston's Pedigree, Theakston's XB, Courage Directors + Guests; Weston's Farm Brand Cider

An older pub refurbished in the usual Wetherspoon style. It has reverted to its original name and function after a period as a Drummonds. There is a large main bar which includes a raised no-smoking area. Panels around the bar illustrate aspects of local history and there is a model train running around the bar. The upstairs bar has a strong railway theme, including a history of the local line. The exterior of the pub is decorated with attractive figurines.

SW16

Pied Bull

498 Streatham High Road, Streatham

Young's
G ML ME SL SE
Opening Hours: normal
Station: Streatham Common BR
Buses: 50, 109, 250, N109
Young's Bitter, Young's Special, Young's Winter Warmer

Probably the best pub in Streatham. This large pub owes its jumbled appearance to the fact that the original coaching inn (c1768) was expanded into the neighbouring premises in 1920 as Streatham grew.

SW17

Castle

38 Tooting High Street, Tooting

Young's
G DA ML ME
Opening Hours: normal
Station: Tooting Broadway
Buses: 155, 219, 355
Younger's Scotch, Young's Special, Young's Winter Warmer

An old Tooting pub, leased by Young's since 1832 and bought outright in 1899. The pub was rebuilt in 1901 in a style much inferior to the building it replaced. The lease to the pub originally included two acres of what is now Tooting Common, a good mile away. Recently refurbished in an unusually light wood colour for Young's, the decor imbues the pub with a yellowy, hazy atmosphere which can be very relaxing, especially on warm days. It is very much a locals' pub, especially at weekends and does good trade since Tooting High Street outside is always thronging.

Kings Head

84 Upper Tooting Road, Tooting

S&N
G CP ML ME SL SE
Opening Hours: normal
Station: Tooting Bec
Buses: 155, 219, 355
Theakston's Best, Theakston's XB, Theakston's OP

Although a pub that has seen better days the King's Head is an extraordinary survival. It was built in 1898 at the height of the property speculation boom that produced so many fine London pubs. There are few survivors from that time which can claim so many original features by way of woodwork, glasswork, mirrors, tiling and overall grandeur. Rather an Irish pub these days and therefore, unfortunately, like many Irish pubs where Guinness is the big brand, it is not a pub that places its emphasis on beer quality. However, it is well worth a visit for those interested in gaining some insight as to what the best London pubs of the 1890s might have looked like.

Leather Bottle

538 Garratt Lane, Tooting

Young's
FR G ML
Opening Hours: normal
Station: Tooting Broadway
Buses: 44, 77, 270, N88
Young's Bitter, Young's Special, Young's Winter Warmer

The pub dates back to at least 1745 and the exterior appearance has changed little in over 150 years. The pub was famous in the eighteenth century for the mock elections of the Mayor of Garratt on the green opposite. These elections, it is thought, were started as a protest against land enclosures. In their heyday, the elections attracted crowds of 100,000. An old leather bottle for carrying beer still hangs in the bar. These are very rare today.

SW18

Alma

499 Old York Road, Wandsworth

Young's
R ML ME SL SE
Opening Hours: normal
Station: Wandsworth Town BR
Buses: 28, 44
Young's Bitter, Young's Special, Young's Winter Warmer

A green, glazed tiled, Victorian pub with an octagonal dome sporting a broken flagstaff, named after the famous Crimean War battle of 1854. It contains many original and unusual features including staircase, woodwork, mosaics and painted mirrors. Of particular interest is the painted plaster frieze in the restaurant area, which was only discovered during renovation work in 1987. The central island bar is unusual in having no superstructure which, combined with the painted mirrors, gives the pub a Continental feel. The restaurant (0181-870 2537) has a deserved good reputation. The pub is directly opposite Wandsworth Town BR station.

Brewers Inn

147 East Hill, Wandsworth

Young's
FR G CP DA R ML ME SL SE
Opening Hours: normal
Station: Wandsworth Town BR
Buses: 28, 37, 39, 45, 77a, 156, 170, 220, 270, 337, N68, N88
Young's Bitter, Young's Special, Young's Winter Warmer

Refurbished pub with recently-added accommodation (16 rooms; tel 0181-874 4128). The Brewers Inn has two bar areas and a restaurant. One bar area is bare boards and wooden tables etc, the other is carpeted with armchair seating. Built in 1800 and until recently called the Two Brewers, the pub changed its name to reflect the addition of accommodation. The inn sign depicts the smiling person of Young's Brewery chairman, John Young.

Country House

2 Groton Road, Earlsfield

Inntrepreneur
ML ME SL SE
Opening Hours: 12-11
Station: Earlsfield BR
Buses: 44, 77, 270, N88
Young's Bitter, John Smith's Bitter, Courage Best Bitter, Courage Directors

Next to the railway line, this pub became known as the 'Fog' back in the days of London's famous pea-souper smogs. Rail users used to pop in at their journey's end and call home to say they were "Stuck in the Fog". This very friendly pub lives up to its name, for it really does have a rural quality to it. There is a rather unusual clock in the middle of the bar and the walls and table tops are festooned with copper. A marvellous example of a small back-street pub doing what they do best. Well worth seeking out.

Grapes

39 Fairfield Street, Wandsworth

Young's
G ML SL
Opening Hours: normal
Station: Wandsworth Town BR
Buses: 28, 44, C3
Young's Bitter, Young's Special, Young's Winter Warmer

A fairly basic but refurbished, medium-sized nineteenth-century pub. A good example of the genre. It started life as a beer shop in 1833, when many beer shops were being built. Beer shops had cheap licences but sold no spirits and were an attempt to counter the rising consumption of gin. Like many beer shops it gained respectability and was granted a full licence in 1849.

Grid Inn

22 Replingham Road, Southfields

Wetherspoon
DA ML ME SL SE
Opening Hours: normal
Station: Southfields
Buses: 39
Younger's Scotch, Theakston's Best, Marston's Pedigree, Theakston's XB, Courage Directors + Guest Beers; Cider

An irrigation of the Southfields' beer desert, this new Wetherspoon pub was again described as 'typical' by the pub surveyor. The bar has a pleasant marble top. There is a mixture of seating types and areas, with an unusual area of bar stool seating. There is the usual Wetherspoon display of local history on the walls.

Old Sergeant

144 Garratt Lane, Wandsworth

Young's

G DA ML SL

Opening Hours: normal

Station: Earlsfield BR

Buses: 44, 77, 270, N88

Young's Bitter, Young's Special

The Old Sergeant existed prior to 1785 and was a watering hole on the London to Brighton road. Little changed, its staging origins can still be seen. A comfortable saloon and a more basic public bar complete the traditional picture of a pub that started life beyond the confines of London and managed to survive as the city gradually surrounded it. Its survival then, as its reputation is now, was probably due to the excellent quality of its beer.

Ship

41 Jews Row, Wandsworth

Young's

G R ML ME SL SE

Opening Hours: normal

Station: Wandsworth Town

Buses: 28, 295, C3

Young's Bitter, Young's Special, Young's Winter Warmer

This pub dates from at least 1809. It contains a large saloon/lounge bar, a restaurant, a small but proper public bar and outside seating by the Thames. Barbecues are a regular event in the summer. A path to the left takes one on a very pleasant riverside walk. The pub is always crowded and is very popular with what used to be called the 'Yuppy set', who, for some reason, largely forswear the public bar, which is by far the best room in the pub. This bar still has a feel of a Thames waterman's pub. If one were to walk in in a roll-neck sweater and oilskin you would not look out of place (except in August perhaps). The restaurant food is first rate and very à la mode but the beer prices are rather higher than can be justified.

Spread Eagle

71 Wandsworth High Street, Wandsworth

Young's
ML ME SL SE
Opening Hours: normal
Station: Wandsworth Town
Buses: 28, 37, 39, 44, 77a, 156, 170, 220, 270, 337, N66, N88
Young's Bitter, Young's Special, Young's Winter Warmer

A hidden gem, albeit on the main road. One of the finest examples of a 'grand London' pub as done in the Young's' style. Recent alterations and refurbishment have been handled sympathetically with the Victorian taste in wood and glass still plainly in evidence. Note in particular the original Victorian entrances and archways onto the High Street. The pub was originally a coaching inn, which will explain its size, and it dates back to at least 1780. Like many London pubs, it was rebuilt in the great pub property boom of the 1890s, in this case 1898. Because of its size it was an important local building and was used for many purposes such as magistrates courts, the collection of rents from the Spencer Estates and the inaugural meeting of the Surrey Iron Railway.

SW19

Hand and Racket

25-27 Wimbledon Hill Road, Wimbledon

Whitbread
DA ML ME SL SE
Opening Hours: normal
Station: Wimbledon
Buses: 57, 93, 131, 155, 156, 163, 164, 200, N68, N87
Boddington's Bitter, Fuller's London Pride, Flowers Original, Marston's Pedigree + Guest Beers

A brand new pub that until April 1995 was a branch of Boots the Chemist. The pub has been designed to appeal to all ages. There is a real fire in winter.

Hand in Hand

7 Crooked Billet, Wimbledon

Young's
FR G ML ME SL SE
Opening Hours: normal
Station: Wimbledon
Buses: 93
Young's Bitter, Young's Special, Young's Winter Warmer

Ironically this pub, an early nineteenth-century bakehouse right by Wimbledon Common, was built on the site of a house owned by the grandfather of the London brewer, Watney. The Hand in Hand was a family-owned beer house before Young's bought it in 1974. It has since been renovated and enlarged but without losing its warmth and intimacy of character, a talent almost peculiar to Young's. In the summer most of the customers like to spill outside.

Old Leather Bottle

277 Kingston Road, Merton

S&N
G CP ML ME SL SE
Opening Hours: normal
Station: Wimbledon Chase BR
Buses: 163, 164
Webster's Yorkshire Bitter, Theakston's Best, Theakston's XB + Guest Beers

Refurbished and reopened in November 1994, the pub has been much improved. Food is very good value and the subdued background music adds to a relaxed and civilised atmosphere.

Princess Royal

25 Abbey Road, Merton

Inntrepreneur
G CP SL
Opening Hours: 11-3, 5.30-11
Station: South Wimbledon
Buses: 57, 152, 200, 293, N87
Courage Best Bitter, Fuller's London Pride, Wadworth 6X, Courage Directors, Morland's Old Speckled Hen

Compact early nineteenth-century corner house, sensitively preserved. Lively local clientele, large enclosed beer garden, relaxed, friendly atmosphere. A great example of a back street pub.

Rose and Crown

55 High Street, Wimbledon

Young's
FR G CP ML ME SL SE
Opening Hours: normal
Station: Wimbledon
Buses: 93, 200
Young's Bitter, Young's Special, Young's Winter Warmer

A spacious yet intimate pub dating back to before 1659. Swinburne drank here when he wasn't at the Green Man; his chair is still there. Leigh Hunt wrote of the Rose and Crown "When I find myself in the little room with the window open and the garden before us and a glass of claret on the table, care seems to be excluded."

Sultan

78 Norman Road, South Wimbledon

Hop Back Brewery
G SL
Opening Hours: 12-11
Station: Colliers Wood
Buses: 57, 152, 155, 200, 219, 293, N87
Hop Back GFB, Hop Back Special, Hop Back Stout, Hop Back Summer Lightning, Hop Back Wheat Beer + Guest Beers

A moderate example of 1950s pub architecture, it is a replacement of a pub bombed during the war. The pub was formerly a Taylor Walker house but was reopened on 27 May 1994 by new owners, the Hop Back Brewery. This pub owes its inclusion as a Hidden Gem entirely to its beers. The public bar (which is actually the more 'saloonier' of the two) is named after Ted Higgins, a CAMRA stalwart and former actor, and one of a very few numbers of people to have a bar named after them during their lifetime. The pub is a fine example of a how a moribund back-street local can be brought back to life by dedicated staff and fine beer.

William Morris

Merton Abbey Mills, 20 Watermill Way

Regent Inns
FR G CP DA ML ME SL SE
Opening Hours: normal
Station: Colliers Wood
Buses: 57, 152, 155, 200, 219, 293, N87
Brakspear Bitter, Theakston's Best, Wadworth 6X + Guest Beers

Opened in 1990 in the restored Liberty silk printing works, it is named after the famous Socialist designer and artist William Morris. His own works were a little downstream on the Wandle and which can be reached by crossing the footbridge near the mill wheelhouse and taking the footpath on the right. The pub has been something of a success, despite not being too close to many homes. It has bars on two floors with ample seating inside and on the roof, overlooking the river Wandle. It serves the Merton Abbey Mills craft centre –

South London's answer to Camden market – which has its market days on Saturdays and Sundays, when car boot sales also take place. Wednesday night is quiz night.

SW20

Cavern

100 Coombe Lane, Raynes Park

Cavern Taverns
G ML SL
Opening Hours: normal
Station: Raynes Park BR
Buses: 57, 131, 265, N87
Young's Bitter, Boddington's Bitter, Fuller's London Pride + Guest Beers

The best pub in SW20 is a Beatles theme pub. Opened in 1991, it manages to recreate a 1960s rock and roll atmosphere with plenty of photos and posters, matched by a good juke box selection. At nights, it takes on a club-like atmosphere.

Croydon – CR0

Builders' Arms

65 Leslie Park Road, Croydon

Fuller's
G ML ME SL SE
Opening Hours: 11.30-3, 5.30-11m-th 11.30-11f 11.30-3, 6.30-11s
Station: East Croydon
Buses: 197, 289, 312
Fuller's Chiswick Bitter, Fuller's London Pride, Fuller's ESB

The Builders' Arms is tucked away in a residential area to the east of Cherry Orchard Road (A222). The building is an unusual shape with the upper floor built out over a yard on one side and a single-storey extension on the other. Inside are two bars, one the former public bar, which houses the food counter; the other, a slightly bigger bar giving access to a surprisingly large garden. Plenty of woodwork is in evidence in both bars which are decorated with artefacts associated with the building trade. Overall, the place has some of the feel of a country pub. Parking is difficult.

Dog and Bull
24 Surrey Street, Croydon

Young's
G ML SL
Opening Hours: 11-11m-s 12-4, 8-10.30su
Station: East Croydon BR
Buses: 154, 157, N88
Young's Bitter, Young's Special, Young's Winter Warmer

An imposing three-storey eighteenth-century Grade II listed building in Croydon's street market. Recent renovation has been done without loss to its character. This included the repossession of part of the ground floor of the premises to provide a larger bar area and a food servery reached by a crooked archway formed by a staircase. The rear yard has been altered to provide a well-equipped outdoor eating and drinking area. There have also been improvements to the upstairs function room. The pace of life here matches that of the market outside. The pub is busy in the daytime on Mondays to Fridays and quieter in the evenings and on Sundays. Very much in the traditional pub style associated with Young's. Darts and a 'joanna' in the rear of the pub, earthenware pots on the ceiling and stone bottles on the picture rail shelf plus a colour scheme of brown and cream make it a pub that would be hard to imagine empty.

Porter and Sorter

Station Road, Croydon

Phoenix Inns
G CP ML
Opening Hours: 11-11m-f 11-3, 7-11s 12-4su
Station: East Croydon
Buses: 64, 130, 197, 312
Courage Best Bitter, Wadworth 6X, Marston's Pedigree, Courage Directors, Young's Special, Ruddles County + Guest Beers

Named to reflect its position tucked between the distinctive 'suspension bridge'-style East Croydon station and the postal sorting office. A modest medium-sized building and one of the few in the area not yet swept away by the eastward march of office development. Used by local office and postal workers, along with homeward bound commuters in the early evenings.

Rose and Crown

124 Church Street, Croydon

Allied Domecq

ML
Opening Hours: normal
Station: West Croydon BR
Buses: 407, 408, 726
Tetley Bitter, Fuller's London Pride, Young's Special + Guest Beers

Originally a mid-eighteenth century building, it now has a three-storey Victorian facade which looks across to the Parish Church in Croydon's Old Town. In France, this would be the setting for a 'place', surrounded by bars and cafes. Do not miss the brass name-board set into the window ledges. Inside there is a J-shaped ground floor bar decorated with prints of old Croydon. An upstairs bar opens in the evenings only.

Royal Standard

1 Sheldon Street, Croydon

Fuller's
G ML SL FR G CP
Opening Hours: 11.30-3, 5-11m-th 11-11f-s
Station: East Croydon BR
Buses: 50, 54, 60, 64, 68a, 109, 119, 130, 154, 166, 194, 198
Fuller's Chiswick Bitter, Fuller's London Pride, Fuller's ESB

A dictionary could not describe an 'alehouse' better than this tiny two-storey street corner building dwarfed by the nearby Croydon flyover and Wandle Road multi-storey car park. Recent sympathetic renovation has extended the back bar but the modest front bar with its etched glass windows remains unspoilt and is the more atmospheric of the two. Across the road, an unusual outdoor drinking area has been created under the flyover. Tongue and groove panelling to shoulder height and plain, nicotine-coloured walls above, coupled with a low ceiling, provide simplicity and plentiful character simultaneously. A carved lintel-piece, fine mirrors and an Art Deco house mirror over a fireplace, give the kind of interesting features that act on the peripheral vision to turn a good pub into an excellent pub. One of the few pubs in London to have never stopped serving real ale in the 1970s.

Mitcham – CR4

Cricketers

340 London Road, Mitcham

Young's
G CP SL

Opening Hours: normal
Station: Mitcham BR
Buses: 80, 93, 154, 293
Young's Bitter, Young's Special, Young's Winter Warmer

A modern replacement of a pub destroyed by a direct hit during the war. There has been a pub on the site since at least 1789. Formerly called the White Swan, by 1823 it had become the Cricketers. Both the pub and the nearby cricket ground have impeccable cricketing credentials. The ground and the Mitcham Club that meet in the pub are supposed to be the oldest in the world. Between 1875-80 the landlord was former England cricketer, James Southerton, and he may well have acted as host to the early Australian touring teams who used to train there. Today the cricketing theme is still very much in evidence.

Morden – SM1

Wetherspoons

Aberconway Road, Morden

Wetherspoon
CP DA ML ME SL SE
Opening Hours: normal
Station: Morden
Buses: 118, 154, 157, 164, 167, 393
Younger's Scotch, Theakston's Best, Marston's Pedigree, Theakston's XB, Courage Directors + Guest Beers; Cider

It may be no accident that this pub, opposite the terminus of the Northern Line, has installed air conditioning, which may be a hit with travellers at the end of a frequently hot and uncomfortable journey. A fairly typical example of the Wetherspoon phenomena, there is a degree of interesting sculpture depicting the local historic themes of snuff production, monastic life and the underground. Notes on the history of the area are displayed on the wall. Food is served all day.

Sutton – SM1

Windsor Castle

13 Greyhound Road, Sutton

Fuller's
G ML
Opening Hours: 11-30-3, 5-11m-f 11.30-11s
Station: Sutton BR
Buses: 80, 151, 164, 213, 280, 407, 408, 413, 520, 726, S1, N68

Fuller's London Pride, Fuller's ESB

The building dates from about 1879 but has been a pub only since the turn of the century. It was formerly a Charrington's house but was gutted and refitted by Fuller's in 1985. Despite being a three-storey building with a two-storey extension, it still offers a remarkably small bar; clearly someone with a sense of humour named it after one of the Royal palaces! The drinking area is effectively a strip a few yards wide facing the L-shaped bar. Not the ideal place to go with the Rugby Team.

Cheam – SM3

Railway Hotel

32 Station Way, Cheam
S&N
ML ME SL SE
Opening Hours: normal
Station: Cheam BR
Buses: 72b, 151, 213, 408,
Theakston's Best, Courage Best Bitter, Theakston's XB, Courage Directors + Guest Beers

Detached two-storey building near the railway bridge and possibly built about 1850 after the railway came to Cheam. Inside there is a comfortable L-shaped lounge where the only noise is the chink of glasses and the buzz of conversation. A well-run comfortable local managed by CAMRA members with no needless, so-called, attractions.

Carshalton – SM5

Greyhound

2 High Street, Carshalton
Young's
FR G CP DA ML ME SL SE
Opening Hours: normal
Station: Carshalton
Buses: 72b, 127, 157, 407, 408 , 627
Young's Bitter, Young's Special, Young's Winter Warmer

A large yet intimate Grade II-listed, hotel pub with 1930s Road House feel, overlooking the Carshalton Ponds. A pub of this name has stood on the site since 1700 and had strong sporting connections. Racehorses were looked over here prior to racing on Banstead Downs. The old inn was rebuilt in 1840 and the pub expanded into neighbouring premises. The weatherboard part of the building houses the saloon bar with original fireplace, long-case clocks, pewter jugs and wood panels. A set of regulars in the saloon prefer to drink their beer from pewter. A larger public bar is in the main body of the building. The pub offers accommodation, children's area and wheelchair access through the rear beer garden. There is a separate function room and the huge car park is capable of accommodating cars for even large functions. The local Round Table has adopted the Greyhound as its home and thoughtfully, the use of mobile phones is banned in the saloon bar.

Wallington – SM6

Duke's Head

6 Manor Road, Wallington **2**

Young's
G CP ML
Opening Hours: normal
Station: Wallington BR
Buses: 72b, 151, 255, 400, 407, 408,
Young's Bitter, Young's Special, Young's Winter Warmer

The present Grade II listed building dates from around 1830 and enjoys a prominent position on The Green at the A232/A237 junction. As well as a wood panelled two room lounge, reached by the side entrance, there is a front entrance to a small, plain, public bar which charges lower prices. The pub's position on The Green gives it a large unofficial outdoor drinking area. A moulded sign on the south wall of the building reads 'Dukes Head Livery and Bait Stables', a reminder of the days of *real* horse-power.

WC1

Cittie of York

22 High Holborn

Sam Smiths
R ML ME SL SE
Opening Hours: 11.30-11m-s closed su
Station: Chantry Lane
Buses: 8, 22b, 25, 501, 521, N8, N21, N76
Sam Smith's OBB, Sam Smith's Museum Ale

A pub has stood on this site since 1430. It was rebuilt in 1695, well back from the road with a garden in front and was called Gray's Inn Coffee Shop. In the next century, it was extended forward and then in the 1890s, the building was partially demolished and rebuilt in its present form. The pub takes its name from a sixteenth-century pub that used to be in the Staple Inn, the timber framed building on the other side of High Holborn. The large rear area (one of three) covers the ground originally occupied by the original coffee house and much of the original fabric is left. There is a long bar counter, handsome screen-work on many small compartments, long rows of vats (holding between 500 and 1100 gallons) and a coal stove dating from the year of the Battle of Waterloo. The stove's smoke escapes by way of a chimney under the floor. Note the high trussed roof. The front bar is more intimate with panelling, an original chandelier and the coats of arms of the cities of York and London. The old cellarage of the Coffee House provides an extensive cellar bar. This is one of London's great pubs.

Enterprise

38 Red Lion St

Bass
ME
Opening Hours: normal
Station: Holborn
Buses: 8, 19, 22b, 25, 38, 55, 68, 91, 168
Highgate Dark, Hancocks HB, Harvey's Sussex Bitter, Draught Bass + Guest Beers

A slightly inept treatment of a fine old Edwardian pub. However, there are enough clues to be able to put together a bit of visual detective work and reconstruct the original floor plan. An original ceiling, wall tiles and bow front (albeit without the original glass) give way to a more modern rear which relies on old photographs to maintain the atmosphere. At least the pictures are properly hung and not merely screwed to the wall as in so many 'traditional' pubs. Bare floors and dark green upholstery give the Enterprise a fairly dark quality of the authentic city pub. The evening menu is on a Tex-Mex theme and the pub is a rare outlet for Highgate Dark, a classic mild and a beer of a style that once was ubiquitous but now is hard to find. The view from the bow window is of another pub, the Dolphin (Whitbread) which has a fine old 'tavern'-style appearance. What better view can there be from a pub, than another pub, though this can give rise to an awful dilemma.

Hansler
133 Kings Cross Road

Free House
SL
Opening Hours: normal
Station: Kings Cross
Buses: 17, 63, 359, N21, N93, N96
Boddington's Bitter, Timothy Taylor's Landlord + Guest Beers

A tiny one-room pub, so cramped for space they have to put the pictures on the ceiling as well as the walls. A hidden gem on the main drag but one that is probably passed over as larger pubs in the area are more likely to catch the eye. Beware, they are nowhere near as good. The Hansler trades on the quality of its beer. The lack of space means food is confined to snacks but these include, at the time of writing, the famous O'Hagan's sausages. All in all a pub for beer-loving locals and office workers, which is quiet when other less good pubs nearby are crowded. Handy for Kings Cross station and the large tourist pubs of the Kings Cross Road.

Kings Arms

11a Northington Street

Bass
G ML ME SL SE
Opening Hours: 11-11m-f closed s-su
Station: Chancery Lane
Buses: 19, 38, 505
Adnams Bitter, Fuller's London Pride, Everards Tiger, Draught Bass

A large local for the area, with a recently added Thai restaurant upstairs. A long bar starts under the stairs and extends along one wall with a food serving area at the other end. The opposite wall is taken up with red plush seating under frosted glass windows. The pub retains plenty of original features, especially glasswork and fireplaces. The Kings Arms is very much a locals' pub, serving one of the few residential areas to extend this far into the heart of the city. The beer quality helps make this a popular pub, as does the very cheerful nature of the bar staff.

Lamb

94 Lambs Conduit Street

Young's
G ML ME SL SE
Opening Hours: normal
Station: Russell Square
Buses: 19, 38, 55, 505, N19, N92, N96
Young's Bitter, Young's Special, Young's Winter Warmer

The Lamb is one of central London's most highly respected pubs. The glazed green tile-fronted authentic Victorian local retains many original features, notably a fine array of snob screens which were used by the class-conscious Victorians to hide themselves from their social betters and social inferiors. There is also a working Polyphon which can be played in aid of charity (visit the pub to find out what it is). There is also a good collection of photographs of Victorian celebrities running along the walls, just above the seating. The pub is split into several parts including a non-smoking 'snug' with bar stools. Walk through the sunken seated area at the back of the pub to find a small secluded outside seating area which gets very popular in summer. The Lamb is a fine Victorian pub and is Grade II listed.

Plough

27 Museum Street

Allied Domecq
ML SL
Opening Hours: normal
Station: Holborn
Buses: 8, 22b, 25, 38, 55, 68, 911, 168
Tetley Bitter, Eldridge Pope Best Bitter, Marston's Pedigree, Ind Coope Burton Ale + Guest Beers

Large inviting corner pub with attractive pink and white frontage on upper floors and a deep red and gilt ground floor, very much in the classic London style. Split into two inside with a church type screen, a green scheme drinking area is separated from a wood-panelled eating area. Popular with visitors to the British Museum and scholars from the British Library wishing to wash the book dust from their throats. It is to be recommended over the nearby and rather better-known Museum Tavern, which is more expensive.

Princess Louise

208 High Holborn

Free House
ML ME SL SE
Opening Hours: normal
Station: Holborn
Buses: 8, 19, 22b, 25, 38, 55, 68, 91, 168
Brakspear Bitter, Greene King IPA, Gales Best, Adnams Old, Wadworth 6X, Draught Bass + Guest Beers

The Princess Louise is a vivid celebration of everything the Victorian pub stood for. At one time it was probably divided by partitions. Every surface is authentic British craftsmanship, from the lyncrysta ceiling to the tiled walls. The cut and gilt mirrors are unparalleled in quality and quantity and even the gents toilets are ranked as national treasures. Behind the long oval bar there is still a publican's office, a very rare feature, which developed from the serving hatches of the seventeenth century that were the precursors of the bar proper and through which pots of beer were originally served. On top of all this, the pub is a free house with a wide range of beers always available. The pub is named after Queen Victoria's fourth daughter who married the Duke of Argyll. It was built in 1872 but current fittings date back to 1891. Refurbished by Arthur Chitty, a famous architect of the day, the tiles were by Simpsons of London. A visit here is to step back in time.

Queens Larder

1 Queens Street

Whitbread
G ML ME SL SE
Opening Hours: normal
Station: Russell Square
Buses: 68, 91, 168, 188, N21, N91
Flowers IPA, Boddington's Bitter, Fuller's London Pride, Wadworth 6X, Marston's Pedigree

Small historic wood-fronted pub in the heart of London's hospital quarter and opposite the church of St George the Martyr, known as the 'sweeps' church' after the charity Christmas dinners for chimney sweeps that were given there. There has been an alehouse on the site since at least 1710 when it was owned by a carpenter named Kenwick. The pub became known as the Queen's Larder as, during the treatment of George III for madness, the

King stayed in Queen's Square under the care of Dr Willis. The doctor's treatment, which was temporarily successful, was helped by Queen Charlotte who rented a small underground cellar beneath the present pub to store delicacies for the King. When the alehouse became a tavern later in the King's reign it was named the Queen's Larder in her honour. This history is displayed on a plaque on the wall of the pub, but contains a serious chronological discrepancy – see if you can spot it. This wood-lined pub, which was originally slightly larger, is a Grade II-listed building.

Skinners

114 Judd Street

Greene King
G ML ME SL SE
Opening Hours: 11-11m-f closed s-su
Station: St Pancras
Buses: 10, 18, 30, 73, 91, N73, N90, N91
Greene King IPA, Greene King Abbot + Greene King seasonal beers

Pleasant corner pub on leafy Judd Street, dominated by a central rectangular bar, younger than the rest of the building, that serves both rooms of the pub. An attractive red and green colour scheme gives the pub a warming feel, making the pub very popular with locals and office workers. Outside there is a small seating area, underneath an attractive display of hanging baskets, giving one a nice view of the Salvation Army Social Services HQ opposite. One must presume that workers from that particular office do not frequent the pub. The pub is one of a number that serve the unusual residential enclave south of St Pancras but is also handy for the Renoir repertory cinema in Brunswick Square, at the south end of Judd Street. It is also close to the Camden Centre in Bidborough Street, which hosts a CAMRA beer festival every March.

Swan

7 Cosmo Place

T&J Bernard
G ML ME SL SE
Opening Hours: normal
Station: Holborn
Buses: 68, 91, 168, 188, N21, N91
Theakston's Best, Courage Best Bitter, Theakston's XB, Courage Directors, Theakston's OP + Guest Beers; Bulmer's Traditional Cider

The Swan in Cosmo place (formerly Fox Place or Little Ormond Street) has been around since at least 1753. The wood- fronted pub is externally very much in the style of a Victorian shop but now sports cafe-style pavement seating on pedestrian Cosmo place which connects Southampton Row and Queen's Square. Done out in what T&J Bernard refer to as their 'kitchen' style (as opposed to the 'classic' style) the recently-refurbished pub has lots of rough wood and small leaded windows, a long bar, bare wood floors and wooden settle seating. Like all T&J Bernard pubs, it serves real cider and has an impressive range of bottled Belgian fruit beers and German wheat beers.

Three Cups

22 Sandland Street

Young's

SL

Opening Hours: 11-11m-f closed s-su

Station: Holborn

Buses: 8, 22b, 25, 501, 521

Young's Bitter, Young's Special

For many years a Charrington house, the Three Cups has now entered the Young's stable. The large one-room pub fronts an old coaching yard which is now home to the Link Theatre and the Holborn Performing Arts Centre, both of which provide the pub with a substantial part of its trade. The pub has the usual Young's treatment and with windows along two sides, has quite a light aspect to it, whilst the ceiling beams and pillars give clues as to how the pub was originally laid out. The pub is part of Young's Verre de Vin group of pubs, which means that the wine on offer is a cut above your average pub plonk. In summer, there are tables and chairs outside for the sunseekers.

Water Rats

330 Grays Inn Road

Inntrepreneur

R ML

Opening Hours: 11-12m-s 7-12su

Station: Kings Cross

Buses: 17, 45, 46,

Young's Bitter, Courage Directors, Young's Special + Guest Beers

Formerly a fringe theatre pub it has now gone over entirely to live music. The pub has a well-known bowed frontage onto the Grays Inn Road and is between the offices of the charitable Ancient Order of Water Rats, from which it takes its name, and the Ear, Nose and Throat Hospital, which probably produces a small amount of medicinal trade. The pub has a late licence to accompany its role as a music venue and to bring in extra daytime trade, there is a new Thai restaurant which just opens for lunches. The pub is so popular as a venue that the bar staff frequently come in on their nights off.

WC2

Angel
61 St Giles High Street

S&N
Opening Hours: 12-11m-f 5.30-11s closed su
Station: Tottenham Court Road
Buses: 14, 19, 24, 29, 38, 176
Theakston's Best, Courage Best Bitter, Theakston's XB, Courage Directors

Old, reputedly haunted, pub near Centrepoint, rebuilt in 1898, lying on the old tumbrel route from Newgate to Tyburn gallows. From the sixteenth century it was known as 'The Bowl' and was the traditional stopping place for the condemned to have a final drink. Like all traditions its roots are based on good sense. One condemned man refused his final drink at the Angel and was thus hanged a few minutes earlier than otherwise, dying moments before his pardon caught up with him. If he had drunk, he would have lived. It was also traditional for the condemned man to make a joke about paying for his drink on the way back. The crowd loved it no matter how often they heard it. There are ornate octagonal ceiling mouldings in the lounge bar, while the public section is more basic with a dart board. Note the attractive tile work in the former side passageway.

Chandos
St Martin's Lane

Sam Smiths
Opening Hours: normal
Station: Charing Cross
Buses: 24, 29, 176
Sam Smith's OBB

Big and dignified, at the foot of St Martin's Lane, this pub has an award-winning interior design and is the definitive rendezvous for groups venturing into theatreland as well as being a fine pub in its own right.

The clientele consists of the whole world. Stay there long enough and you're bound to meet someone you know. Handy for pigeon fanciers visiting Trafalgar Square, and art lovers visiting the National Gallery and National Portrait Gallery. Downstairs, the wood- floored bar is surrounded with Tudoresque booths, whilst upstairs is a more relaxed lounge with sofas and the food area. Children are permitted only until the early evening and the beer is remarkably good value for central London.

Cross Keys

31 Endell St, Covent Garden

Inntrepreneur
G ML ME SL SE
Opening Hours: normal
Station: Covent Garden
Buses: 8, 25
Webster's Yorkshire Bitter, Courage Best Bitter, Courage Directors

Small side-street pub just off the main Covent Garden beaten track. In summer, the frontage is nearly obscured by an abundance of foliage, hiding the cross keys depicted in relief over the door. The single bar is decorated with a varied collection of prints and bric-a-brac which has resulted from many years of tenancy occupation. The pub memorabilia includes a signed Australian cricket bat from the 1932/4 bodyline era, as well as a sign from the Isleworth Brewery. The Grade II-listed building was rebuilt in 1848. Worth walking the extra few yards to find, this small and cosy pub makes a change from some of the larger more touristy pubs on Bow Street and Long Acre.

George IV

28 Portugal Street

Bass
ML ME SL SE
Opening Hours: 11-11m-f closed s-su
Station: Temple
Buses: 1, 68, 91, 168, 171, 188, 501, 505, 521, X68
Charrington IPA, Fuller's London Pride, Draught Bass, Morland's Old Speckled Hen

Imposing and ornate corner pub, first licensed in 1825, rebuilt in 1898/9 by Hoare and Co (the Red Lion Brewery, now defunct) at a cost of £7,440 and designed by the architects Perry and Reid. The pleasant wood-panelled and mirrored bar has an upstairs pool room. Custom comes mostly from the nearby Law Courts and the

London School of Economics. The Old Curiosity Shop is just around the corner. The pub is well worth a visit, even if it is just for a look.

Lamb and Flag

Rose St, Covent Garden

Inntrepreneur
ML SL
Opening Hours: 11-10.45f-s
Station: Leicester Square
Buses: 24, 29, 176
John Smith's Bitter, Courage Best Bitter, Wadworth 6X, Courage Directors

Close to Covent Garden Market, Theatre Museum, London Transport Museum and Opera House, this seventeenth-century wood-panelled pub was originally known as the Coopers Arms and has been referred to as the Bucket of Blood. The bar counters of this old pub are inlaid with metal tags bearing the names of old regulars. The bars have different opening times, the roomier upstairs bar is open only in the evenings and for jazz on Sunday nights. On summer evenings, the customers spill out onto Rose Street, which is a great place to watch Covent Garden life go by.

Marquess of Anglesey

39 Bow St, Covent Garden

Young's
ML ME SL SE
Opening Hours: normal
Station: Covent Garden
Buses: 6, 9, 13, 23, 77a
Young's Bitter, Young's Special, Young's Winter Warmer

Modern-post war pub with bars on two levels. The upper bar/restaurant is less crowded and more comfortable. Very popular and busy in the evenings and weekends. It was first licensed in 1663 under the Coffee House Act of that year. By the following century a tavern called the 'Green Man' occupied the site. By 1815 it was renamed in honour of William Henry Pagett, 2nd Earl of Uxbridge, who was created 1st Marquis of Anglesey after his exploits at the Battle of Waterloo, where he lost a leg. The previous pub, rebuilt in 1881, was destroyed in the war. The present building was erected in 1955/6. Ironically when it was reopened the licence was held by Nicholson's, who now run the 'Globe' next door. Very handy for the Covent Garden Area, the Opera House, London Transport Museum, Theatre Museum and the Strand.

Nags Head

James Street

McMullen

ML

Opening Hours: normal

Station: Covent Garden

Buses: 6, 9, 13, 23, 77a

McMullen's AK, Draught Bass, McMullen's Country, McMullen's Gladstone

Busy Covent Garden pub, just a few yards from the tube station. You pass it as you walk towards the market. The smallish one-bar pub is always crowded, with the seats in the small annexe to the rear of the bar at a premium. The pub is comfortably furnished with frosted mirrors. Very much at the heart of Covent Garden, it is not nearly as pretentious as some of the pubs to the south of the Market towards the Strand. Also close to Jubilee Market, Royal Opera House, Adelphi Theatre.

Opera Tavern

21 Catherine Street

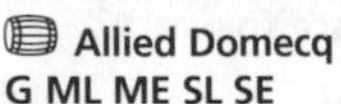

Allied Domecq

G ML ME SL SE

Opening Hours: 11-11m-s closed su

Station: Covent Garden

Buses: 6, 9, 13, 23, 77a

Tetley Bitter, Young's Bitter

Small pub crammed with theatre posters, memorabilia and with a fine decor facing the Theatre Royal, Drury Lane. The present pub was rebuilt in 1879 and was the work of the celebrated pub architect George Treacher. It is much used by theatre-goers and performers alike. The upstairs bar is known variously as the Aldwych (after the theatre) or the Raddeley (after the actress).

Roundhouse

1 Garrick Street, Covent Garden

S&N

Opening Hours: normal

Station: Leicester Square

Buses: 24, 29, 176

Theakston's Best, Younger's IPA, Theakston's OP + Guest Beers

First S&N pub in London to get the T&J Bernard treatment – that is to be remodelled as S&N's version of the bare-board alehouse pioneered by the Firkin chain. This pub is, unfortunately, more expensive than can really be justified but as it is quite small and enough people are prepared to pay over the odds, S&N are not unduly concerned. One of the major pubs in Covent Garden, however, and its round frontage and central location make it a popular meeting place.

Salisbury

90 St Martins Lane

S&N
ML ME SL SE
Opening Hours: normal
Station: Leicester Square
Buses: 24, 29, 176
Eldridge Pope Dorchester, Tetley Bitter, Theakston's Best, Ind Coope Burton Ale

A superb example of a late Victorian 'Gin Palace' with brass, polished woodwork, glasswork, mirrors and Art Nouveau light fittings. It featured in the 1961 Dirk Bogarde film *Victim* where it appeared as the Shaftesbury. A haunt of theatrical types until driven out by tourists, it was called the 'Coach and Horses' until 1866 and the 'Salisbury Stores' until the 1960s. It was rebuilt in 1892 but closed within a year, becoming a restaurant until it was relicensed and refurbished in 1898. Handy for Theatreland, Trafalgar Square and the National Gallery and National Portrait Gallery.

Seven Stars

53 Carey Street

Inntrepreneur
ML SL
Opening Hours: 11-9m-f closed s-su
Station: Temple
Buses: 4, 11, 15, 23, 26, 76, 171a
Courage Best Bitter, Courage Directors

Historic old-world pub built in 1602 with an unspoilt interior. Popular with the legal profession from the Royal Courts of Justice (the Law Courts) which are opposite. To reach this pub from the Strand, go up Bell Yard which is almost opposite St Clement Danes church and Carey Street is the first turning right. If you do not have any business in the Law Courts, the pub is also handy for Lincolns Inn Fields and the Sir John Soanes Museum.

Sherlock Holmes

10/11 Northumberland Street, Westminster

Whitbread

G R ML ME SL SE
Opening Hours: normal
Station: Embankment
Buses: 3, 11, 12, 24, 53, 77a, 88, 109, 159, X53
Brakspear Bitter, Boddington's Bitter, Flowers Original

Under its previous name, 'The Northumberland Arms', the pub was featured in one of Sir Arthur Conan Doyle's Sherlock Holmes stories and was given a 'Sherlockian' theme for the 1951 Festival of Britain, although it did not take its present name until 1957. As well as Holmes memorabilia downstairs, the upstairs contains a replica of Holmes' Baker Street study. Definitely a tourist pub, indeed it is probably the quintessential London tourist pub, catering for coach parties and walking pub tours and is very busy at all times. Built in 1846 it was called 'The Northumberland Hotel' to avoid confusion with another 'Northumberland Arms' at No. 18 which was pulled down along with the whole of the west side of Northumberland Street in the late 1860s. The pub was partially rebuilt and a red brick frontage added in 1891.

Wellington

351 Strand

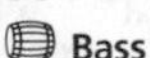

ML ME SL SE
Opening Hours: normal
Station: Temple
Hancocks HB, Fuller's London Pride, Draught Bass

Ornate-fronted corner pub facing Waterloo Bridge with a narrow split-level bar and traditional decor. Being busy and narrow gives it a rather intimate and cosy effect. Licensed in 1848 and rebuilt in 1903 by architects Bird and Walters, in an era when very little pub refurbishment was being carried out, it used to be part of the George Whitehead '199' free house chain until the group was bought out by Bass for £7m in the 1980s. Renovations revealed an original marble wall that had been covered in less tasteful times. Handy for Drury Lane Theatre and other Strand theatres.

White Hart

191 Drury Lane

ML ME SL SE
Opening Hours: normal
Station: Holborn
Buses: 1
Worthington Best Bitter, Draught Bass

Attractive, narrow fronted pub with a deceptively large interior. Popular with postal workers, unsurprisingly, as it is situated behind the West Central Sorting Office. The large rear bar area has an impressive vaulted, clerestory lit, Tudor roof in a baronial style. Rebuilt in 1911 by the Red Lion Brewery (Hoare and Co) it is an early example of the 'Brewers Tudor' style that was to become quite popular in the inter-war years. The architect was George Cranham. If the pub's inn sign is to be believed (AD 1201) it could be one of the oldest surviving tavern sites in London. Before it was rebuilt the White Hart was smaller than the nearby Sun at 21 Drury Lane.

Fitzrovia – W1

Albany

240 Great Portland Street
Allied-Domecq
ML ME SL SE
Opening Hours: normal
Station: Great Portland Street
Tetley Bitter, Adnams Broadside + Guest Beers

A big olde worlde single-bar pub that was once a hotel. The cellar hosts a resident comedy club five nights a week and stays open to midnight (1am Fri/Sat). The cellar is also a venue for house music on Sunday night. Sunday night's customers are clubbers but during the rest of the week are a mix of tourists and office workers.

Bricklayers Arms

31 Gresse Street
Sam Smith
ML ME SL SE
Opening Hours: 11-11m-f 12-11s 7-10.30su
Station: Goodge Street
Buses: 10, 24, 29, 73, 134
Sam Smith OBB

Small neat Sam Smith's pub in Fitzrovia. The Bricklayers Arms has won a best pub refurbishment award from CAMRA, an award never given unless a high standard is achieved. The narrow frontage is just wide enough for the doorway and a seat on either side. The door opens onto a small front room with enough seating for about 20 people. A small passage to the side of the bar takes you into the public bar which has a further small number of seats, a darts board and a small half bar no more than three feet long. Upstairs is a lounge bar with more generous upholstery, a broad gas-effect fire in a wide chimney piece, an alcove seat in the window and low coffee tables to give it a bit of a hotel lounge feel. Food is served all sessions but the pub is not open Sunday lunchtimes.

George
55 Gt Portland Street

Greene King
ML ME SL SE
Opening Hours: 11-11m-f 11-6s closed su
Station: Oxford Street
Buses: 135, C2
Greene King XX Mild, Greene King IPA, Rayment's Special Bitter, Greene King Abbot

Ornate-fronted corner pub which, apart from its 'snug' bar partitions, has retained almost all of its Victorian panelling, woodwork and glass. The original pub, dating from 1744, was given the nickname the 'glue pot' by the famous conductor Sir Henry Wood, as most of his musicians spent their spare time drinking there. The present pub, rebuilt in 1878, was designed by the architects Bird and Walters and cost £4,470 at the time.

Newman Arms

23 Rathbone Street

Bass
G ML ME SL SE
Opening Hours: 11-11m-f 5-11s closed su
Station: Goodge Street
Buses: 10, 73
Hancocks HB, Fuller's London Pride, Draught Bass

Small and cosy, panelled bar with a nautical theme, including a superb model sailing ship in a glass case. The first floor boasts 'The Pie Room', a smart restaurant, which also doubles as a function room. It has a collection of lepidoptera (four-winged insects). First licensed in 1863 as a beer house, it is one of the smallest bars in the region north of Oxford Street that, due to its Bohemian and literary connections, became known as Fitzrovia. The pub menu also includes vegetarian dishes. Well worth a visit.

Ship

134 New Cavendish Street

Bass
SL

Opening Hours: 11.30-11m-f, s-su closed
Station: Goodge Street
Buses: 135, C2
Worthington Best Bitter, Draught Bass

A true classic and not to be missed. The interior's original maritime theme has gradually given over to a shrine dedicated to the Wenlock Brewery which was taken over by Charrington's (now part of the Bass group) in 1961 and closed down. The small bar is crowded with Wenlock and Bass bar fittings and mirrors etc. Note the unique Wenlock, Charrington and Bass mirror, made specially for the landlord to express his opinion as to what the merged Bass Charrington group should have been called. A collection of barrel bushes chart Bass's takeovers and closures of breweries. The upstairs snooker room was first licensed as 'The Centurion' in 1772 after the ship of that name which was the first vessel to try out the new sea-going chronometer. This enabled the first accurate measurement of latitude to be made and so revolutionised the art of navigation. The pub was renamed 'The Ship' in 1815 and was rebuilt in 1887.

Tottenham

6 Oxford Street

Allied Domecq
DA ML ME SL
Opening Hours: normal
Station: Tottenham Court Road
Buses: 7, 8, 10, 24, 25, 29, 55, 73, 98, 134, 176
Adnams Bitter, Adnams Broadside, Marston's Pedigree, Ind Coope Burton Ale, Morland's Old Speckled Hen

Amazingly, the Tottenham is the only pub left along the whole length of Oxford Street (in 1852 there were at least 38 and by 1955 there were only eight). Called 'The Flying Horse' until it was rebuilt in 1892 by its owners, the Baker Bros, at a cost of £12,120, it was designed by the architects Saville and Martin. The deep bar has five painted ceiling bosses and elaborate murals on the walls. Always busy, the beer is much better kept than in many central London pubs.

Marylebone – W1

Barley Mow

8 Dorset Street

Nicholson
G ML ME SL SE
Opening Hours: 11-11m-s closed su

Station: Marble Arch
Buses: 2, 13, 30, 74, 82, 113, 139, 159, 274
Brakspear Bitter, Tetley Bitter, Wadworth 6X, Adnams Broadside, Marston's Pedigree

The sixth oldest surviving pub in Marylebone dating from 1791/2. It retains most of its woodwork and matchboarding from the last century, along with two small private cubicles (with seats) fronting one side of the bar counter. These were originally used for privately conducted pawnbroking transactions – a secondary occupation of an early landlord. His customers, both for the purposes of drinking and borrowing, were mainly employees of the Portman estate. There is a second bar area hidden away at the back of the pub. Darts and board games are available. Well worth a visit.

Beehive

7 Homer Street

Whitbread
G ML SL
Opening Hours: 11-3, 5-11m-th s 11-11f 12-3, 7-10.30su
Station: Edgware Road
Buses: 18, 27
Boddington's Bitter, Fuller's London Pride

Small and very popular side-street bar (the second smallest in Marylebone) with 1960s tankard doors and etched glass windows fronted with a floral window box display. There is a large display of sepia photographs of bygone Marylebone around the walls and over the bar counter. Trade is mainly locals, office workers and the occasional, more adventurous tourist. Licensed as a beer house from 1840-1952 and rebuilt in the early days of this century, it is rather surprising that the pub was not called 'The Coopers' Arms' as it operated a small cooperage at the back from 1858-1869. A fine pub with a friendly and welcoming atmosphere.

Golden Eagle

59 Marylebone Lane

Free House
SL SE
Opening Hours: 11-11m-f 11-3,5.30-11s
Station: Bond Street
Buses: 3, 25, 53, 55, 176, X53
Brakspear Bitter, Fuller's London Pride, Draught Bass

Tiny pub just off Marylebone High Street, with handsome back bar mirrors. There is a piano player on some evenings and food often includes locally made sausages.

Windsor Castle

29 Crawford Place

Bass
G DA ML ME SL SE
Opening Hours: normal
Station: Edgware Road
Buses: 6, 7, 15, 16, 16a, 23, 27, 36, 98
Adnams Bitter, Draught Bass

Here is a good example of how a keen licensee has built up a theme decor, in this case British Royalty, with walls covered in photographs and newspaper cuttings going back over the years. Amongst the memorabilia is a model of a ship called the 'Windsor Castle' in a glass case. Built in 1832 and first licensed in 1850 as a home-brew beer shop (although brewing was short-lived, lasting only about two years), the pub only got its full beer, wine and spirit licence in 1949. Like a growing number of London pubs it has formed an association with Thai food.

Worcester Arms

89 George Street

Regent Inns
FR G ML ME SL SE
Opening Hours: normal
Station: Marble Arch
Buses: 2, 6, 7, 13, 15, 16, 23, 30, 36, 74, 82, 98, 113, 139, 159
Brakspear Bitter, Adnams Bitter, Courage Best Bitter, Draught Bass, Theakston's XB

Built and licensed in 1777, this is one of the few remaining mid-Georgian taverns in this part of London. A smallish, narrow bar, it has some decorative bar fittings. A Regent Inns outlet since the 1980s, it has been a regular feature in the Good Beer Guide for some years, although a clue as to the nature of its regular custom can be gleaned from the fact that the choice of beer is often reduced at weekends. This is a sign of good quality as the landlord will clearly reduce the choice of what is on offer, rather than allow beer to deteriorate over slack periods. Most commendable.

Mayfair – W1

Audley

41 Mount Street

Inntrepreneur
G DA R ML ME SL SE
Opening Hours: normal

Station: Marble Arch
Buses: 2, 10, 1, 36, 73, 74, 82, 137, 137a
John Smith's Bitter, Theakston's Best, Wadworth 6X, Courage Directors

A marvellous late-Victorian edifice in red brick and pink terracotta, designed by architect Thomas Verity. It was built in 1889 on the site of a pub with an unsavoury reputation called 'The Bricklayers Arms'. The Grosvenor Estate, who owned the land, insisted that it be pulled down and rebuilt with a new name if the lease were to be renewed. All the costs were borne by Watneys. The inside is equally impressive with fine polished wood and plasterwork. Note the double-faced clock in the centre of the bar. Tourists tend to form the bulk of the trade, but there is an excellent sandwich service as well as a restaurant and wine bar in the cellar.

Coach and Horses

2

5 Hill Street

Bass
ML SL
Opening Hours: 12-11m-f
Station: Green Park
Buses: 2, 10, 16, 36, 73, 74, 82, 137, 137a
Greene King IPA, Hancocks HB, Fuller's London Pride, Robinsons Best, Draught Bass

Eighteenth-century corner pub (licensed in 1744) with an unusual feature. Its side porch extends out to the kerbside and is part of the lounge bar. Set in the most fashionable part of Mayfair, it unusually retains its dart board. The pub was partly altered in 1899 when London pub architects Birn and Walters had a go at it.

Guinea

3

30 Bruton Place, Mayfair

Young's
R ML ME SL
Opening Hours: 11-11m-f 11-3, 7-11s closed su
Station: Green Park
Buses: 8
Young's Bitter, Young's Special, Young's Winter Warmer

Small intimate mews pub. A tavern has stood here since 1423 and was for many years called the One Pound One. The present building dates from 1675. There is an exclusive restaurant to the rear and the licensee has won several awards for the quality of his food. The pub can get very busy due to its small size and the clientele spill out into the Mews on warmer days. Very well worth sniffing out.

Punch Bowl

41 Farm Street

S&N
ML ME SL SE
Opening Hours: 11-11m-f 11-3s 12-3su
Station: Bond Street
Buses: 2, 10, 1, 36, 73, 74, 82, 137, 137a
John Smith's Bitter, Theakston's Best, Theakston's XB, Courage Directors

The second oldest pub in Mayfair after 'The Guinea', it has stood here since at least 1732 and, in its early days, it also served as a magistrates court for such offences as sheep stealing. In the 1970s it was nearly lost to redevelopment but was thankfully saved. It is a Grade II listed building, has the only public bar in Mayfair, and what is probably one of only two darts boards in Mayfair, the other is in the Coach and Horses (q.v.).

Red Lion

1 Waverton St, Mayfair

Inntrepreneur
DA R ML ME SL SE
Opening Hours: normal
Station: Marble Arch
Buses: 2, 10, 1, 36, 73, 74, 82, 137, 137a
Greene King IPA, John Smith's Bitter, Theakston's XB, Courage Directors

Pleasant secluded pub dating from the mid-eighteenth century (licensed in 1749), hidden away in a Mayfair backwater. Old-world atmosphere with a counter serving several different drinking areas, including the exclusive restaurant with waiter service. Although it has not sold keg bitter for years, the old Red Barrel set into a window is a reminder of the old days. Upmarket and well known on the tourist trail, well worth a visit.

Shepherd's Tavern

Shepherd's Market, Mayfair

Inntrepreneur
ML ME SL SE
Opening Hours: normal
Station: Green Park
Buses: 8, 9, 14, 19, 22, 38
John Smith's Bitter, Theakston's Best, Courage Best Bitter, Courage Directors

Atmospheric Shepherd's Market has four pubs, all worth a visit. The Tavern has recently been restored as a traditional London alehouse, which means woodwork and bric-a-brac. The Market still has a Victorian look to it more associated with Whitechapel and indeed its side streets are reputed to house the prostitutes' lodgings that exist to serve the needs of wealthy Mayfair.

Woodstock

11 Woodstock Street

S&N
ML ME SL SE
Opening Hours: normal
Station: Oxford Street
Buses: 7, 8, 10, 25, 55, 73, 98, 176
Younger's Scotch, Theakston's Best, Marston's Pedigree, Theakston's XB, Younger's IPA, Theakston's OP + Guest Beers

A small olde worlde pub, just off Oxford Street, opposite Debenhams, which is a real Mecca for beer hunters – well maybe not Mecca exactly. The pub serves wheat beers and fruit beers from all over Europe as well as one draught Belgian beer. The pub hosts occasional beer festivals and its home-made pies are a speciality. Wide range of bottled beers from Belgium, including fruit beers, Bavarian wheat beers and draught Leffe Blond.

Soho – W1

Argyle Arms

18 Argyle Street

Nicholson
G ML ME SL SE
Opening Hours: 11-11m-s closed su
Station: Oxford Street
Buses: 7, 8, 10, 25, 55, 73, 98, 176
Samuel Allsopp's Stout, Adnams Bitter, Cains Bitter, Wells Bombardier

Well-preserved Nicholson's house which still retains its internal snugs, etched glasswork, decorated mirrors and moulded ceiling. The pub's attractive exterior can be viewed from the paved drinking area out front. Its famous snugs are London's finest surviving examples of this style of pub interior that was very popular in the 1880s but which rapidly fell foul of the licensing authorities who disliked hidden corners where visual supervision was impeded. Most pubs with Argyle Arms-type interiors were refurbished from the 1890s onwards and much fine woodwork and glass destroyed. Just off London's busiest shopping thoroughfare, Oxford Street, it is frequented by locals and tourists in roughly equal numbers. It dates back to 1743 and is named after one of the Duke of Marlborough's generals who was also a local landowner.

Carlisle Arms

2 Bateman Street

Bass

SL

Opening Hours: 11-11m-s closed su

Station: Tottenham Court Road

Buses: 10, 24, 29, 73, 134

Worthington Best Bitter, Draught Bass

Small side-street pub with a curved counter and friendly staff. The entire rebuilding in 1877 cost only £1,300. One of the smallest bars in Soho, it is popular with office workers at lunchtimes and early evenings. The pub is taken over by a younger, trendy set later on.

Coach and Horses

29 Greek St, Soho

Allied Domecq

SL

Opening Hours: normal

Station: Leicester Square

Buses: 14, 19, 24, 29, 38, 176

Tetley Bitter, Young's Bitter, Ind Coope Burton Ale

One of the few Soho pubs retaining some character. Made famous by regular customer and Spectator columnist Jeffrey Bernard, it is one pub where celebrities may be seen. Favoured by the Private Eye set, the walls are decorated with a series of 'Jeff bin in' (Jeffrey Bernard) cartoons by Eye regular Michael Heath, also a local. Rebuilt in 1847 the pub is rather small and tends to fill up with people desperate to be seen.

Crown and Two Chairmen

31 Dean St, Soho

Nicholsons

ML ME SL SE

Opening Hours: normal

Station: Leicester Square

Buses: 14, 19, 38

Tetley Bitter, Ind Coope Burton Ale + Guest Beers

A cosy, traditional two-bar Soho local which is popular with all the beautiful people from the surrounding media and music industry's district. The pub takes its name from the Sedan Chair, introduced into Britain in the 1630s. The second bar is upstairs.

De Hems

11 Macclesfield St, China Town

Allied Domecq
ML ME SL SE
Opening Hours: normal
Station: Piccadilly Circus
Buses: 14, 19, 38
Tetley Bitter, Marston's Pedigree, Ind Coope Burton Ale

A large busy continental-style bar with a strong Dutch influence (signs are in both English and Dutch). Licensed in 1685 as 'The Horse and Dolphin', it was rebuilt in 1898 and renamed 'The Macclesfield Arms'. In 1959, it was again renamed the De Hems Restaurant (becoming just De Hems in 1974) after a famous Dutch landlord famed for his ale and oysters. At one time the wall of the alcove at the back of the pub was inlaid with oyster shells. In the summer, the front of the pub is opened and jazz is played on Sundays at both lunchtimes and evenings.

Dover Castle

43 Weymouth Street

Sam Smiths
G ML ME SL SE
Opening Hours: normal
Station: Regent's Park
Buses: 135, C2
Sam Smith's OBB, Sam Smith's Museum Ale

Small snug mews pub licensed in 1777. The bar is divided into three areas; the rear one has a sliding door which is useful when it is used for private functions. The front etched windows show the position of the original layout. The mirror strips under the dividing ceiling beam enabled the ostlers (coachmen) to see when their passengers were ready to depart from the adjacent bar. For many years, it was nicknamed 'Mooney's' after a particularly long-serving landlady. After a period as a free house, it is now part of Yorkshire brewers Sam Smith's London estate.

George

D'Arblay St, Soho

Free House
Opening Hours: normal
Station: Tottenham Court Road

Buses: 7, 8, 10, 25, 55, 73, 98, 176
Tetley Bitter, Friary Meux Best Bitter, Wadworth 6X, Ind Coope Burton Ale

Tiny, traditional street-corner alehouse with big gilt mirrors but which blasts out the latest in house and techno music. It is unusual in that it does no food. The clientele wear their jeans baggy, their baseball caps the wrong way round but still love their real ale.

Jack Horner

Tottenham Court Road

Fuller's
ML ME SL SE
Opening Hours: normal
Station: Goodge Street
Buses: 24, 29, 134
Fuller's Chiswick Bitter, Fuller's London Pride, Fuller's ESB

Don't be misled by the apparent age of this pub. It is, in fact, a modern pub built into the fabric of an old bank. Fuller's have developed an excellent style for their "Ale and Pie Houses" and this pub is a superb and overdue addition to the Tottenham Court Road which once contained a large number of very fine Victorian public houses.

John Snow

39 Broadwick St, Soho

Sam Smiths
ML ME SL SE
Opening Hours: normal
Station: Piccadilly Circus
Buses: 3, 6, 12, 13, 15, 23, 53, 88, 94, 139, 159, X53
Sam Smith's OBB, Sam Smith's Museum Ale

Well restored back-street pub with historical connections. Licensed in 1721 and called the Newcastle-upon-Tyne until 1954. The renaming commemorated the centenary of the 1854 cholera epidemic when Dr John Snow chained up the water pump outside the pub and subsequently proved that the disease was water borne. He died in 1858. The present pub, rebuilt in 1867, has recently had a refurbishment which has given it a public bar, a rarity in Soho. There is an additional bar and function room upstairs.

Lyric Tavern

37 Great Windmill St, Soho

Inntrepreneur
ML ME SL SE
Opening Hours: 11-11m-s 7-10.30su
Station: Piccadilly Circus
Buses: 14, 19, 38
Ruddles Best, John Smith's Bitter, Courage Directors

Tiny bow-fronted pub with a tiled exterior just off Piccadilly Circus. Trade is mainly local and caters for theatre employees. The small and snug wood-panelled bar gives it a cosy atmosphere. It was formed by two eighteenth-century taverns merging, hence its old name: the Windmill and Ham. It was rebuilt in 1890, at the then fabulous expense of £2,000 and renamed after the nearby Lyric Theatre that was then being built.

Old Coffee House
Beak Street

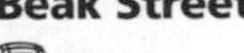

Inntrepreneur
ML
Opening Hours: normal
Station: Oxford Circus Tube
Buses: 3, 6, 12, 13, 15, 23, 53, 88, 94, 159, X53
Courage Best Bitter, Marston's Pedigree, Courage Directors

One-bar early Victorian pub near Carnaby Street. Originally, as its name suggests, it was a coffee house. Busy decor with plenty of brass, posters, nick-nacks etc. at the comfy end of the scale. The clientele consists of tourists searching for the 1960s and ponytails from surrounding advertising and media offices. Soho Pub of the Year 1986.

Pillars of Hercules
Greek St, Soho

S&N
ML SL
Opening Hours: normal
Station: Tottenham Court Road
Buses: 7, 8, 10, 5, 55, 73, 98, 176
Theakston's Best, Marston's Pedigree, Younger's IPA, Younger's No 3, Theakston's OP + Guest Beers

A single long, narrow room with a bar running all down one side. There are wood-panelled walls and bare floorboards for a traditional alehouse look. It has the usual Soho schizo clientele, workers by day, partyers by night. Not too many years ago it did no real ale.

Spice of Life

38 Romilly St, Soho

McMullen
ML ME SL SE
Opening Hours: normal
Station: Leicester Square
Buses: 14, 19, 24, 29, 38, 176
McMullen's AK, McMullen's Country, McMullen's Gladstone

Large, well-restored pub facing Cambridge Circus and well placed for the theatre trade. The plush split-level bar is in an Edwardian style with a cellar bar come function room. Originally, the site was occupied by two separate taverns, the George, Moor Street and the Thirteen Cantons, Silver Street (renamed Romilly Street in 1937). The pubs merged in 1756 to become the George and 13 Cantons. The present pub was built in 1898 by Reids Brewery, Clerkenwell (they merged with Watneys and Combes the same year) and was renamed the Scotch House in 1908. It was renamed again in 1975 after the maxim of William Cowper (1731-1800) that "Variety is the Spice of Life."

W2

Archery Tavern

4 Bathurst Street

Hall & Woodhouse
G ML ME
Opening Hours: normal
Station: Lancaster Gate
Buses: 12, 94
Wells Eagle, H & W Badger Best Bitter, Wadworth 6X, H & W Tanglefoot, Gribble Plucking Pheasant

A secluded outside drinking area with wooden benches surrounded by plants welcomes one to this cosy wood-fronted pub. It dates from c1840 and was built close to the site of archery butts from which it takes its name. Hanging hops and a large leaded-glass figure of an archer on high above the main entrance area, opens onto an elongated U-shaped bar with a corridor-type drinking bar leading to a bare floorboarded bar complete with dart board. The other bar opens onto a working stables in a mews. The mid-height dado, wood-panelled walls and ornate cornices and ceiling roses, along with the display of plates and pictures, make the tavern a joy to visit. A daily selection of national papers are available, along with an assortment of board games.

Situated near Hyde Park and Kensington Gardens near the Bayswater Road, this pub is a very central hidden gem.

Bridge House

13 Westbourne Terrace Road

Bass
G DA ML ME SL SE
Opening Hours: normal
Station: Warwick Avenue
Buses: 7, 23, 27, 36
Worthington Best Bitter, Draught Bass + Guest Beers

A pleasant, nineteenth-century canalside pub overlooking Little Venice. There is a small garden at the front and it can get pretty crowded, especially during the annual London Inland Waterways Association jamboree, which is usually held on the 'Mayday' bank holiday weekend. There is a fringe theatre (The Canal Cafe Theatre) upstairs, with its own bar which stays open until 11.30 during performances. A pub has stood on this site since Georgian times.

Fountains Abbey

109 Praed Street, Paddington

T&J Bernard
ML ME SL SE
Opening Hours: normal
Station: Paddington
Buses: 15, 27, 36
Theakston's Best, Courage Best Bitter, Theakston's XB, Courage Directors, Theakston's OP; Bulmer's Traditional Cider

Large airy pub recently renovated and much improved, it has reverted to its original name (from Tavistocks). The pub is opposite St Mary's Hospital and the window of Sir Alexander Fleming's room, through which penicillin drifted and killed the bacteria on his culture dishes, allowing him to discover antibiotics. Who knows, the penicillium mould may have drifted out of the window of the pub first?

Royal Exchange

26 Sale Place

Whitbread
G ML ME SL SE
Opening Hours: normal
Station: Paddington
Buses: 7, 15, 23, 27, 36
Brakspear Bitter, Boddington's Bitter

The Royal Exchange is an extremely popular local pub. It has an eclectic mix of clientele drawn from local businesses (advertising/BT/BR) and institutions (St Mary's Hospital) as well as local residents. The pub has a sporting inclination and the satellite TV is usually on to keep punters abreast of what is happening in the world of sport. The beers are well kept and the food comes in enormous portions. Especially recommended are the hot salt beef sandwiches (Fridays only) and home-cooked roast dinners. The pub is sometimes described as male-dominated but women are very welcome and old-fashioned gentlemanly behaviour is to the fore. The pub is always busy and although fairly small, rarely becomes claustrophobic. The staff are extremely friendly and welcoming and after a couple of visits you will be on first name terms. The architecture is reminiscent of the pub's front-room origins. The fish tank and racing memorabilia make interesting features. There is a juke box but no machines.

Swan Tavern

66 Bayswater Road

1

Inntrepreneur
G ML ME SL SE
Opening Hours: normal
Station: Lancaster Gate
Buses: 12, 94
John Smith's Bitter, Theakston's XB, Courage Directors

Busy and usually very crowded tourist haunt facing Hyde Park. There is a beer garden at the front with a glass canopy. The separate 'Birds' Nest' drinking area at the back, with an ornate skylight, usually has a pianist in the evenings for 'sing-alongs'. Although there has been a Swan Tavern here since at least the beginning of the eighteenth century, the present one dates from the following century. The pub comes into its own at weekends when the park railings opposite double up as a picture gallery – Montmartre style. The quality of some of the pictures is very high indeed and a slow stroll along Bayswater before or after a visit to Speaker's Corner is an ideal way to spend a Sunday lunchtime.

Victoria

10a Strathern Place

3

Fuller's
ML ME
Opening Hours: normal
Station: Paddington

Buses: 12, 94

Fuller's Chiswick Bitter, Fuller's London Pride, Fuller's ESB

A self-enclosed outside drinking area protected by a small brick wall, welcomes you to this splendid Victorian drinking house, reputedly visited by the doughty monarch when opening nearby Paddington Station. The dumb-bell shaped bar with a fireplace at each end, the wood-panelled walls with embossed ceiling, chandeliers and bare wood floors throughout give a real Victorian feeling. The bar has the history of the pub painted in stages along the outside top fascia. Behind the bar is a large semi-circular coloured mirror situated virtually opposite a full-sized embossed central glass window pane denoting the words *Dieu Et Mon Droit*. The bar also boasts a framed copy of a newspaper of 28th June 1838 recording Queen Victoria's coronation along with many prints and period pictures. The small upstairs bar, with an ex-Gaiety Theatre style decor is available for private functions and the cellar may be changed into a restaurant in the near future. A selection of national daily papers is available and the tavern, situated close to Hyde Park, the Bayswater Road and Paddington is a real ale-lovers' 'haven'.

W3

Castle

2

140 Victoria Road, Acton

Fuller's
G CP ML ME SL SE
Opening Hours: normal
Station: North Acton
Buses: 187, 260, 266

Fuller's Chiswick Bitter, Fuller's London Pride, Fuller's ESB

A large and welcoming pub on the edge of the North Acton industrial estate and opposite the tube station (Central line). The pub is a beer oasis in a desert. The comfortable lounge is decorated with old *Radio Times* covers and other memorabilia of the BBC radio era. The pub is often frequented by broadcasters using the nearby BBC rehearsal studios and the occasional famous face can be spotted.

Duke of York

86 Steyne Road, Acton

Inntrepreneur
FR G ML ME

Opening Hours: normal
Station: Acton Central BR
Buses: 7, 70, 207, 260, 266
Webster's Green Label, Webster's Yorkshire Bitter, Courage Best Bitter, Wadworth 6X, Young's Special, Morland's Old Speckled Hen

A former Watney's house, the Duke of York is now on a much quieter road following recent traffic-flow alterations. The pub now acts as a haven from the nearby bustle of the High Street and the recent supermarket development. The superb garden has won a number of awards.

George and Dragon
183 High Street, Acton

Inntrepreneur
ML ME SL SE
Opening Hours: normal
Station: Acton Central
Buses: 7, 70, 207, 266, N23, N89
Fuller's London Pride, Courage Directors

This former coaching inn is the oldest pub in Acton and retains the look and atmosphere of its origins. The bar is busy and welcoming and the yard and gates survive to remind you of its coaching days.

King's Head

214 High Street, Acton

Fuller's
G DA ML SL
Opening Hours: normal
Station: Acton Town
Buses: 7, 70, 207, 260, 266
Fuller's Chiswick Bitter, Fuller's London Pride, Fuller's ESB

A large single-bar corner pub located in a rather boisterous part of central Acton. There are several dining areas and a function room upstairs. After loosening up your tongue with a couple of excellent Fuller's beers you could always try striking up a conversation with Jasper the parrot.

Red Lion and Pineapple

281 High Street, Acton

Wetherspoon
G DA ML ME SL SE
Opening Hours: normal

Station: Acton Town
Younger's Scotch, Theakston's Best, Wadworth 6X, Theakston's XB, Courage Directors; Westons Old Rosie Cider

Formerly a Fuller's tied house, this huge pub has been converted from a three-bar pub to just one large circular bar plus a no-smoking area. Known locally as the 'Goldfish Bowl' from its all round glass frontage, the decor here is standard Wetherspoon identikit with facilities and service to match.

W4

Bell and Crown

72 Strand-on-the-Green

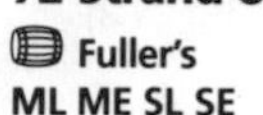 **Fuller's**
ML ME SL SE
Opening Hours: normal
Station: Kew Bridge
Buses: 65, 391
Fuller's Hock, Fuller's Chiswick Bitter, Fuller's London Pride, Fuller's ESB

Attractive and characterful riverside pub rebuilt by Fuller's in 1907. The patio/conservatory area overlooks the river and allows the visitor to enjoy a quiet pint even when the pub is quite busy. The beer is very well kept and this is one pub not to miss.

City Barge

27 Strand-on-the-Green

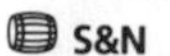 **S&N**
G CP ML ME SL SE
Opening Hours: normal
Station: Kew Bridge
Buses: 65, 391
Theakston's Best, Wadworth 6X, Theakston's XB, Courage Directors, Theakston's OP

Upmarket and popular riverside pub, part of which dates back to 1484 as the 'Navigators Arms'. It has a 500-year charter granted to it by Queen Elizabeth I. It has 'old' and 'new' bars and can get very busy, especially on Sunday lunchtimes when customers spill out onto the towpath. Called the 'Bohemia Head' until 1786 when it was renamed the 'City Navigation Barge' and the 'City Barge' two years later. The pub name is derived from the Lord Mayor's barge which had its winter mooring nearby.

George and Devonshire

8 Burlington Lane, Chiswick

Fuller's

G

Opening Hours: normal

Station: Turnham Green

Buses: 190, 415

Fuller's Chiswick Bitter, Fuller's London Pride, Fuller's ESB

Large two-bar pub, the 'other' brewery tap for the next-door Fuller, Smith and Turner Brewery. The broad Georgian-style frontage faces the notorious Hogarth Roundabout but the 190 bus from Hammersmith to Richmond passes the door. There is a small garden at the back and the bar hosts occasional live music. An attractive journey's end after a riverside walk. The pub is convenient for the home of the famous English painter William Hogarth as well as the house and grounds of Hogarth's neighbour and virtual enemy, the champion of the un-Hogarthian Italianate style, Lord Burlington.

W5

Duffy's

122-124 Pitshanger Lane, Ealing

Free House

G R ML ME SL SE

Opening Hours: normal

Station: Hanger Lane

Brakspear Bitter, Fuller's London Pride, Draught Bass, Gales HSB

A very small pub in a converted shop on the northern side of Ealing, with a restaurant downstairs at the rear. The shop belonged to United Dairies from 1910 and was converted to a pub in 1985 by the owner Tommy Duffy. It serves a wide range of beers to an appreciative clientele.

Fox and Goose

Hanger Lane, Ealing

Fuller's

G CP ML

Opening Hours: normal

Station: Hanger Lane

Buses: 83

Fuller's Chiswick Bitter, Fuller's London Pride, Fuller's ESB + Guest Beers

The tiny public bar, large and comfortable saloon and the

garden at the rear, all combine to offer a very welcome refuge from the infamous Hanger Lane gyratory system nearby. The pub gets very busy at lunchtimes as there are a large number of business premises nearby.

Plough

297 Northfield Avenue, Ealing

Fuller's
G CP ML ME
Opening Hours: normal
Station: Northfields
Buses: E2, E3
Fuller's Chiswick Bitter, Fuller's London Pride, Fuller's ESB

A busy and friendly two-bar pub on the corner of Northfields Avenue and Windmill Road. The lounge extends through a conservatory to a small garden at the rear and features several alcoves. Seriously damaged by a fire in 1991, the Plough was restored to its former glory by means of the original set of plans.

Red Lion

13 St Mary's Road, Ealing

Fuller's
SL SE
Opening Hours: normal
Station: Ealing Broadway
Fuller's Chiswick Bitter, Fuller's London Pride, Fuller's ESB

An absolute gem of a pub between the Thames Valley University and the Ealing Film Studios. The latter gave the Red Lion its alternative name, Stage 6. Many studio-related pictures jostle for the limited available space on the walls with various certificates. Several of these are for the garden, which comes highly recommended in summer when it is occasionally the venue for live music. Other than this all you will hear is the buzz of conversation, there being no electronic racket here, terminated all too soon by the bell for time. There should be more pubs like this one.

Wheatsheaf

41 Haven Lane, Ealing

Fuller's
G ML ME SL SE
Opening Hours: normal
Station: Ealing Broadway
Buses: 83, 207
Fuller's Chiswick Bitter, Fuller's London Pride, Fuller's ESB

A busy and deceptively large two-bar pub to the north of Ealing town centre. An extensive refurbishment in 1993 introduced much wood and exposed brickwork in addition to creating a separate public bar. There is frequently live music.

W6

Blue Anchor

13 Lower Mall, Hammersmith

Inntrepreneur
G ML ME SL SE
Opening Hours: normal
Station: Hammersmith
Buses: 9, 9a, 33, 72, R69
Courage Best Bitter, Wadworth 6X, Courage Directors

Delightful pub on the riverside with excellent views of the highly decorative Hammersmith Bridge and the rowers from the club next door. It is one of the most famous and oldest ale houses in London – first licensed in 1722. Gustav Holst wrote his Hammersmith Suite in the pub. Inside there is an interesting pewter bar top and the typical stubby handpumps of a Victorian beer engine. The walls are covered with lots of bric-a-brac. If the weather is good customers tend to spill outside by the river. In the summer, the pub puts on barbecues and vegetarian food is a speciality.

Dove

19 Upper Mall, Hammersmith

Fuller's
G ML ME SL SE
Opening Hours: normal
Station: Hammersmith
Buses: 9, 10, 27, 33, 72, 190, 211, 220, 266, 267
Fuller's London Pride, Fuller's ESB

A famous riverside pub which dates back to the seventeenth century and has considerable charm. It is claimed that Charles II and Nell Gwynne drank here. It has also attracted many literary types in the past including A.P. Herbert and James Thompson who composed 'Rule Britannia' in one of the upstairs rooms. The bar areas are wood panelled and the tiny 'public' bar has been listed in the Guinness Book of Records as London's smallest. There is a terrace overlooking the River Thames and a conservatory with a fruit bearing vine. The Dove is one of an increasing number of pubs offering Thai food, which is available weekday evenings. The pub can get very busy, especially in summer.

Hope and Anchor

20 Macbeth Street

Inntrepreneur
G DA ML SL
Opening Hours: normal
Station: Ravenscourt Park
Buses: 27, 190, 237, 267, 391, H91, N97
Webster's Yorkshire Bitter, Fuller's London Pride

Entering the saloon bar is like going back in time as nothing seems to have changed since it was rebuilt in 1934 (except for the Truman's doormat, now gone). There is superb wood panelling throughout, recommending Truman's Burton- brewed beers. There is a real fire in a brick fireplace and draught curtains around the doors. Tied to the Kilburn brewers, Mitchell and Aldous, until their takeover by Truman's in 1920, it is definitely worth a visit.

Salutation

15a King St, Hammersmith

Fuller's
G ML SL
Opening Hours: normal
Station: Ravenscourt Park
Buses: 94, 190, 237, 267, 291, H1, N97
Fuller's Chiswick Bitter, Fuller's London Pride, Fuller's ESB

A former coaching inn with an interesting tiled exterior located opposite Hammersmith Town Hall. Inside is a large bar featuring a fine fireplace. Beyond is a pleasant conservatory and an award-winning garden. On the conservatory wall are a number of certificates and photographs chronicling the history of the pub, including the visit of HM The Queen Mother in July 1989.

White Hart

383 King St, Hammersmith

Allied Domecq
ML ME SL SE
Opening Hours: normal
Station: Stamford Brook
Buses: 27, 190, 237, 391, H91
Tetley Bitter, Ind Coope Burton Ale

Big Victorian pub with three live music nights every

week. A speciality is the South African band on Fridays. There is a separate pool room with four tables. The office crowd at lunchtimes gives way to a 25-40 year old local crowd in the evenings. Friday nights are exceptionally busy, requiring a staff of 10 to keep the beer flowing.

W7

Fox

Green Lane, Hanwell

Free House
G CP ML
Opening Hours: 11-3, 5.30-11m-f 11-11s
Station: Hanwell
Buses: E8
Courage Best Bitter, Marston's Pedigree, Courage Directors

An unspoilt local serving good quality food and beer. Its location at the junction of the Grand Union Canal and the River Brent means that it is very popular with boaters either ascending or descending the flight of twelve locks nearby (thirsty work). The pub was built in 1807 and added to in 1909 by the Royal Brewery, which was brewing in nearby Brentford from 1880 to 1923.

W8

Britannia

1 Allen Street

Young's
G ML SL
Opening Hours: normal
Station: High Street Kensington
Buses: 9, 9a, 10, 27, 28, 31, 49
Young's Bitter, Young's Special, Young's Winter Warmer

A deservedly popular pub just off the western end of the fashionable Kensington High Street shopping area close to the Commonwealth Institute. The long wood-panelled bar leads to a larger bar and seating area down a few steps and a conservatory. The latter serves as a non-smoking area during lunchtimes. There is also a small public bar. The pub was once the brewery tap of the William Wells Britannia Brewery (established in 1903 and now demolished) until it was taken over by Young's in 1924.

Catherine Wheel

23 Kensington Church Street, Kensington

Nicholsons
G ML ME SL SE
Opening Hours: normal
Station: High Street Kensington
Buses: 27, 28, 31, 52, 70
Brakspear Bitter, Tetley Bitter, Wadworth 6X, Marston's Pedigree

Well-placed Nicholsons house handy for shoppers in Kensington High Street. The mock-Victorian interior contains ornate mirrors, prints, pots on shelves and plenty of woodwork. The pub was rebuilt in 1870 by the architect W.E. Williams and underwent a major refurbishment exactly 100 years later. It has been owned by Nicholsons since 1948.

Churchill Arms

119 Kensington Church Street

Fuller's
FR DA ML ME SL SE
Opening Hours: normal
Station: Notting Hill Gate
Buses: 27, 28, 70
Fuller's Chiswick Bitter, Fuller's London Pride, Fuller's ESB

An excellent multi-bar pub with great character located at the upper end of Kensington Church Street. The low-ceilinged rooms are decorated with a framed collection of over 1,500 butterflies, plus the expected photographs and prints of the great Prime Minister after whom the pub takes its name. A recent addition is a rear conservatory eating and drinking area, attractively hung with foliage, which in the evenings doubles as a Thai restaurant. The pub is liable to get extremely crowded.

Hillgate

39 Hillgate Street

Inntrepreneur
G DA R ME SL SE
Opening Hours: normal
Station: Notting Hill Gate
Buses: 94
Webster's Yorkshire Bitter, Fuller's London Pride, Ruddles County

Popular two-bar back-street local attractively decorated on the outside with hanging baskets. The main bar is cosy, with some sectioned seating areas and it features a collection of ceramics and, on the wall, an old brewery map of Britain. The pub was built in 1854 as the Johnson Arms, Johnson Street. The pub and street were originally named after a family of local landowners and builders. A member of the family was elected Lord Mayor of London in 1846.

Windsor Castle

114 Campden Hill Road, Notting Hill

Bass

G ML ME SL SE

Opening Hours: normal

Station: Notting Hill Gate

Buses: 94

Adnams Bitter, Worthington Best Bitter, Fuller's London Pride, Draught Bass

Picturesque and unspoilt corner pub which still retains its original three dark-wood-panelled bars. The small, pleasant beer garden also has a servery. The pub clientele is varied but the pub is popular with Irish rugby fans. It was built in 1845 and named after the fact that in those days it was still possible to see Windsor Castle from that part of Campden Hill.

W9

Prince Alfred

5a Formosa Street

Allied Domecq

ML SL

Opening Hours: normal

Station: Warwick Avenue

Buses: 46, 6

Tetley Bitter, Young's Bitter, Ind Coope Burton Ale

Built in 1863, this pub is one of the finest surviving examples of the London pub as it was at the period; most others having been rebuilt or refurbished in the 1890s. The pub still retains its five original bars complete with partitions and stoop-through doors – one bar was a ladies only bar. Snob screens and a fine stillion as well as decorative external faience and floor mosaics complete the picture. The large etched auriel windows at the front are advisedly well insured. Prince Alfred (1844-1900) was the second son of Queen Victoria and he was created Duke of Edinburgh in 1862. The Greeks elected him as their King but he tactfully declined the offer. Architecturally one of the finest pubs in London, though the large back room is nothing special and more could be done with the whole.

Warrington Hotel

93 Warrington Crescent, Maida Vale

Free House
ML ME SL SE
Opening Hours: normal
Station: Warwick Avenue
Buses: 16, 16a, 46, 98
Brakspear Bitter, Fuller's London Pride, Marston's Pedigree, Young's Special, Fuller's ESB

Large Victorian 'Gin Palace' type pub, dating from 1859, with semi-circular marble-topped bar, florid decorations and ornate woodwork. It contains original Art Nouveau stained and etched glass. Once the resort of jockeys and racing men, one of whom is said to have ridden a horse up the stairs for a bet, and they are easily wide enough to take it. A lovely ornate pub and yet another to feature a Thai restaurant upstairs. Note the decorated exterior pillars.

W11

Portobello Star

171 Portobello Road, Notting Hill

Whitbread
ML SL
Opening Hours: normal
Station: Notting Hill Gate
Buses: 23, 52, 302, N23, N52
Whitbread Castle Eden Ale, Flowers Original

A pub as pubs were 30 years ago. A linoleum floor and Formica-topped tables; this pub has miraculously escaped the dead hand of refurbishment. Wooden settle seating lines the walls under pictures of old Portobello, disguising a mock-Tudor decor that was once all the vogue in pub design. Very much a locals' pub, even on busy market days with the famous Portobello Road street market right outside the front door. Most market visitors and tourists tend not to enter the Portobello Star, preferring the modern-style pubs they are more used to. Perhaps, if anything, this authentic pub is a little intimidating. Not an Irish pub, by any means, it nevertheless has a feel about it found in many small bars in Ireland.

Star

46 Queensdale Road

Inntrepreneur

G DA

Opening Hours: 11-11m-f 11-4, 7-10.30s 12-3, 7-10.30su

Station: Shepherd's Bush

Buses: 295

Webster's Yorkshire Bitter, Ruddles Best, Young's Bitter, Wadworth 6X

An excellent, quiet and well-run back-street local with two interconnecting comfortable bars. Both are lined with wooden curtain-fold panelling and topped with highlighted, wave pattern, moulded covering. Decorative bric-a-brac, including stuffed animal heads, uniforms and civilian head-gear resides above the bar. There is also an unusual dart game played here. In the summer, there is a barbecue in the garden and live music is played on Friday and Saturday nights. The original Star, a Ford and Woodbridge 'Stingo' beer house, dated from the 1850s. The pub was rebuilt in 1937 by Watney Combe Reid, who had taken over the Stingo Brewery in 1907.

W13

Foresters

2 Leighton Road, West Ealing

S&N

G

Opening Hours: 11-3, 5-11m-s

Station: Northfields

Buses: E2, E3

John Smith's Bitter, Courage Best Bitter, Wadworth 6X, Courage Directors

A four-bar Grade II-listed Edwardian building of imposing proportions which was built for the Royal Brewery (1880-1923) of Brentford. Many original features are still in evidence and the exterior boasts a wood and tiling facade. There are four bars, each with its own character. The pub is an all too rare outlet for Russian Stout.

Kent

2 Scotch Common, West Ealing

Fuller's

G CP ML

Opening Hours: normal

Station: Castle Bar Park BR

Buses: E4, E7

Fuller's London Pride, Fuller's ESB

A large and imposing pub next to Cleveland Park which was built in 1929 (the pub not the park). The actor Graham Moffat (the fat boy in Will Hay films) ran this pub for several years when he retired from acting. He went to run another pub elsewhere in his later years, using his celebrity to good effect in the days when pubs were closed in the afternoons. A lot of locals of a certain age were said to look strangely like Mr Moffat! Perhaps the same is true of West Ealing! The pub's garden is exceptionally large and is an ideal place to bring children.

W14

Colton Arms

187 Greyhound Road

Inntrepreneur
G SL
Opening Hours: 11-3, 5.30-11m-f 11-4, 7-11s
Station: Baron's Court
Buses: 74, 220, C4, N9
Webster's Yorkshire Bitter, Fuller's London Pride, Ruddles County

Upmarket regulars' pub built on the site of a bone-yard dating from the Great Plague of London of 1665. The decor is in the cottage style with a fine copper bar. Located behind the Queen's Club tennis courts near Baron's Court tube station. It can be a bit expensive but is worth seeking out.

Warwick Arms

160 Warwick Road

Fuller's
G ML ME SL SE
Opening Hours: normal
Station: Earls Court
Buses: 9, 9a, 10, 27, 28, 49, N9, N31
Fuller's Chiswick Bitter, Fuller's London Pride, Fuller's ESB

A fine one-bar pub dating from 1828, located just around the corner from the Olympia Exhibition Centres. The pub is divided into two sections, the front having a dart board and the rear section having exposed brickwork and a real coal fire. The bar also sports attractive Wedgwood handpump handles. Close to the Hilton Hotel, its fine well-kept beers make it very popular with the staff from CAMRA's Great British Beer Festival which takes place each August in Olympia.

Kingston – KT1

Cocoanut

16 Mill St, Kingston

Fuller's

G CP ML

Opening Hours: 11-3, 5-11m-f 11-11s 12-10.30su

Station: Kingston BR

Buses: 71, 281, 46, 465, 479, N14

Fuller's Chiswick Bitter, Fuller's London Pride, Fuller's ESB

More a community than a pub. A warm welcome and good food with vegetarian options and a children's menu on request. Don't upset Benjy, the pub dog, by leaving before closing time. The Cocoanut, which sells Fuller's seasonal beers as well, was CAMRA's Greater London Pub of the Year 1992.

Two Brewers

19 Wood St, Kingston

Free House

ML SL SE

Opening Hours: normal

Station: Kingston

Buses: 57, 65, 71, 85, 111, 131, 213, 281, 285, 371, 406, 411

Courage Best Bitter + Guest Beers

Enterprising free house in centre of Kingston on main 'race track' as the town's ludicrous one-way system is known. The pub is suitably close to the station, the river Thames and Kingston's historic market and shops. The guest beers change monthly and the pub also hosts occasional live music evenings and theme nights. The pub was the Kingston and Leatherhead CAMRA branch Pub of the Year 1995.

Kingston – KT2

Boaters Inn

Lower Ham Road, Kingston

Regent Inns

G R ML ME SL SE

Opening Hours: 11-3, 5-11m-th winter 11-11f, s summer

Station: Kingston BR

Buses: 65, 371, 465, K6, N9

John Smith's Bitter, Wadworth 6X, Shepherd Neame Spitfire + Guest Beers

Attractive, modern pub pleasantly situated in gardens alongside the River Thames. The pub has its own moorings and it is very popular in the summer. Boaters Best Bitter is Hancocks HB rebadged. The pub can be approached along the riverside from Kingston town centre and is about three-quarters of a mile from Kingston Bridge. Sunday evenings are jazz nights. The Jerome K Jerome classic Three Men in a Boat was set near here. There is no food on Sunday and Monday evenings.

Canbury Arms
49 Canbury Park Road, Kingston

Inntrepreneur
G CP DA ML ME SL SE
Opening Hours: normal
Station: Kingston BR
Buses: 57, 85, 131, 213, 371, 511, 718, K3, K5
John Smith's Bitter, Courage Best Bitter, Courage Directors, Gales HSB, Morland's Old Speckled Hen + Guest Beers

Bar containing a huge library of fact and feat for settling all manner of disputes. The good value lunchtime meals attract lots of custom. There is no food on Sunday evening. The pub has the feel of a rural house in an urban setting, with a friendly and international mix of customers. There is also secure motor-cycle and cycle parking.

Fighting Cocks

56 London Road, Kingston

CCC Leisure
ML SL SE
Opening Hours: normal
Station: Norbiton
Buses: 57, 85, 131, 213, 371, K3, K5, K6, N14, N87
Courage Best Bitter + Guest Beers; Cider

Small pub with weekly rotating guest beers, handy for Kingston Fairfield Bus Station. The interior is spartan but comfortable, with wooden floors. The pub sports a collection of cinema memorabilia and Belgian bottled beers, the latter of which are for sale.

Norbiton and Dragon

16 Clifton Road Kingston

FR G R ML ME SL

Opening Hours: 11-3, 5-11m-f 11-11s 12-10.30su
Station: Norbiton BR
Tetley Bitter, John Smith's Bitter, Wadworth 6X, Marston's Pedigree

A big, one-bar Victorian pub in a mixed residential street off the Kingston Hill. It was the Norbiton Hotel until a 70-cover 'oriental' restaurant was added, which has contributed to providing a lively atmosphere. It is packed with office workers at lunchtimes and with a younger clientele during the evenings and at weekends.

Park Tavern

19 New Road, Kingston
Free House
G SL SE
Opening Hours: 10.30-11m-s 12-10.30su
Station: Norbiton
Buses: 57, 85, 213, K3, K5, K6, K8, K10, N14
Brakspear Bitter, Young's Bitter, Boddington's Bitter, Young's Special + Guest Beers

Fronted by an arch of greenery, this whitewashed pub has painted shutters and climbing wisteria. It is small and comfortable and close to the Kingston Gate of Richmond Park (turn second right from the park). On summer evenings, when the front door is open, a golden glow suffuses the front patio at dusk. The inn sign suggests a sunset in Richmond Park and after a long evening walk, the tavern is an ideal retreat. The U-shaped pub carries photos of the 1995 England Rugby World Cup squad (the landlord is very much a rugby fan) and a set of horseshoes that belonged to Shergar. Dogs are very welcome and a bowl of water and a few biscuits are likely to be offered by the friendly staff. The quality of the beer is superb. Parking close to the pub can be difficult but the term hidden gem was coined to describe pubs just like this.

Wych Elm

93 Elm Road, Kingston
Fuller's
G ML SL
Opening Hours: 11-3, 5-11m-f 11-11s
Station: Kingston BR
Buses: 371
Fuller's Chiswick Bitter, Fuller's London Pride, Fuller's ESB

Friendly pub with what the locals regard as the best pint of Fuller's in London, which gives the pub a large following. In the evening, the pub glows in an otherwise dark street, like a hedge of luminous foliage. In summer, the front of the ground floor is a riot of colour, a fantastic glory of flowers, as is the immaculate back garden. The pub's floral displays have won several prizes. Inside, the public and saloon bars are separated by a very basic partition. The saloon bar decor is an example of how pub decor can be done tastefully and is an object lesson to the many pub interior designers who insist that modern pub interiors must be vulgar. The public bar is plain, yet neat and smart. The whole is presided over by a very enthusiastic licensee. Fuller's seasonal beers are also available but food is limited at weekends.

New Malden – KT3

Royal Oak

90 Coombe Road, New Malden

Allied Domecq
G CP ML
Opening Hours: normal
Station: New Malden BR
Buses: 213, K10
Benskins Best Bitter, Tetley Bitter, Young's Bitter, Ind Coope Burton Ale + Guest Beers

A large corner pub with an equally big garden. The function room occasionally features live music or theatre. The pub has won the local authority's 'prettiest pub' competition on the strength of its floral displays. The guest beers are chosen from the Carlsberg-Tetley Tapster's Choice approved list. The pub hosts a comedy night on Mondays and a quiz night on Tuesdays. No food is available in the evenings.

Woodies

Thetford Road, New Malden

Free House
G CP ML SL SE
Opening Hours: normal
Station: New Malden BR
Buses: 213, 265, 726, K1, K9
Young's Bitter, Boddington's Bitter, Courage Best Bitter, Fuller's London Pride, Flowers Original, Courage Directors, Young's Special + Guest Beers

An amazing pub in an old sports pavilion. A staggering montage of old sporting programmes, theatrical and film mementoes greet the visitor. The pub can get busy in the evenings, especially in summer.

Surbiton – KT6

Denby Dale

84 Victoria Road, Surbiton

Fuller's
DA ML ME SL SE
Opening Hours: normal
Station: Surbiton BR
Buses: 71, 465, 501, 511, K1, K3, K4
Fuller's Chiswick Bitter, Fuller's London Pride, Fuller's ESB

A new pub converted from former bank premises. It is virtually in Surbiton BR Station car park. The pub is ornately decorated with lots of varnished wood and a marble floor, with snob screens at the far end of the bar. Fuller's seasonal beers are sold in this Ale and Pie badged house with a good line in home-cooked food.

Wagon and Horses

1 Surbiton Hill Road

Young's
G ML SL SE
Opening Hours: 11-3, 5-11m-f 11-11s 12-10.30su
Station: Surbiton BR
Buses: 71, 281, 46, 465, 479, K1, K2, K3, N14, 501, 511
Young's Bitter, Young's Special, Young's Winter Warmer

Although not that well hidden, this pub is still a gem in that it retains its multi-roomed interior, which is a rarity in this day and age. Fine dark-wood panelling throughout, with many pictures on the walls along with the many awards that the licensees have picked up in their 28 years of running this pub. Many of these are for charity efforts. The pub can get busy, particularly at weekends. Summer barbecues. No food Saturday lunchtime. The pub was Kingston and Leatherhead CAMRA 'Pub of the Year 1993'.

Hampton Court – KT8

Albion

34 Bridge Road, East Molesey

Bass
R ML ME SL SE
Opening Hours: normal
Station: Hampton Court BR
Buses: 411
Fuller's London Pride, Draught Bass, Marston's Pedigree,

Morland's Old Speckled Hen

Close to Hampton Court Palace, this characterful pub has comfortable seating and an impressive clock. The architecture has a Jacobean flavour throughout and the pub has a cosy drawing room atmosphere, especially on cold winter evenings.

King's Arms
Hampton Court Road, Hampton Court

Hall and Woodhouse
G R ML ME SL SE
Opening Hours: normal
Station: Hampton Court
Buses: 111, 267, 411, 726, R68, X55, 216
H & W Badger Best Bitter, Wadworth 6X, H & W Tanglefoot, H & W Hard Tackle, Gribble Black Adder II + Guest Beers

An historic pub backing onto Hampton Court maze. It has three separate bars, the public having a sawdust-strewn floor, basic seating, dart board and jukebox. The other two are quieter, the smaller having a fine trilogy of stained glass coats-of-arms, while the larger boasts some original floor mosaics. There is a good range of bar food in addition to fine dining in the separate restaurant. A private dining room can seat up to 12. A deservedly popular pub, which also offers breakfasts on weekdays and afternoon teas.

Chessington – KT9

North Star

271 Hook Road, Chessington

Bass
G CP ML ME SL SE
Opening Hours: 12-11m-f 11-11s
Station: Ewell West
Buses: 479, 5, 468, K8, K9
M & B Highgate Dark, Charrington IPA, Hancocks HB, Draught Bass, M & B Highgate Old

Nearest decent pub to Chessington World of Adventures on the A243. A popular and lively pub, serving beers that are a rarity in the area. Menu offers choices for vegetarians and children. No food Tuesday or Sunday evening.

Hounslow

Queens Head
123 High St, Cranford

Fuller's
FR G CP ML ME
Opening Hours: normal
Station: West Hounslow
Buses: 111
Fuller's Chiswick Bitter, Fuller's London Pride, Fuller's ESB

The first pub in the country to obtain a liquor licence (1604), it was attractively rebuilt in 1936 in the Tudor style. This was probably because mock Tudor was then the height of architectural vogue for pubs rather than out of deference to its late Elizabethan origins. One bar serves two distinct drinking areas and a lounge to one side is used as a dining area (the home cooked food is not available weekends). The pub has real fires. Crib, dominoes and darts are played – a darts team uses the pub in winter. The pub has been in the Good Beer Guide regularly for many years now and its reputation as the best pub in the area is augmented by its policy of reasonable prices.

Esher – KT10

Bear

71 High St, Esher

Young's
FR G CP R ML ME SL SE
Opening Hours: normal
Station: Esher BR
Buses: 218
Young's Bitter, Young's Special, Young's Winter Warmer

Town centre pub near Sandown Park racecourse. Pleasantly situated on Esher Green, it retains several different drinking areas, providing a cosy atmosphere. The restaurant area has several cubicles for small parties. The pub used to be the posting house and second stage on the London to Portsmouth road. It was also once home to Clive of India.

Byfleet – KT14

Plough

104 High Road, Byfleet

Free House
G CP ML SE
Opening Hours: normal
Station: Byfleet
Courage Best Bitter + Guest Beers

This pub offers most of what a pub-goer requires – a truly friendly atmosphere, interesting and comfortable surroundings plus an ever-changing range of five or so guest beers. Weekend beer festivals are held every six months or so. Apart from lunches (not Sundays), food is not an obtrusive feature until Wednesday night when the landlady prepares 20 or so set supper meals which offer value and quality. The single horseshoe bar manages to achieve at least three areas with different atmospheres, having beams and 'implements' and a wood fire in winter. No obtrusive music, and conversation is only interrupted by the hubbub of other conversation. Not far from the famous Brooklands historic racetrack.

Twickenham – TW1

Fox

39 Church Street, Twickenham

Inntrepreneur
G ML SL
Opening Hours: normal
Station: Twickenham
Buses: 33, 90, 290, H22, R70, N9
H & W Badger Best Bitter, Wadworth 6X, Marston's Pedigree, Ruddles County, Morland's Old Speckled Hen

Attractive seventeenth century coaching inn, located in one of Twickenham's oldest and most picturesque streets. The large single-room bar has many original features and old wooden beams. A collection of plates and prints adds to the general ambience. A corridor leads to the original coaching areas and beyond this a small garden has just been completed. To find Church Street walk to the centre of Twickenham and follow the signpost beside the bank. The prices are normal for this upmarket area of Twickenham. However, the regular local trade shows that the small premium is well worth paying in return for a friendly atmosphere, attractive surroundings and an enthusiastic landlord, who takes a personal interest in the quality of all his ales.

Whitton – TW2

White Hart

121 Kneller Road, Whitton

Free House
G CP ML ME SL SE
Opening Hours: normal
Station: Whitton BR
Buses: H22
John Smith's Bitter, Smiles Best Bitter, Wadworth 6X, Marston's Pedigree

A former seventeenth century coaching inn which was destroyed by fire before being bought and sympathetically rebuilt by the current owner in 1991. The rebuilding incorporated some 300-year-old former roof timbers into the wall behind the bar servery. One of the nearest pubs to Twickenham Rugby Stadium, so it is best to get there early to secure a beer and a seat on match days. The pub is a rare London outlet for Smiles' beer which is served in over-size glasses, to ensure full measure. Some accommodation is available and the food is value for money.

Isleworth & Osterley – TW7

Bridge Inn

457 London Road, Isleworth

Inntrepreneur
R ML ME SL SE
Opening Hours: normal
Station: Isleworth
Buses: 116, 117, 237, H37
John Smith's Bitter, Wadworth 6X, Marston's Pedigree

Virtually under the bridge after which it is named, this pub (formerly called the 'Iron Bridge') was built by the Isleworth Brewery originally to slake the thirsts of the railway construction workers. Although the pub may have changed since then (it was refurbished in 1993), the railway bridge has not and all the trains have to cross at minimum speed. Now a family-run locals' pub it is also popular with students from the nearby training college. The Bridge Inn has turned one of its rooms into a successful Thai restaurant which is still going strong when other similar ventures in the area have failed. Excellent food, and very reasonably priced, although the restaurant is not open on Saturday lunchtimes or Sundays. There is impromptu Irish music on alternate

Tuesday evenings and the pub is home to the Twickenham Cardinals football team. The pub offers accommodation by way of six double bedrooms for those who feel that they just do not wish to leave.

Hare and Hounds
Windmill Lane, Osterley

Fuller's
G CP ML ME SL SE
Opening Hours: normal
Station: Osterley
Buses: H28
Fuller's London Pride, Fuller's ESB

Relatively isolated, being surrounded by parkland, a gardening centre and a golf course, the Hare and Hounds does not seem to notice and gets quite busy, especially with car-borne trade. Walkers are also drawn to the pub, not least by the food as hot meals are offered during all seasons.

London Apprentice
62 Church Street, Isleworth

Inntrepreneur
G R ML ME SL SE
Opening Hours: 11-11 except winter
Station: Syon Lane
Buses: H37
John Smith's Bitter, Courage Best Bitter, Wadworth 6X, Courage Directors

Historic and picturesque riverside pub dating from 1724. The outside drinking area overlooks the Thames and Isleworth Ait, and Syon Park is within easy walking distance. It has a no-smoking dining area on the ground floor as well as upstairs dining and function rooms. Bar billiards and darts are available. The nearest public transport is the H37 bus (Richmond to Hounslow) which stops nearby.

Brentford – TW8

Brewery Tap
47 Catherine Wheel Road, Brentford

Fuller's
G ML SL SE
Opening Hours: normal
Station: Brentford

Buses: 116, 117, 237, 267
Fuller's London Pride, Fuller's ESB

Small hidden pub in a short road off Brentford High Street. The name refers to the William Gomm Brewery which was acquired by Fuller's in 1908 but subsequently closed. Very much a local with a regular clientele supplemented by others enjoying Trad Jazz nights on Tuesdays and Thursdays, when the smallness of the pub means that you have to appreciate the music – or leave! The pub often has quizzes on Monday nights but on other (non-music) evenings it is a quiet haven. The pub's weekday lunches are popular. It is convenient for Brentford football ground, the Watermans Arts Centre and Brentford Lock and the Grand Union Canal. Darts are available.

Express Tavern

56 Kew Bridge Road, Brentford

Free House
G DA ML ME SL SE
Opening Hours: normal
Station: Kew Bridge
Buses: 7, 65, 237, 267, 391
Young's Bitter, Draught Bass, Young's Special

Incredibly well-preserved building dating from 1797 which has been run by the Aldington family since 1882 and owned by them since 1921. A few months' closure in 1994 saw essential structural repairs undertaken and the addition of indoor toilets and wheelchair access at the rear. Conversation is prominent. There are no obtrusive games machines or jukebox and only the faintest background music is heard. Now a managed house, the Express offers a comprehensive food menu Monday-Friday but its reputation is founded mainly on its Draught Bass which has been offered since 1921 when the tie to Hawkes and Co (now defunct) was severed. CAMRA's first London meetings were at The Express in 1973 and it has been in the Good Beer Guide virtually every year since. The pub is near the Kew Steam Museum and the famous Royal Botanical Society's gardens are just over the bridge.

Kew, Richmond & Twickenham – TW9

Coach and Horses

8 Kew Green, Kew

Young's

G CP ML ME SL
Opening Hours: normal
Station: Kew
Buses: 65, 7, 391
Young's Bitter, Young's Special, Young's Winter Warmer

A coaching inn on Kew Green dating from 1831, the Coach and Horses contains many traditional features including large Worthington and Wenlock Brewery mirrors – in a Young's pub too! Its original role is perpetuated by the availability of six first-floor bedrooms and the excellent meals served lunchtimes daily and up to 9.30pm in the evenings (Sundays excepted). The pub has a garden at the rear and a few tables out front facing the southern end of the green. A social club at the rear contains three snooker tables but darts and board games are available in the bar area. Darts matches take place Monday and Wednesday, with Mondays also being quiz night. The pub's location makes it convenient for Kew Gardens, and it is therefore the perfect place to which to adjourn after a long stroll.

Orange Tree

2

Kew Road, Richmond

Young's
R
Opening Hours: normal
Station: Richmond
Buses: 65, 90, 190, 290, 371, 391, H22, H37, R61, R68, R70, N9
Young's Bitter, Young's Special, Young's Winter Warmer

An historic pub sandwiched between two theatres. It has a basement wine bar/restaurant that can be a bit 'luvvie', but the ground floor bar is rather sportier. The pub dates from at least 1780 and its name is *supposed* to be connected with the introduction of orange trees to nearby Kew Gardens. Young's converted their lease to outright ownership in 1897 and rebuilt the pub in the popular Flemish brick and terracotta style of the day. It achieved fame in the 1970s through the lunchtime theatre it accommodated in its function room. The audience were seated on old church pews, which were not then the fashionable choice of pub seating they are now. Some of its productions went on to bigger things in the West End and the pub was the first licensed pub/theatre of its kind. The theatre expanded out in 1990. The Orange Tree is best avoided on international rugby match days as the shuttle buses to and from Twickenham operate from there.

Triple Crown

15 Kew Foot Road, Richmond

Corporate Catering
ML ME SL SE FR
Opening Hours: normal
Station: Richmond
Guest Beers

A thriving back-street local, drawing its customers from the surrounding area. There are four regularly changing real ales (around 300 in a year), almost entirely from independent breweries which has led to the Triple Crown being voted 'Pub of the Year' in 1994 and 1995 by the local CAMRA branch. Although small and narrow, the single bar area has room for darts at the far end. The pub is usually packed for the Tuesday night quizzes, which feature a running jackpot. A truly 'hidden gem', the Triple Crown is nevertheless only a short walk from Richmond Station (District Line and South-West Trains). Turn right on leaving the station to the roundabout, cross the main road on the left, and follow the pathway a few metres to the left. The pub is right by Richmond Athletic Ground (home of London Scottish RFC) and close to Old Deer Park and Kew Gardens. An upstairs function room with its own small bar (including handpump) and balcony is available. No meals on Sunday but snacks prepared to order.

White Cross Hotel

Riverside – Water Lane, Richmond

Young's
G ML SL
Opening Hours: normal
Station: Richmond
Buses: 33, 65, 90, 190, 290, 337, 371, 391, H22, H37, R681, R68
Young's Bitter, Young's Special, Young's Winter Warmer

'Beware – Road Liable to Flooding' say the signs leading to the White Cross, the most famous of Richmond's riverside pubs. The imposing building is a prominent feature of the waterfront and attracts uncountable hordes on summer evenings, practically taking over the promenade which becomes an unofficial extension of the outside patio. The White Cross dates from 1835 and is on the site of a former 'Monastery of the Observant Friars'. Inside is a single island bar, with a separate food counter under the stairs. Note the open fire below the window in the bar area, an unusual and unique feature. A separate room is up a short staircase and can be hired for functions. At busy times a basement level garden bar is used – river level permitting. When it is hectic they do have to resort to plastic glasses for outside drinkers. Do not be put off if it seems impossibly crowded – you will still be served quickly.

White Swan
Riverside, Twickenham

Inntrepreneur
G ML ME SL SE
Opening Hours: Normal
Station: Twickenham BR
Buses: 33, 90, 290, H22, R70, N9
Webster's Yorkshire Bitter, Wadworth 6X, Marston's Pedigree + Guest Beers

Picturesque, unspoilt seventeenth century riverside inn, located in one of the most pleasant areas of Twickenham. The bar is on the first floor and is accessed by an outside stairway. The balcony provides fine views of the Thames and a riverside patio area is popular in the summer. The pub boasts many original features and the traditional wooden floor is especially appreciated by the locals. It is well worth walking to the pub from the Embankment towpath at Twickenham. As you pass down Riverside, look out for the statues behind the walls of York House Gardens and as you near your destination, you pass under a delightful old foot-bridge. Depending on the tides, small boats can be used to access the pub as there are slipways nearby. Being in an expensive area the prices are slightly above average but the general ambience and good-value food make this unique building well worth a visit.

White Swan
26 Old Palace Lane, Richmond

Inntrepreneur
G ML ME SL SE
Opening Hours: 11-3, 5.30-11m-f 11-4, 6-11s 12-10.30su
Station: Richmond
Buses: 33, 65, 90, 190, 290, 337, 371, 391, H22, H37, R61, R68
Courage Best Bitter, Courage Directors

A country-style pub set in an historic and very upmarket area off Richmond Green. The White Swan is just what the overseas visitor expects of an English Inn. Dating from the early eighteenth century, with a beamed ceiling, attractive conservatory and garden and copper bric-a-brac, the pub attracts many visitors. The pub is rather small but it was originally only half the size. The single bar has a food servery at one end from which meals are always available. The Sunday lunches in particular are very popular and occasionally the upstairs function room is called upon to take the overflow of customers. Friday night barbecues are offered in summer and on special occasions. A quiet pub, the hubbub of conversation is the only noise, apart from the Monday night quizzes.

Richmond – TW10

Duke's Head

42 The Vineyard, Richmond

Inntrepreneur
G ML SL SE
Opening Hours: normal
Station: Richmond
Buses: 35, 65, 90, 190, 290, 33, 371, 391, H22, H37, R68, R70
Courage Best Bitter, Marston's Pedigree, Courage Directors, Morland's Old Speckled Hen

Olde worlde, two-bar pub in a narrow street halfway up Richmond Hill with a 55-seater theatre club upstairs offering professional productions five nights a week. It is still largely a locals' pub although there are a smattering of 'luvvies' to be seen and a lorra, lorra wanna-be luvvies. It has Irish music on Tuesday nights and a quiz on Thursday nights. Parking for four cars is available behind the rear patio.

Teddington – TW11

Queen Dowager

49 North Lane, Teddington

Young's
G ML SL
Opening Hours: 11-3, 5.30-11m-th 11-11f-s 12-10.30su
Station: Teddington
Buses: 33, 281, 285, 592, N9
Young's Bitter, Young's Special, Young's Winter Warmer

Superb local in a side street just off Teddington High Street and within five minutes of Teddington BR station. A quiet lounge bar contrasts with the more basic public bar, one of the few left in this part of London. It has a lovely garden. The friendly landlord and landlady have created a pub well worth seeking out. In 1993 it was the local CAMRA branch's pub of the year.

Tide End Cottage

8 Ferry Road, Teddington

Magic Pub Co
FR G CP DA ML ME SL SE
Opening Hours: normal
Station: Teddington
Buses: 281, 185, R68
Webster's Green Label, Boddington's Bitter, Draught Bass + Guest Beers

An intimate and cosy local by Teddington Lock, the upper limit of the tidal Thames. A 'pet friendly' pub whose outside patio can be crowded in summer. In keeping with Magic Pub Co. policy, the food portions are generous and keenly priced and the Websters is at a promotional level. Darts, cards and dominoes are available. Occasional guest ales are served straight from the cask behind the bar.

Hampton – TW12

Railway Bell

Station Road, Hampton

Inntrepreneur
G ML SL
Opening Hours: normal
Station: Hampton BR
Buses: 111, 216, 592
Courage Best Bitter, Courage Directors

Delightful little pub within two minutes walk of Hampton BR station. Known locally as the 'dip', the pub started life as three cottages built in 1711 as servants quarters for a local member of the gentry. It was known as the Farriers Arms until 1862 when the railway reached Hampton. The pub comprises a pleasant, basic public bar and a comfortable lounge with many interesting photographs of Hampton in bygone days. There are also some interesting drawings and paintings of the pub in a variety of guises. Very good value food is served at lunchtimes (not Sundays) with barbecues in the award-winning garden in summer. Now run by the third generation, it has been in the same family since 1933.

White Hart

70 High St, Hampton

Free House
DA ML ME SL SE
Opening Hours: normal
Station: Hampton BR

Buses: 267, 592, R68
Boddington's Bitter, Flowers Original, Greene King Abbot

A real Free House with eight handpumps and a regularly changing selection. Real ale lovers visiting Hampton Court Palace will be well rewarded by a detour to visit this pub in Hampton Village. Traditional, with a real fire in winter, its history goes back to at least 1730, although it was known as the Six Bells until 1780. It would have been around this time that the pub was owned by the famous actor David Garrick. The pub was rebuilt in 1898. Dickens chose it as the place for Bill Sykes and Oliver Twist to take refreshment prior to a burglary in Chertsey. Food is always available but the real appeal is the best range of ales in the area. A few minutes walk from Hampton station, the pub is a regular entry in the Good Beer Guide and was given a 'Full Measure' award by the local CAMRA branch in 1995.

Hatton – TW14

Green Man

Green Man Lane, Hatton
S&N
G CP ML ME SL SE
Opening Hours: 11.30-11m-f 11.30-3, 7-11s 12-3, 7-10.30su
Station: Hatton Cross
Buses: 90, 285
John Smith's Bitter, Theakston's Best, Theakston's XB, Courage Directors + Guest Beers

It is hard to imagine that a typical village inn dating back to 1627, and a Grade II listed building to boot, exists almost at the eastern end of Heathrow Airport's southern runway but that is where the Green Man is; quite close to Hatton Cross tube station. As would be expected in a pub of this age, the 'olde worlde' atmosphere prevails and legend has it that there was a hiding place for highwaymen behind the fireplace in the bar. The huge garden caters for families and has a children's play area. This, and the tables at the front of the pub, can get very busy in summer. A visit is likely to explain why air crew refer to the pub as the 'finals bar' and why it is popular with plane spotters. No meals on Saturdays.

Uxbridge – UB

Crown and Treaty House

90 Oxford Road, Uxbridge

Whitbread
G CP ML ME SL SE
Opening Hours: normal
Station: Uxbridge BR
Buses: 305, 331, 335, 392, R1, 705, W4
Wethered's, Boddington's Bitter, Marston's Pedigree, Morland's Old Speckled Hen + Guest Beers

A Grade I listed building originally called the 'the place' when it first appeared in 1575. It changed its name to the Treaty House in 1645 when Charles I used it as a venue to sue for peace at the end of the English Civil War. Historically, one of our most important pubs. Three guest beers always on gravity at the back of the bar.

Southall – UB1

Hambrough Tavern

The Broadway, Southall

Free House
G CP SL SE
Opening Hours: normal
Station: Southall BR
Buses: 207, 607, N89
Guest Beers

Along with many other pubs in Southall, the Hambrough owes its existence to the coming of the canal at the turn of the eighteenth century. The current building dates from only 1982 replacing one that burnt down during the Southall riots. Real ale is available only in the saloon bar but the range of four ales changes constantly and includes several rare to the neighbourhood. A former Watney's house, it was originally known as 'Frankey Newell's' after a former landlord and local 'brickmaster', some of whose bricks were used in the construction of Buckingham Palace.

Norwood Green – UB2

Plough

Tentelow Lane, Norwood Green

Fuller's

G CP ML
Opening Hours: normal
Station: Southall BR
Buses: 111, 120
Fuller's Chiswick Bitter, Fuller's London Pride, Fuller's ESB

The oldest inn in Fuller's tied estate, the Plough is a largely locals' pub. It can often appear much more crowded than it really is due to the large space devoted to the bar. The former function room can be used as an overspill area when the pub is really busy. Lunch is served on weekdays only.

Greenford – UB6

Black Horse

425 Oldfield Lane, Greenford

Fuller's
G CP ML
Opening Hours: normal
Station: Greenford BR
Buses: 92
Fuller's Chiswick Bitter, Fuller's London Pride, Fuller's ESB

A busy and friendly waterside pub with moorings on the Paddington arm of the Grand Union Canal. From the lounge bar, a set of steps leads down to a very pleasant beer garden which comes thoroughly recommended. The beer is of consistently high quality and the Black Horse has appeared in the majority of Good Beer Guides, as the stickers covering the back windows will prove.

Harefield – UB9

Breakspear Arms

Breakspear Road South, Harefield

Morland
FR G CP DA R ML ME SL SE
Opening Hours: normal
Buses: 331, R1
Morland's Independent IPA, Morland's Original Bitter, Morland's Old Masters, Morland's Old Speckled Hen + Guest Beers

A real family pub which is one of the few to have been granted a full children's licence under the government's less than successful scheme. It features a number of children's attractions, such as a bouncy castle in the garden and lots of ice cream. Recommended if you have children and you like Old Speckled Hen.

Plough

Hill End Road, Harefield

Free House
G CP ML ME SL SE
Opening Hours: 11-3, 6-11m-s
Buses: 331, R1
Ruddles Best, Fuller's London Pride, Timothy Taylor's Landlord, Wadworth 6X + Guest Beers

An excellent, if isolated, single-bar Free House near the famous Harefield Hospital. The largest range of beers for miles around. There is a regular turnover of four guest beers as well as the five regulars, which may go part way to explaining its popularity, especially during the summer. The food, which is not served on Sundays, is also very good value.

White Horse

Church Hill, Harefield

Greenalls
G CP ML ME
Opening Hours: 11-3, 6-11m-s
Buses: 331, R1
Greenall's Bitter, Shipstone's, Wadworth 6X, Greenall's Original + Guest Beers

This Grade II listed building, located on the south side of Harefield village, is reputed to be some 500 years old. In 1709 it was recorded as being one of only two alehouses in the village. Summer sees frequent barbecues in the garden. Traditional pub games include comparative rarities: Shove Ha'penny and Shut the Box.

Harrow – HA1

Castle

30 West St, Harrow

Fuller's
G SL SE
Opening Hours: normal
Station: Harrow on the Hill
Buses: 114, 140, 182, 183, 186, 258, 340, H10, H14, H15, H17
Fuller's London Pride, Fuller's ESB

The Castle is located near the top of Harrow on the Hill,

tucked away in cottaged back streets. There is a small public bar at the front with the lounge accessed by a passage down the left of the pub. However, these two bars will not prepare you for the superb wood-panelled room at the rear. This is twice the size of the two other bars put together and is usually the preserve of the passing trade; the lounge and public bar being left to the regulars. The Castle is definitely a conversation pub and one topic under virtually constant discussion is rugby union, as many regulars are avid fans of the game. If you enjoy solitude, choose your moment carefully as it is more often busy than not and the conversation can rise to a raucous level.

Harrow Weald – HA3

Case Is Altered

Old Righting, Harrow Weald

Allied Domecq

G ML ME SL SE

Opening Hours: normal

Buses: 258

Benskins Best Bitter, Tetley Bitter, Marston's Pedigree + Guest Beers

The Case Is Altered is very close to the edge of Greater London and is handily placed for investigating the many nature trails on Harrow Weald Common. With no nearby railway station, the only way of reaching it other than by car, is to take the 258 bus and get out at the Hare public house on Brookshill. The Case was refurbished in July 1994 and is much airier than it was and is considerably extended inside. The refurbishment has largely been sympathetic and several drinking areas have been created within the single bar. Prior to the refurbishment the Case Is Altered was not what you would call a beer drinkers' pub. However, the range of beers has been enlarged and the pub now attracts a wide range of social groups. Many people are attracted by what must be the largest beer garden in the area which is also well furnished with things for the kids to climb on. The pub also attracts diners in droves. The neighbourhood historically has more than its fair share of pubs with this name. For an explanation of the origin of the name see The Case is Altered, Eastcote HA5.

Royal Oak
60 Peel Road, Wealdstone

Allied Domecq
G CP ML
Opening Hours: normal
Station: Harrow and Wealdstone
Buses: 140, 182, 186, 258, 340, N18
Tetley Bitter, Ind Coope Burton Ale + Guest Beers

An imposing pub which dates from 1932 and features a very pleasant conservatory. There are two separate bars, the lounge being split into several drinking areas and boasting a large collection of miniatures behind the bar. The house beer, Oak Bitter, is brewed by Eldridge Pope.

Seven Balls

749 Kenton Lane, Harrow Weald

Allied Domecq
G CP ML ME SL SE
Opening Hours: normal
Station: Kenton
Buses: 258
Tetley Bitter, Ind Coope ABC Bitter, Eldridge Pope Best Bitter, Eldridge Pope Hardy Country + Guest Beers

A good mixture of locals and passing trade make for a pleasant atmosphere in this 250-year-old pub. The ceiling in the public bar is rather low and anyone over six feet tall should bear this in mind if they do not want the fact brought abruptly to their attention.

Eastcote – HA5

Case is Altered

High Road, Eastcote

Allied Domecq
FR G CP ML ME SL SE
Opening Hours: normal
Station: Eastcote
Buses: H13
Benskins Best Bitter, Tetley Bitter, Marston's Pedigree, Ind Coope Burton Ale, Young's Special

This excellent country-style hostelry is a Grade II listed building and is the house of the Clutterbucks of Stanmore. There is a fine stone-flagged floor in the public bar, which was once the floor of the stables attached to the farmhouse. The pub gets very busy and is popular with Pinner's fashionable set. There are a number of pubs of this name throughout the country and it is often assumed that the name is usually a landlord's joke to refer to some upturn in his fortunes that have removed his creditors from his back and allowed him to keep the pub. It is also the name of a Ben Johnson comedy circa 1599. The Harrow and Pinner area actually had a large number of pubs with this name, which gave rise to the theory that the name is a corruption of Casa Alta (high house) and was connected with soldiers returning from the Peninsular War. However, there is no evidence for this theory.

Stanmore – HA7

Malthouse

7 Stanmore Hill, Stanmore

Free House
G ML ME SL
Opening Hours: normal
Station: Stanmore
Buses: 142
Boddington's Bitter + Guests; Cider

The Malthouse was opened in October 1994 and in its first seven months sold over 200 different real ales. It is split into two levels, with the room to the right available for meetings. There are always things going on here, though not all may appeal to the traditional drinker. He or she will, however, be treated to superb quality beer from breweries all over England. There are usually at least four real ales available and more when the frequent beer festivals are held. Beer festivals will either consist of up to a dozen different ales or will feature a particular brewery. There is a proposal that CAMRA members will get a 20 per cent discount off real ales on Monday evenings.

Vine

154 Stanmore Hill, Stanmore

Allied Domecq
G CP
Opening Hours: 11-3, 5-11m-s
Station: Stanmore
Buses: 142
Benskins Best Bitter, Tetley Bitter, Ind Coope Burton Ale + Guests

Single bar, former coaching inn, located at the top of Stanmore Hill. Separate drinking areas have been retained and part of the original bar can still be seen in the rear room.

Edgware – HA8

Blacking Bottle
122-6 High Street, Edgware

Wetherspoon
DA ML ME SL SE
Opening Hours: normal
Station: Edgware
Buses: 32, 79, 107, 113, 142, 186, 204, 221, 240, 288, 303
Younger's Scotch, Theakston's Best, Theakston's XB, Courage Directors + Guests

Large single-bar shop conversion, opened in April 1993 in a former supermarket. It is situated on the historic roman road, Watling Street, which runs from Marble Arch to Holyhead. The unusual name is to commemorate Charles Day, a local shoe polish manufacturer whose house was built in the shape of a bottle. Familiar, and abundant, Wetherspoon wood panelling is bedecked with prints of old Edgware and its public transport. A homely atmosphere is engendered in this music-free pub with comfortable seating and subtle lighting. Good-value food served all day. The pub puts on several beer festivals during the year.

Change of Hart

21 High Street, Edgware

Allied Domecq
G CP DA ML ME SL SE
Opening Hours: normal
Station: Edgware
Buses: 32, 79, 107, 113, 142, 186, 204, 221, 240, 51, 288, 303
Benskins Best Bitter, Adnams Bitter, Tetley Bitter, Ind Coope Burton Ale + Guests

Formerly the White Hart, a miraculous transformation is the only way to describe what has happened to this pub. It was left to run into the ground but has now been brought back from the brink. Although some of the internal work has opened up the old bars, the overall effect has worked well. The only thing to be heard is the murmur of conversation broken by the occasional swoosh of the handpump being pulled. Disabled access means just that, level access throughout, disabled toilets, reserved floodlit parking spaces etc. Add home-made food and room for up to eight beers on a rota, plus a house beer called Hart Bitter at a promotional price and you have to congratulate Allied Domecq on a job very well done.

Middlesex

De Burgh Arms

High Street, Yiewsley, Middx

Allied Domecq
G CP DA ML ME
Opening Hours: 11-11m-s 12-3, 7-10.30su
Station: West Drayton
Buses: 222, U5
Adnams Bitter, Tetley Bitter, Eldridge Pope Best Bitter

A tourist pub, used by people staying near the airport. It has an island bar, with regularly changing beers, friendly staff and atmosphere.

Load of Hay

33 Villiers St, Uxbridge

G CP ML ME
Opening Hours: 11-3, 5.30-11m-f 11-3, 7-11s
Station: Uxbridge BR
Buses: 207, U3, U4, U5
Guest Beers + Ciders

Originally built as the Officers' Mess for the Elthorne Light Militia, the Load of Hay is a cosy local near to Brunel University. The pub is not the easiest place to find but it is worth the effort for the range of beers, including some rare to the area, as well as for the food. There is also a small front bar which opens as a restaurant on Saturday evenings.

Plough

Mandeville Road, Northolt

Fuller's
G CP ML
Opening Hours: normal
Station: Northolt
Buses: 90, 120, 140, 282, N89, 398
Fuller's London Pride, Fuller's ESB

London's only thatched pub looks like it has been there since the year dot. In fact it dates only from the 1940s. Situated on the edge of Northolt village, between the tube station and the A40 junction, it is easily accessible. It is not as large inside as the exterior view suggests.

Prince of Wales

1 Harlington Road, Hillingdon

Fuller's
G CP ML
Opening Hours: 12-11
Station: Hillingdon
Buses: U4
Fuller's Chiswick Bitter, Fuller's London Pride, Fuller's ESB

This curiously-shaped pub on the corner of Harlington and Uxbridge roads, is a real locals' local. There is a lively public bar and a quieter saloon. Built over 100 years ago, the pub was originally three cottages knocked together and for many years had a beer and wine licence only.

Queen's Head

High Street, Pinner

Allied Domecq
G CP ML SL
Opening Hours: 11-4, 5-11
Station: Pinner
Buses: H11, H12, H13
Benskins Best Bitter, Tetley Bitter, Marston's Pedigree, Ind Coope Burton Ale + Guests

This Grade I-listed pub is 400 years old but stands on the site of an earlier alehouse first granted a licence in 1336 to serve the people visiting the first 'Pinner Fair'. The current inn sign shows a Stuart Queen, Queen Anne, rather than Elizabeth. The pub has a ghost of a lady in white which has been sighted on several occasions. It is reputedly the daughter of Lady Hamilton, who was knocked down and killed by a coach outside the inn. Many original timbers and real fires make this a not-to-be-missed pub.

Companies Operating Public Houses in London

Allied Domecq

Allied Domecq owns 50 percent of the Carlsberg-Tetley Group, which was formed by the merger of Allied Lyons breweries with Danish giant, Carlsberg. Allied was established in 1961 by the amalgamation of Ansells, Tetley-Walker and Ind Coope. Questions hang over the fate of a number of its breweries as the company is plagued by over-capacity. The company's biggest brand is Tetley.

On the pub front, Allied is keen to keep its local brewery image with traditional brewery liveries prevailing. These include Friary Meux, Benskins, ABC and Halls in the South. In London, the Taylor Walker brand is complemented by the small chain of upmarket Nicholson's pubs. Allied also owns the Firkin chain (q.v.). In total, there are around 4100 pubs across the country.

Friary Meux Best Bitter ABV 3.7 percent, Tetley Bitter ABV 3.7 percent, Ind Coope Burton Ale ABV 4.8 percent

Bass

Until the recent takeover of Courage by S&N, Bass was the biggest brewer in Britain. It commands 23 percent of all beer production and draught Bass is the biggest premium cask ale. Following closures at Edinburgh (Heriot), Sheffield (Hope) and Wolverhampton (Springfield), Bass now brews on only nine sites, with three (Alton, Belfast and Tadcaster) producing no real ale.

Bass owns 4100 pubs (74 percent sell real ale) of which 2600 are managed. Many pubs bear the liveries of former trading divisions eg Charrington (London), Tennents (Scotland), M&B (Midlands) and Welsh Brewers. In recent years Bass has sold over 2700 pubs to comply with the 1990 Supply of Beer Orders. The free trade represents about half of Bass' sales and the tied trade about a third; the rest is take home.

Hancock HB ABV 3.6 percent, Worthington Best Bitter ABV 3.6 percent, Draught Bass ABV 4.4 percent

Courage

When Courage attempted to purchase S&N a few years ago, S&N described it as a potential disaster for brewing. The reverse was apparently not the case as S&N purchased Courage in 1995. Courage was a brewer with no pubs, having sold them in 1991 to Inntrepreneur Estates, a company owned jointly by Fosters and Grand Metropolitan. This was to avoid the full implications of the government's Supply of Beer Orders. Unfortunately, it left Courage very exposed. As part of the deal, Courage took over all Grand Met's breweries (ex Watneys).

Webster Yorkshire Bitter ABV 3.5 percent, John Smiths Bitter ABV 3.8 percent, Courage Best Bitter ABV 4 percent, Courage Directors ABV 4.8 percent

Eldridge Pope & Co

A well respected Dorset brewer with 200 pubs, a handful of which are in London. Dating from 1837, the brewery has stood on its current site since 1880 and is still run by the Pope family. Its Thomas Hardy's Ale is well known as being the UK's strongest bottle-conditioned beer. The brewery made a controversial decision a few years ago to serve its beer through Northern style swan neck handpumps. As a result, there is a fair amount of debate as to whether its beer has suffered as a result. It has recently split the brewing from the pub-owning side and what this means for the future is yet to be determined.

Dorchester Bitter ABV 3.3 percent, Best Bitter ABV 3.8 percent, Blackdown Porter ABV 4 percent, Thomas Hardy Country Bitter 4.2 percent

Firkin

Now owned by Allied Domecq (q.v.). Set up by David Bruce in 1979 in South London, there are now Firkins all over the country. Note that beers brewed on the premises are often kept under gas although those that are not, are not!

Mild ABV 3.4 percent, Bitter ABV 3.5 percent, Best Bitter ABV 4.3 percent, Dogbolter ABV 5.6 percent

Fuller, Smith & Turner

London's largest brewery has seen continuous brewing on the site for over 325 years. John Fuller joined Henry Smith and John Turner in 1845 and descendants of the original partners are still on the board today. The brewery recently completed a £1.6 million brewhouse redevelopment to cope with growing demand. It owns around 200 pubs and all bar one sell real ale. Fuller's can also be found regularly in the free trade. The shop is open 8-4 Mondays to Thursdays; 8-3 Fridays; tours by arrangement.

Hock ABV 3.2 percent, Chiswick Bitter ABV 3.5 percent, London Pride ABV 4.1 percent, ESB ABV 5.5 percent

Greenalls

Former brewing giant that purchased and closed many fine independent Midland breweries before it stopped brewing in 1991. During the 1980s Greenalls closed Wem, Davenports, Simpkiss and Shipstones. After Greenalls closed their own brewery in Warrington, Carlsberg-Tetley took over the brewing of the Greenall brands. The company is also infamous in Manchester for bulldozing the famous Tommy Duck's pub during a night in 1993. This totally ignored local planning legislation. The recent acquisition of the Boddington pub chain, who also stopped brewing (after selling the brewery to Whitbread), has added another 475 pubs to its 2000 strong estate, which is mainly in the North West.

Bitter ABV 3.8 percent

Greene King

Established in 1799, Greene King is East Anglia's largest regional brewer, producing cask conditioned beers at Bury St Edmunds. Its other brewery, at Biggleswade, is lager only. Having acquired 85 new pubs from Bass, its tied estate is now 900 pubs and covers London, Kent, Surrey and Sussex as well as East Anglia. Ninety percent of them take cask ale.

XX Dark Mild ABV 3 percent, IPA ABV 3.6 percent, Rayment Special Bitter ABV 4 percent, Abbot Ale ABV 5 percent

Grosvenor Inns

Grosvenor run around 47 pubs in the Midlands, South and (mainly) in London. The majority are leased from Inntrepreneur (q.v.) or other companies and are tied to Courage beers. The other pubs take, in addition, Whitbread, Fuller's and Wadworth. Once known as Cromwell Inns, it is now a publicly quoted company with plans to develop its estate, including more Slug & Lettuces (now 15). It also owns seven Hedgehog and Hogshead and a subsidiary company of seven free house catering outlets, Belcher's Pubs Ltd. David Bruce is a member of the board (see Firkin).

Hall & Woodhouse

Founded as the Ansty Brewery in 1777 in Dorset by Charles Hall. The partnership of Hall & Woodhouse came into being in 1847. Often known as Badgers, the brewery serves cask ale in all its 160 pubs as well as supplying around 300 free trade outlets in the South.

Best Bitter ABV 4 percent, Hard Tackle ABV 4.6 percent, Tanglefoot ABV 5.1 percent

Hop Back Brewery

Originally the Wyndham Arms home-brew pub in Salisbury, a five-barrel plant was set up in 1987 but it switched most of its production to a new brewery in Downton in 1992. This was added to in 1995 to cope with increased demand. A fourth tied house and brew pub (Hop Leaf, Reading) was opened the same year. Hop Back also sells to 85 free trade outlets.

GFB ABV 3.5 percent, Special ABV 4 percent, Entire Stout ABV 4.5 percent, Summer Lightning ABV 5 percent

Inntrepreneur

Formed by Fosters and Grand Metropolitan as part of the pubs-for-breweries swap in 1991. Grand Met took on 330 pubs and subsequently sold them to S&N. The changes saw many tenants leave the trade. Inntrepreneur currently operates 4330 pubs, some of which are free houses, although most are tied to Courage until 1998. In 1994, it was clarified that these pubs had the right to stock a guest beer of their choosing outside the Inntrepreneur list. However, this may well change with S&N's takeover of Courage as there is no longer a direct tie with a UK brewer.

Magic Pub Co

Pub group established in June 1994 with the purchase of 260 pubs from S&N (former Chef and Brewer pubs). The pubs are mostly managed and are mostly within the M25. The beer list features ales from national and regional brewers.

McMullen

Hertfordshire's oldest independent brewery, founded in 1827 by Peter McMullen. The Victorian tower brewery was built on the site of three wells and houses the original oak and copper lined fermenters which are still in use. Real ale is served in all 145 pubs in Hertfordshire, Essex and London and to 200 free trade outlets. Seasonal beers are brewed for a limited period under the banner of McMullen's Special Reserve. In April 1995, head brewer, Tony Skipper, was voted Brewer of the Year by the Parliamentary Beer Club.

AK ABV 3.7 percent, Country Best Bitter ABV 4.3 percent, Gladstone ABV 4.3 percent, Stronghart ABV 7 percent

Morland

Established in Abingdon in 1711, Morland is the second oldest independent brewer in the UK and has been on its present site since 1861. In 1992, it survived a takeover bid by Greene King. Nearly all Morland's 350 pubs serve cask ale and the company supplies around 500 free trade outlets around the Thames Valley and Surrey. Old Speckled Hen is a popular guest.

Old Speckled Hen ABV 5.2 percent

Pubmaster

Formed in 1991 to take over the pub estate of Brent Walker (ex Camerons and Tolly Cobbold pubs). In 1992, 732 pubs were leased from Allied and 174 pubs from Whitbread. Pubmaster currently runs 1750 pubs across the country, 1650 are tenanted. Its most famous trading name is Tap & Spile, a growing chain of traditional alehouses (75 aimed for by the end of 1996) offering a good choice of beers. There is also a new chain of European style bars specialising in continental beers. Other Pubmaster pubs stock beers from Bass, Carlsberg-Tetley, Whitbread and regional independents. The company shares control of 170 Maple Leaf Inns with Labatts.

Regent Inns

Company founded in 1980 and now owning 49 managed houses in London and the Home Counties. In 1994, a rationalisation took place with 10 pubs sold off and 17 acquired. Further pubs are being sought. The pubs are allowed to preserve their individual identities and sell a wide range of beers.

Sam Smith

Yorkshire's oldest brewery (1758) based in Tadcaster. Unlike the other brewery in Tadcaster, John Smith's, this brewery is still in family hands. Beers are brewed from well water without the use of adjuncts. All the cask beer is fermented in Yorkshire stone squares and racked into wooden casks provided by the brewery's own cooperage. Real ale is sold in fewer and fewer of its 27 or so London pubs. The brewery says it is to ensure high quality which is a shame when their prices are very competitive.

Old Brewery Bitter ABV 3.8 percent, Museum Ale ABV 5 percent

Scottish & Newcastle

S&N were founded in 1960 as a merger between Scottish Breweries Ltd (the former Younger and McEwan breweries) and Newcastle Breweries Ltd. The company runs approximately 2750 pubs including some former Chef & Brewer houses purchased from Grand Met in 1994 and which gave S&N a foothold in Southern England. In

1995, S&N took over Courage and the brewing operation is now known as Scottish Courage. This has massively increased its presence in London and elevated it to the status of Britain's largest brewer, having one quarter of the beer production in this country. S&N own Theakstons, which they acquired when they purchased and closed Matthew Brown of Blackburn. Although there is a Theakston's brewery in Masham, Yorkshire, the majority of this beer is brewed in Newcastle.

Younger's Scotch ABV 3.7 percent, Theakston's Best Bitter ABV 3.8 percent, Theakston's XB ABV 4.6 percent, Theakston's Old Peculier ABV 5.7 percent

Shepherd Neame

Shepherd Neame is the oldest continuously brewing concern in Britain (since 1698) but records show brewing commenced as far back as the twelfth century and the same water source used. Steam engines have been brought back into use and the mash is produced in two teak tuns which date from 1910. Its tied estate of some 370 pubs is mostly in Kent with a few in Surrey, Sussex, Essex and London. Another 1000 outlets are supplied directly from the brewery. The brewery has been at the forefront against cross Channel smuggling. The shop is open 8.30-4.

Master Brew Bitter ABV 3.7 percent, Best Bitter ABV 4.1 percent, Spitfire Ale ABV 4.7 percent, Bishops Finger ABV 5.2 percent, Porter ABV 5.2 percent

Taylor Walker - see Allied Domecq

JD Wetherspoon Organisation

Ambitious group, founded by Tim Martin, which opened its first pub in 1979 and went public in 1992. It currently owns 103 pubs in and around London, plus a few elsewhere, all managed. The company continues to add about an extra 25 pubs each year, many of which are conversions from shops. It tends to feature identikit decor and use common names incorporating 'Moon'. No music is played in any of the pubs and all offer no smoking areas and food all day. The six standard beers are: Theakston's Best and XB, Younger's Scotch, Courage Directors, Wadworth 6X and Greene King Abbot Ale. Recent changes have allowed a greater choice to liven up this list.

Whitbread

Whitbread has a history of brewery closures: Strongs of Romsey, Wethereds of Marlow, Chesters of Salford,

Higsons of Liverpool and, latterly, Exchange of Sheffield in 1993. Since then Whitbread seems to have rediscovered cask conditioned ale and has been investing heavily in its cask ale portfolio. The retail side of the company has turned a number of pubs into ale houses to support this initiative and there have been some special brews worthy of praise, involving limited edition beers brewed in Cheltenham and Castle Eden. Whitbread's 4700 pubs are controlled by Whitbread Inns (managed houses) and Whitbread Pub Partnerships (pubs leased out, usually on 20 year leases).

Wethereds ABV 3.6 percent, Flowers IPA ABV 3.6 percent, Boddingtons Bitter ABV 3.8 percent, Castle Eden Ale ABV 4 percent, Flowers Original ABV 4.5 percent

Young's

The quintessential London brewing firm was founded in 1675 by the Draper family and bought by Charles Young and Anthony Bainbridge in 1831. Their partnership was dissolved in 1884 and the business was continued by the Young's family who run it today. It was the only London brewer not to join the keg revolution in the 1970s. Young's still brew in the traditional way and use horse-drawn drays to deliver to pubs close to the brewery. The brewery supplies around 400 free trade outlets, mostly within the M25 although the brewery is spreading westwards. The estate has increased to 188 but it is still under-represented in South-east London.

Bitter ABV 3.7 percent, Special ABV 4.8 percent, Winter Warmer ABV 5 percent

CAMRA BEER FESTIVALS

CAMRA runs many beer festivals around the country; all offer a discount to CAMRA members and all serve the beer in over sized glasses to ensure the customer gets a full pint.

The beer festivals in and around Greater London are:

February	Battersea
March	North London (opposite King's Cross)
April	Ealing
May	Ongar
June	Catford
	Thurrock
	Surrey, Dorking
July	Kent, Canterbury
August	Great British Beer Festival, Olympia
September	Chappel, Essex
	Watford
	Feltham
October	Croydon
November	Pigs Ear, Stratford
	Woking

For further details contact CAMRA 01727 867201 or buy the *London Drinker Magazine* from many good pubs

OR JOIN CAMRA
for a full listing of all CAMRA's UK beer festivals.

CAMRA MEMBERSHIP

If you enjoy real ale and good pubs, then help protect them. For only £1 a month you can become a member and gain many benefits:

- As a CAMRA member you will get generous discounts on CAMRA products and discounts to all CAMRA beer festivals.
- A monthly newspaper, What's Brewing, which will keep you updated on beers, pubs and breweries.
- The opportunity to become involved with local CAMRA activities including brewery visits.
- The knowledge that you are helping to save today's heritage for tomorrow's drinkers.

JOIN CAMRA & PROTECT YOUR PLEASURE, OVER 45,000 MEMBERS CAN'T BE WRONG!

Single Membership £12 Joint Husband & Wife £14
Life Membership £144 Joint Life Membership £168

From January 1st, 1997 rates will be:
Single Membership £14 Joint Husband & Wife £17
Life Membership £168 Joint Life Membership £204

Please delete as appropriate
I/We wish to become members of CAMRA and agree to abide by the Memorandum and Articles of Association of the company

I/We enclose a cheque/p.o. for
£__________________ (payable to CAMRA Ltd)

Name(s) ______________________________

Address ______________________________

____

________________________Postcode____________

Signature(s)______________________________
To pay by Access or Visa, please contact the Membership Secretary on 01727 867201.

CAMRA Ltd, 230, Hatfield Road, St Albans, Herts AL1 4LW

The CAMRA Books range of guides helps you search out the best in beer (and cider) and brew it at home too!

Buying in the UK

All our books are available through bookshops in the UK. If you can't find a book, simply order it from your bookshop using the ISBN number, title and author details given below. CAMRA members should refer to their regular monthly newspaper *What's Brewing* for the latest details and member special offers. CAMRA books are also available by mail-order (postage free) from: CAMRA Books, 230 Hatfield Road, St Albans, Herts, AL1 4LW. Cheques made payable to CAMRA Ltd. Telephone your credit card order on 01727 867201.

Buying outside the UK

CAMRA books are also sold in many book and beer outlets in the USA and other English-speaking countries. If you have trouble locating a particular book, use the details below to order by mail or fax (+44 1727 867670).

Carriage of £3.00 per book (Europe) and £6.00 per book (US, Australia, New Zealand and other overseas) is charged.

UK Booksellers

Call CAMRA Books for distribution details and book list. CAMRA Books are listed on all major CD-ROM book lists and on our Internet site:
http://www.cityscape.co.uk/users/al96/beer/html

Overseas Booksellers

Call or fax CAMRA Books for details of local distributors.

Distributors are required for some English language territories. Rights enquiries (for non-English language editions) should be addressed to the managing editor.

Good Beer Guides

These are comprehensive guides researched by professional beer writers and CAMRA enthusiasts. Use these guides to find the best beer on your travels or to plan your itinerary for the finest drinking. Travel and accommodation information, plus maps, help you on your way and there's plenty to read about the history of brewing, the beer styles and the local cuisine to back up the entries for bars and beverages.

GOOD BEER GUIDE TO MUNICH AND BAVARIA

by Graham Lees

206 pages Price: £8.99

This guide tells you where to find the best beers and the many splendid bars, beer halls and gardens, and the food to match. You'll also find all the background information for the world's most famous beer extravaganza, the Munich Oktoberfest. Author Graham Lees, a founder member of CAMRA, has lived and worked in Munich for several years and has endlessly toured Bavaria to compile this book.

Use the following code to order this book from your bookshop: ISBN 1-85249-114-0

GOOD BEER GUIDE TO BELGIUM AND HOLLAND

by Tim Webb

286 pages Price: £9.99

Discover the stunning range and variety of beers available in the Low Countries, our even nearer neighbours via Le Tunnel. There are such revered styles as Trappist Ales, fruit beers, wheat beers and the lambic and gueuze specialities made by the centuries-old method of spontaneous fermentation. Channel-hopping Tim Webb's latest edition of the guide offers even more bars in which an incredible array of beers can be enjoyed. There are maps, tasting notes, beer style guide and a beers index to complete the most comprehensive companion to drinking with your Belgian and Dutch hosts.

Use the following code to order this book from your bookshop: ISBN 1-85249-115-9

GOOD BEER GUIDE

edited by Jeff Evans

546 pages Price: £10.99

Fancy a pint? Let CAMRA's *Good Beer Guide* lead the way. Revised each year to include around 5,000 great pubs serving excellent ale – country pubs, town pubs and pubs by the sea.

Fully and freshly researched by members of the Campaign for Real Ale, real enthusiasts who use the pubs week in, week out. No payment is ever taken for inclusion. The guide has location maps for each county and you can read full details of all Britain's breweries (big and small) and the ales they produce, including tasting notes.

KNOWN GEMS & HIDDEN TREASURES – A POCKET GUIDE TO THE PUBS OF LONDON

by Peter Haydon

224 pages **Price: £7.99**

If you live in or visit London, then you need this guide in your top pocket! It will take you to the well-known and historic pubs you must not miss, but also to the pubs which are tucked away. The grass roots organisation of CAMRA and beer journalist Peter Haydon have brought London's pubs alive through their descriptions of ale, food, entertainment, history and architecture. These pubs have a story to tell. The pubs in this pocket, portable, guide are listed by locality with a street address and London postal code districts heading pages so that you can easily match your location with the nearest pub. The guide covers pubs which are near tube and railway stations and gives relevant bus route numbers. It covers central London out to the commuter belts of Bushey and Surbiton.

Use the following code to order this book from your bookshop: ISBN 1-85249-118-3

CAMRA GUIDES

Painstakingly researched and checked, these guides are the leaders in their field, bringing you to the door of pubs which serve real ale and more...

GOOD PUB FOOD

by Susan Nowak

448 pages **Price: £9.99**

The pubs in these pages serve food as original and exciting as anything available in far more expensive restaurants. And, as well as the exotic, you will find landlords and landladies serving simple, nourishing pub fare such as a genuine ploughman's lunch or a steak and kidney pudding.

You'll discover cooking from a new wave of young chefs who would prefer to run a pub than a restaurant. Many pubs are producing the traditional dishes of their regions, building smokeries, keeping cattle and goats, growing vegetables and herbs, creating vibrant, modern cuisine from fresh ingredients. Recipes from some of them are dotted about this guide so you can try them at home.

Use the following code to order this book from your bookshop: ISBN 1-85249-116-7

Room at the Inn

by Jill Adam

242 pages Price: £8.99

From the first pub claiming to have sold Stilton cheese to travellers in 1720 to old smugglers haunts in Dorset, *Room at the Inn* gives details of pubs up and down the country offering generous hospitality. Travellers and tourists looking for a traditional British alternative to bland impersonal hotels need look no further than this guide.

The guide contains almost 350 inns – plus some hotels and motels – which provide overnight accommodation and a wholesome English breakfast. You'll also find a good pint of real ale on your arrival. Room at the Inn is a must for the glove compartment of the family car and vital reading for anyone planning a bed and breakfast break, sports tour or business trip.

Use the following code to order this book from your bookshop: ISBN 1-85249-119-1

Guide to Real Cider

by Ted Bruning

256 pages Price: £7.99

Cider is making a major comeback and Real Cider is worth seeking out wherever you are. This guide helps you find one of Britain's oldest, tastiest and most fascinating drinks. Reading this guide makes your mouth water as you leaf through details of more than 2000 pubs selling the real stuff. There are also many farmhouse producers from all over the country and outlets for Cider's equally drinkable cousin, Perry – if you bring a container.

Use the following code to order this book from your bookshop: ISBN 1-85249-117-5

Brew Your Own

Learn the basics of brewing real ales at home from the experts. And then move on to more ambitious recipes which imitate well-loved ales from the UK and Europe.

Guide to Home Brewing

by Graham Wheeler

240 pages Price: £6.99

The best way to learn successful home-brewing basics is over the shoulder of expert Graham Wheeler, in this second edition of his popular guide. Equipment, ingredients, yeast, water, boiling and cooling, fermenting, finishing, bottling, kits, measurements and calculations. These are just some of the subjects fully covered in this definitive beginner's guide.

Use the following code to order this book from your bookshop: ISBN 1-85249-112-4

Brew your own Real Ale at Home

by Graham Wheeler and Roger Protz

196 pages Price: £6.99

This book is a treasure chest for all real ale fans and home brew enthusiasts. It contains recipes which allow you to replicate some famous cask-conditioned beers at home or to customise brews to your own particular taste. Measurements can be used world-wide.

Use the following code to order this book from your bookshop: ISBN 1-85249-113-2

Brew Classic European Beers at Home

by Graham Wheeler and Roger Protz

196 pages Price: £8.99

Keen home brewers can now recreate some of the world's classic beers. In your own home you can brew superb pale ales, milds, porters, stouts, Pilsners, Alt, Kolsch, Trappist, wheat beers, sour beers, even the astonishing fruit lambics of Belgium… and many more. Recipe measurements are given in UK, US and European units.

Use the following code to order this book from your bookshop: ISBN 1-85249-117-5